I0814460

OLIVIER MESSIAEN

OLIVIER MESSIAEN

A CRITICAL BIOGRAPHY

ROBERT SHOLL

REAKTION BOOKS

In memoriam
Lindsay O'Neill (1924–2002) and Dennis Hunt (1931–2014)

Published by
Reaktion Books Ltd
Unit 32, Waterside
44–48 Wharf Road
London N1 7UX, UK
www.reaktionbooks.co.uk

First published 2024

Printed and bound in Great Britain by TJ Books Ltd, Padstow, Cornwall

A catalogue record for this book is available from the British Library

ISBN 978 1 78914 865 7

CONTENTS

Harawi (song x): 'Amour oiseaux d'étoile', order of service from Messiaen's funeral, 14 May 1992.

Introduction: 'All the birds of the stars'

'I compose because I wish to make music.'[1]

'My work is addressed to all who believe – and also to all others.'[2]

'The Catholic religion is a veritable fairy tale – but with this difference: *it is all true*.'[3]

This autograph example opposite, from Olivier Messiaen's song cycle *Harawi* (1945), was printed in the order of service for his funeral and later placed on his headstone (which is shaped like a bird). Messiaen's second wife, the pianist, teacher and composer Yvonne Louise Georgette Loriod-Messiaen (1924–2010), was interred with her husband near their summer house at Petichet in Isère (Auvergne-Rhône-Alpes), in the graveyard of the Église Saint-Théoffrey. In the service booklet, this musical example was followed by a short text by Messiaen:

> After death, during the necessary purification that precedes the definitive vision of God, one cannot remember the joys and pains of this life. One remembers only the good and bad actions. At this moment, I will be upset with all the evil that I have done. But I will also rejoice in all the good I have been able to do, and this final memory permits me progressively to understand at last the invisible.[4]

The prescience of these words, accompanying the legacy of Messiaen's music at his funeral, was apposite. Messiaen understood that his task was to shape contingent material towards permanence, to make it necessary, and in this he would be a judge and be judged.[5] His life and work were marked by 'the truths of the Catholic faith [as] the first aspect of my work, the noblest, and no doubt the most useful and most valuable – perhaps the only one I won't regret at the hour of my death'.[6] Through music he attempted to manifest the real presence of Christ to humanity and to realize a vision of human destiny after death.

This was an audacious mandate for music, made possible in part by other historical and ideological musical projects, notably those of Richard Wagner (1813–1883). Messiaen's Christian message was preached to believers and non-believers alike through a music that is constructed to be religious. Messiaen, echoing the theologian Jacques Maritain (1882–1973), and following the Symbolist artist and theorist Maurice Denis (1870–1943), stated that there is 'no style specific to religious music'; religious music is a reflection of 'God who exists before all, and after all, and is beyond time and the eternal'.[7] The liminal quality of Messiaen's thought and music was founded in his own participation in and translation of God's real presence: music was his way of making a transcendent God empirical and sensate while retaining the mystery, numinosity and venerable qualities of the sacred.[8] However, despite being a composer who spent much time explaining his music, Messiaen also believed that it could be experienced without these commentaries, 'in all its freshness'.[9]

More critically, Messiaen's music exposes both the fragility and the strength of faith by its evocation through art of what is beyond the threshold of death. Yet death had no sting, only a sweetness;[10] his music functioned as a rite of passage that was refigured throughout his life, and as an imaginative preparation for death and what would come after. Messiaen's music should also be thought of as an aid to bind human subjects to each other beyond the objective strictures of the world, and as illuminating an awareness of ourselves as contingent beings searching for forms of worldly emancipation.[11]

Messiaen often compared the effect of his music to looking at stained glass: light shines onto the viewer and they are dazzled, overwhelmed by the profusion of colours rather than merely entranced by specific figures in the glass.[12] This metaphor implies a transcendent form of experience, but also a deeply personal one – through Messiaen's music, it follows, God addresses each person both uniquely and collectively. Implicit here is the notion of God (as white light) as broken into its spectral components through the glass (dissonant, modernist music), thus saturating and breaking into that part of the onlooker below that is, as St Augustine defines God, 'more inward to me than my most inward part'.[13] Music, and especially modernist dissonance, becomes understood as a call to humanity that is cathartic and emancipatory, and that necessitates a response. Both God and humanity are left to seek and create meaning (and knowing) from the construction of this experience. This is the enduring legacy of Messiaen's music.

Messiaen's importance and his position in the twentieth century is defined not only by his contribution to French culture but by the way his music provided a potent and profound redescription of the understanding of the human condition as temporal, corporal and sensate, and as contingent but aspiring to the divine. Messiaen's music offered the opportunity for believers and non-believers alike to try to feel (not just to know intellectually) what the possibility for human transformation might be. His work created a space and capacity for others to experience what he himself felt: joy, bliss and the sweetness of God's redeeming presence expressed through the human medium of music. The excessive and sensuous qualities of Messiaen's music seem appropriate for the already cognitively overloaded nervous system of twentieth-century humanity. His music searches for new liminal, contemporary experiences, and it creates conditions for forms of religious and social participation through enjoyment and beauty. It exhorts humanity, as Loriod put it, to 'drink at the same source of light and joy that he [Messiaen] sang all of his life'.[14]

Messiaen was once asked why his music did not comment on the 'situation of modern man': alienated, facing the noise of the mechanized world and reckoning with historic and natural catastrophes. He countered that he was inspired not by 'frightful, sad, sorrowful, black, grey, ominous things' or 'suffering', but rather by 'light, joy, and glory': 'joy is a great deal more difficult to express than pain.'[15] It could be argued that Messiaen's music explored a rather narrow emotional bandwidth, but he did not ignore or forget human suffering; nor was it only a form of redirection or of fugitive theology through music, understood as fleeing from the real world.

Messiaen's music comes to fulfil a particular vision of art as a conduit to, and revelation of, God. For the listener, it suggests answers to unanswerable questions: Is there a God? What is God (made man) like? How should we respond to this mystery? Arguably, Messiaen's art did not provide definitive answers but rather further complicated and enriched the symbolism and thought around such issues. For those of the Christian faith, this usually represents a personal relationship with God and the belief, even 'certainty', as Messiaen put it, of absolute truths: that 'the invisible exists more than the visible' and that 'joy is beyond sorrow.'[16] For Christians, Christ is the son of God sent to redeem humanity from sin through his death. By his death and resurrection, humanity is also granted salvation and eternal life. Messiaen's music looks beyond the absolute sign of the empty cross to the resurrection of Christ and the promise of what this holds for humanity.[17] The absence of the divine as much as the desire for its presence have been inspirations for centuries of religious music. Messiaen belongs to and extends this tradition.

Messiaen's music acts as a deeply human response to religion and personal faith that embodies contemplation, exploration, supplication, praise, celebration, pathos and expiation as much as inspiration, aspiration and the search for affirmation beyond the ontological breach symbolized in the cross. In part it attempts to escape the cultural immanence of French Catholic thought and symphonic French organ music, for example, yet it amplifies and creates a wider diaspora for these loci. It imagines its own unique form of insight and desire for a connection to the divine as an act of private devotion and faith and as public witness. This form of renewal through art was the task that animated Messiaen's life.

To attempt this renewal, Messiaen employed the alterity, radicalism and complexity of modern music. Modernism was already a loaded term for Catholics; it concerned the eighty 'errors' for Catholics enumerated by Pope Pius IX in 1864 that represented a fear of new liberal ideologies and systems of thought. In 1907 Pope Pius X condemned it as 'delirium' and a 'monstrosity'. The works of Père Alfred Loisy were sanctioned, and he was excommunicated for his modernist reforming ideas on the Church and its attributes.[18] Modernism was understood to be undermining the Church's divine imprimatur and traditional authority. For philosophers, writers and artists inside and outside the Church it had exposed fissures of authority, belief and doctrine that represented a fragmentation of religion and a reinscription of religious coherence in other, secular systems of thought, which in turn generated equally powerful forces reintegrating traditional theological authority and doctrinal thought.[19] The critical task, then, is to examine the quilting points in these competing ideologies and to understand Messiaen's existence within a polarized modernist culture of both innovation and recovery in the wake of the First World War.

Messiaen can therefore already be understood as an epigonic figure: a modernist reinscribing and contributing to previous fields of debate, reviving faith and mystery through modern music and advocating for a

Christian ideology founded in a search for apocalyptic fulfilment. This recovery of Christianity is founded not merely in mourning (after the First World War) but in a form of eschatological need that is both a personal form of Catholicism, informed by a desire to affirm traditional faith, and to do so in a radical and contingent manner.[20] Blindness and insight coalesce here. Messiaen's form of musical modernism might seem to be synthetic and contingent – even contrived – and one that arguably speaks to the few rather than the many, but the sense of transparency, purposefulness and intention in his music allows the listener (wherever they are on the spiritual spectrum) to sense the force of the catalyst for his work through its musical realization.

The source of Messiaen's joy does not resist being found but is instead manifested throughout his music. It is not a refreighting of the positivist narratives of the Enlightenment,[21] nor is his music the puppet of religion. In this book, I seek to show that his work provides a unique, idealist yet universalist vision, a scaffolding and pathway to a form of knowledge of God. Messiaen's pieces are iconic and performative; they are generative and a continuing force in the world. In articulating its apocalyptic trajectory, his work embraces metaphysical, spiritual and emotional concerns: it acts as a deep-seated panacea to the ills of the world and as a reassurance that these are to be taken up, like ourselves, and transformed in a way that we do not yet know. Through engagement with this music, we are given to understand our place in this telos and to set ourselves on the pathway, like Messiaen, to an appreciation of the invisible within the realms of the visible.

It is tempting to think of Messiaen's art as affirmative, confirmatory of a religious status quo or a reconsigning of a familiar old story. In an interview, the French philosopher Alain Badiou stated: 'My own work is a search for a formalism adequate to the challenge of thinking the possibility of an effective break in the contexts of forms.'[22] Messiaen's work can be thought of in a similar vein within and outside an event horizon. In a private note from sometime between 1941 and 1944, he advised himself to 'Write unheard chords . . . write unheard melodies . . . write everywhere unheard rhythms', ideas that he would later impart to his students.[23] His life and work have a critical, constructed dimension. What is 'unheard' arises from a set of circumstances – a background in French Catholicism, his parents, his teachers – but it also emerges from a voracious capacity to understand and exceed his own environment, imagining new forms, parameters, resources, content and colours.

Messiaen's life was not that of a saint, or of someone extricated from worldly issues. It was informed by specific cultural and national references, by the enduring presence and troubles of family, by a realization of his own originality and mortality, by war, by invective, and by personal tragedy and illness. It was also configured by the public and private photographic images and aesthetic concepts that Messiaen and others created. In them, he ranges from the angelic, dreamy child to the bespectacled adolescent, to the intense and studious young man. There are family photographs and intimate portraits of Messiaen holding his baby, Pascal. In his apparel, there is a move from neck ties to open-necked shirts with large lapels after the Second World War; there is the beret for outdoors, and the notable change in glasses throughout his life. Later in his life, there is the man of brightly coloured shirts and a coloured scarf. There are the countless location shots (the touristic Messiaen), and photographs with composers, performers and his students.[24] There was also a natural change in Messiaen's appearance and voice as he grew older.

Recent biographies of Messiaen have detailed the composer's life through his diaries, but this book tells his story in a different way.[25] My approach here moves between biographical, musical, theological, philosophical, psychoanalytic and aesthetic thinking, and I have used sketches and archival material that often pose more questions than they answer. Crucially, this book details and evaluates the ways in which other musicians, including Messiaen's contemporaries and students, have assessed the composer.

This biography begins with an understanding of Messiaen's background. Chapter One discusses Messiaen's parents, teachers, intellectual inheritance and cultural environment. Chapter Two continues this through an examination of Messiaen's evolving life in the 1930s and his burgeoning originality. Chapter Three details Messiaen's life during the Second World War, his works and the controversy that they caused. The fourth chapter then examines Messiaen's engagement with Surrealism, as well as his students and the works he created immediately after the war.

Chapter Five focuses on the evolution of Messiaen's use of birdsong, contextualized in his life and works in the long 1950s, and Chapter Six examines the presence of and reciprocal interaction with certain students, especially Pierre Boulez (1925–2016), Iannis Xenakis (1922–2001) and Karlheinz Stockhausen (1928–2007). The penultimate chapter discusses the monumental works of the 1960s onwards, which culminated in the opera *Saint François d'Assise* (1975–83), and the final chapter examines Messiaen's late music and style, his renewed invention of his religious-modernist vision and his legacy.

1

On Beginnings

Olivier Eugène Prosper Charles Messiaen was born in Avignon, France, on 10 December 1908. Later in life, Messiaen wrote: 'I was born a believer.'[1] His parents were Pierre Léon Joseph Messiaen (1883–1957), a teacher and translator, and his wife, the poet Cécile Anne Marie Antionette Sauvage (1883–1927). Both had typically Catholic educations.[2]

Cécile Sauvage died prematurely of tuberculosis just as Messiaen's career was commencing. The last part of her collection of poems *Tandis que la terre tourne* (As the World Turns) is a cycle of poems titled *L'Âme en bourgeon* (The Burgeoning Soul). These twenty poems were addressed to and about her unborn male child.[3] They are full of joy, anguish and euphoria but above all a sense of the impending loss of a close maternal bond. *Tandis que la terre tourne* was published in 1910 (five hundred copies were printed but fewer than fifty were sold)[4] and re-edited posthumously in 1929 by her husband. The 1929 edition of *L'Âme en bourgeon* was dedicated to Messiaen, and eight of the poems were set to music in 1937 by the violinist and composer Louise-Justine Delbos, known as Claire (1906–1959), Messiaen's first wife. His sense of predestination to be a composer and his religious-artistic mission owed much to his mother, whom he described as 'guiding my hand or my spirit'.[5] In the preface to the 1987 edition of these poems, Messiaen stated: 'I am very proud of this book. More than all of the concerts which have marked out my career as a composer of music, *L'Âme en bourgeon* is the most beautiful and glorious title, because it was for me, during 1908, as my mother waited for me.'[6] He continued:

> Psychoanalysis and modern medicine tell us that the embryo already possesses all future characteristics. But more, he [the

> child] receives from his Mother an exterior exhalation, which instructs and prepares him, and renders the tragedy of birth less difficult. I am persuaded that the lyrical expectation of *L'Âme en bourgeon* had influenced my career and my destiny. The surprise is that my Mother never doubted for an instant what I would be: a boy, an artist, and a musician (the only one in my family!).[7]

In the following lines from Sauvage's poem 'Tu tettes le lait pur...' ('You suck the pure milk...', poem VI) there is a premonition of the colours and birds that would feature in Messiaen's music, including, as he noted in 1987, his transcriptions of Japanese birdsong:

> The plot of brightness there, is the window
> Where the sun seats his globe of sunbeams
> There all the Orient sings in my being
> With its blue birds, with its butterflies.[8]

Messiaen made an LP vinyl disc of organ improvisations on 3 June 1977, which included Sauvage's poems recited by the French actress Gisèle Casadesus. He stated his desire to

> surround them, to accompany them, and to prolong them through an improvised musical commentary . . . I wanted to be discrete, the most discrete possible, that one should hear me without hearing me, and, in the end, to leave the poems in their light and darkness, adding only here and there my humble colours. A man may not say these things in a high voice: that is the property of women, and Cécile Sauvage who had the knowledge to say it. My only excuse was to have been the awaited child . . . But the musician of 1978 remembers himself always to have been the infant of 1908, and it is his purest pride to have inspired *L'Âme en bourgeon*.[9]

These lines from Sauvage's 'Enfant, pâle embryon' ('Child, pale embryo', poem V) addressed to the unborn composer, were important to Messiaen:

> I am around you like a green almond
> Which closes its husk around the milky little almond
> Like the soft pod with cotton-like folds
> Covering the childlike silky seed.[10]

He read this when he was eight years old and proclaimed: 'Mother . . . you are also a poet like Shakespeare. Like him you make the suns, the planets, the ants and the skeletons that create fear. I prefer all that makes fear.'[11] He may not have understood much of her poetry, but he stated that it 'gave me a sense of wonder'.[12] Other prophetic lines became meaningful to the adult Messiaen, such as 'I suffer from a distant unknown music,' and a strange observation of his birth made by his mother: 'He is born, I have lost my young beloved.'[13] Messiaen stated: 'This is quite incredible. I don't think that most mothers feel like this.'[14] He also commented that 'Birth, a terrible separation, leaves the mother withdrawn into herself, and the child almost alone, having forgotten everything.'[15] At the beginning of his diary each year, the composer recopied this verse by Sauvage:

> I shall love you more [from] under the earth
> I shall love you with all my bones
> As here below I was your Mother
> I will watch over your rest.[16]

Messiaen was with his mother when she died in a hotel in Montlhéry, near Paris.[17] She died at around 4.35 a.m. on Friday, 26 August 1927. According to Pierre, she had had a 'great cold' and 'pulmonary congestion . . . At 2 a.m., I asked her: "Do you recognize us?" She smiled, and said, "Yes, it is Pierre, Olivier and Alain."'[18]

Cécile was one of three children (including André and Germaine). Her father, Gal Prosper Sauvage (1847–1915), was a history and geography schoolteacher and had been posted to Digne in Alpes-de-Hautes-Provence. He married her mother, Marie Eugénie Jolivet (1857–1936), on 4 October 1882 in Avignon.[19] Through her study of poetry at the Lycée and the encouragement of Frédéric Mistral, the winner of the Nobel Prize in Literature in 1904, Cécile submitted a poem in May 1905 to the *Revue forézienne*, a literary journal in Saint-Étienne, just southwest of Lyon. Pierre Messiaen was the editor of the journal, and he described Sauvage's poem 'Les trois muses', published in October 1905, as 'swarming with realism and the quivering of the countryside'.[20]

Pierre Messiaen was born near Wervicq-Sud, north of Lille, but his family of seven children – three boys, including Paul and Léon, who both died in the First World War, and four girls, Marie, Marthe, Madeleine and Agnès – moved in 1900 to the village of Fuligny, east of Troyes, where his parents, Charles Adolphe Messiaen (1841–1904) and Marie Flavie

Cécile Sauvage (Messiaen's mother, bottom right), her sister and brother (Germaine, seated and André, standing) and their parents (immediately behind), with extended family and friends(?) in 1889.

Demytteneare (1853–1932), became tenant farmers.[21] Pierre became a student in law and letters at the Catholic University of Lille, obtaining his *license* (bachelor's degree) in 1903.[22] He would later recall times at Fuligny in this 'charming country house . . . holidays filled with sunshine and siestas beneath the trees . . . intellectual work with the large windows open and the perfume of roses and the songs of warblers . . . Olivier studying Beethoven and Chopin on old Erard piano . . . and rereading the *Georgics* [Virgil] with my son Alain'.[23]

Through their correspondence Pierre discovered that he shared similar origins to Cécile through his maternal grandparents. They met for the first time over three days in Lyon in November 1905. Pierre was undertaking an *agrégation* (a competitive teacher's exam)at the University of Lyon at the time, an examination that gave him the right to teach his subject – English. He described her as 'petite [*menue*], lively, pink, with gold-brown eyes that are exquisitely soft, black hair with bluish reflections; her large, rounded forehead made up half of her face; her hands were very little, and her little feet were light like those of a silent cat,' and he affectionately described her easy sense of humour.[24] They shared an admiration for French poetry and Shakespeare.[25] In July 1906, Pierre spent around fifteen days in Digne with the Sauvage family, and visited again at Christmas that year.[26] Further correspondence confirmed their prospective union, and they were married on 9 September 1907 in the Église des Sieyes in Digne.[27] The couple settled in Avignon a month later, and Pierre began his military service. Cécile became pregnant and wrote a letter to Pierre:

> It seems to me that I am helping to form a tiny planet and that I am kneading the frail globe from it . . . I dream of a young day full of flutes, wakened bees, of dew, coloured, and agitated within me. If you only knew what spring freshness and what youthfulness this burgeoning soul [*cette âme en bourgeon*] makes in my heart![28]

Pierre Messiaen and Cécile Sauvage.

Olivier Messiaen at one year old on his mother's knees.

In a fragment written in Avignon (August–September 1908), she writes of '*L'Âme en bourgeon* [Messiaen himself] whose little heart continues to beat. It is above all at twilight that it manifests itself. Tonight, his tic-toc is a little quicker, this little gentleman who makes a fist inside. This makes me laugh.'[29]

After his birth, Olivier was baptized on Christmas Day in the medieval Église Saint-Didier.[30] He is sometimes called 'Olivette' in his mother's letters,[31] and their contents reveal the intimacy of her relationship with him. On 2 February 1909, Sauvage wrote to Pierre, whom she refers to as 'mon cher Pierrot' and 'Pio' (a diminutive used by Messiaen later in his diaries):

> For Olivier, I am searching for verses with new and soft rhythms which express the little rage of maternal tenderness. It's amusing [*drôle*]; I need to cuddle [*cajoler*] this little one in my head. The

Messiaen family (from left to right): Pierre, Olivier, Cécile and Alain.

> more I think about him, the more I love him. I just went to see him; he sleeps from midday most peacefully . . . This morning, he smiled at me, without me claiming his smile.[32]

On 4 February 1909, she wrote: 'Olivier . . . his smile is divine . . . it is like the first hesitant brightness of his little luminous soul.' When she ran her hand through his hair, 'he purrs like a little cat.'[33]

The family moved to Ambert (Puy-de-Dôme) in 1909, where Pierre was appointed as an English teacher, and then to Grenoble (Auvergne-Rhône-Alpes, l'Isère) in 1912, the city of Cécile's maternal grandparents and where her brother André, whom Cécile and Olivier nicknamed 'frangin', was a surgeon.[34] Sauvage returned to Ambert to give birth to Messiaen's younger brother, Alain André Prosper Messiaen, who was born on 30 August 1912, and then she returned to Grenoble. In a letter to Pierre of 12 October 1912 she described him as 'becoming more and more beautiful . . . He makes the most wonderful smiles; he is wise, wiser than Olivier when he was little. Olivier seems to love his little brother, but when he cries, Monsieur covers his ears. A bientôt.'[35] Talking to Alain later, she told him that even in her own childhood, 'You were in my heart.'[36] Alain became a poet whose work showed a wide interest in modern music especially, and a profound sense of Catholic spirituality.[37] He died on 10 May 1990, two years before his older brother.

Pierre passed his *agrégation* and was appointed to a school in Nantes between 1913 and 1914, where the family moved. In January 1913, Cécile published her second book of poetry, *Le Vallon* (1909–13), which included a verse about a field lark much treasured later by Olivier Messiaen.[38] Sauvage also began her poetry collection *Primavère* in summer 1911, presented as unfinished in the 1929 edition of *L'Âme en bourgeon*.[39] Pierre

Olivier Messiaen, Alain Messiaen and Cécile Sauvage.

described this poetic cycle as the 'summa of Cécile Sauvage's work – perhaps the masterpiece of feminine poetry'.[40]

Sauvage's poetry was much encouraged by Jean de Gourmont (1877–1928), the younger brother of the poet Remy (1858–1915), one of the founders of Mercure de France. Jean was an editor at the *Revue forézienne*. He published Sauvage's first two collections of poems, *Vers l'azur* and *L'Âme universelle*, in 1906.[41] Sauvage met Jean in Paris shortly before the First World War, and a relationship between them began in spring 1914 (or possibly earlier), at a time when she was in Nantes and could visit him in Paris.[42] Her cycle of poems *Le Vallon* was dedicated to him and published by Mercure de France in 1913, but Pierre removed this dedication for the 1929 collection of her poems and replaced it with the name of his son Alain (the dedication to de Gourmont was restored in the 2020 edition).[43] Sauvage was separated from de Gourmont because of the war; she and her two children lived in Grenoble at her brother André's house (from summer 1914 to autumn 1918), leaving Pierre in Nantes before he was mobilized in the First World War as a 'soldier-interpreter' for the British army.[44] In Grenoble, Sauvage wrote two volumes of love poetry, *L'Etreinte mystique* and *Prières* (1915), and then a drama in poetry (in two parts) *Hémérocalle et la guerre* and *Hémérocalle et l'amour* (1916–19), that enshrined her love for de Gourmont.[45]

Olivier Messiaen later confided to his second wife, Yvonne Loriod, that he was brought up by his maternal grandmother during the war, rather than by his troubled mother.[46] He would regularly act out plays by Shakespeare for his younger brother at this time, making costumes and scenery and even improvising some music on the piano: 'Shakespeare formed me; it is strange, but it is like that.'[47] Through this experience of fantasy, enchantment and terror (also derived from the fairy tales of Charles Perrault and Madame d'Aulnoy, loved by his mother) he discovered the fantastical and supernatural, and later connected this to the 'real' in Christianity.[48] Messiaen's intellectual development can also be understood as a form of psychic defence mechanism (repression, denial, displacement, sublimation and introjection, for example) that can in hindsight be attributed to his experience of his mother's personal issues and his somewhat cloistered environment during the war.

Messiaen was certainly a curious and gifted child, and his burgeoning artistic and intellectual needs were satisfied by his mother. There was an old upright piano in the family home, and Messiaen taught himself to play. His mother read books and poems to him (including her own), notably Tennyson's Arthurian poem 'The Lady of Shallot' (1832), which became the title of Messiaen's first acknowledged composition for piano, *La Dame de Shalott* (1917). Cécile referred to Messiaen as 'Mon beau chevalier rose' (my beautiful pink cavalier).[49] She also read opera stories to Messiaen. Aged seven and a half, he sat on a bench in the Jardin de Ville in Grenoble with a copy of Gluck's opera *Orfeo ed Euridice* (1762), bought from the music shop Deshairs, and discovered that he could hear the music he was seeing: 'So, I was a musician.'[50]

For Christmas 1916, Messiaen asked for Gluck's *Alceste* and Mozart's *Don Giovanni*. Opera scores of Berlioz and Wagner followed, Debussy's *Estampes*, Ravel's *Gaspard de la nuit* and Grieg's *Peer Gynt*, which gave Messiaen a love of melody. These works remained in his consciousness as a composer and teacher.[51] They may well have been too difficult for the young Messiaen to understand, but an investment and belief in him had been made. Pierre noted that 'Olivier had the gift of music: he sightread at the piano everything that fell into his hands, and with his youthful [*fraîche*] little voice [he sang and played] entire opera scores,' and he observed that both boys had a 'true passion for [church] ceremonies and religious music'.[52] Cécile also understood Messiaen's burgeoning interest in religion. As with his budding artistic vocation, inspiration, affirmation and confirmation did not require full comprehension, but an artistic trajectory had been created, with sage support and guidance.

Cécile, Olivier and Alain moved to Nantes in 1918, where Olivier received professional tuition from, among others, Jean de Gibon (1873–1952), a harmony teacher at the Conservatoire de Nantes.[53] He advised Messiaen's parents to enrol Messiaen at the Conservatoire de Paris.[54] Pierre, having finished his military service, was reunited with Cécile and Alain in Nantes and began a teaching post at the Lycée Clemenceau. Messiaen was confirmed in the Catholic faith on 22 June 1919, and he received his first solemn communion. Messiaen's parents followed de Gibon's advice, and Olivier went to Paris in September 1919, the beginning of the school year.

As a tenth birthday or Christmas present, de Gibon gave Messiaen the vocal score of Claude Debussy's *Pelléas et Mélisande* (1893–1902), an opera that Messiaen later said 'decided my vocation as a composer'.[55] This opera was important to Messiaen likely because of its engagement with darkness and light, its fatalistic, Gothic love story (perhaps something that Messiaen saw mirrored in his own parents' turbulent relationship), its use of silence, its harmonic narrative and flux, its poetry (Debussy changed little of the Belgian Symbolist playright Maurice Maeterlinck's text, first performed in 1893 in Paris, and attended by Debussy), its metric subtlety and its sense of rhythmic and formal control and liberty.

In July 1919, Messiaen's father was appointed to the Lycée Charlemagne in the Marais district of Paris, a school with a distinguished history of directors and alumni, and then at the Institut Catholique from 1929 to 1956.[56] The Messiaen family lived initially on the Quai de Bourbon and then at 67 rue Rambuteau, at the intersection with rue Quincampoix in Les Halles, from 1919 to 1929. This house was, by Messiaen's account, cramped and troublesome for the family.[57] From this period came Messiaen's piano prelude *La Tristesse d'un grand ciel blanc* (1921), which he later described as 'assez moderne' and Stravinskian. This was not a religious work, and he commented that, despite his desire, he was not capable at this stage of expressing his religious beliefs in the way that he wanted.[58]

From 1925, Messiaen's mother showed signs of the tuberculosis to which she would succumb on 26 August 1927, a disease that Messiaen may also have been afflicted with in his youth.[59] In a letter written two days after her death to his future second wife, Marguerite Élie, Pierre described a letter written to Cécile's brother André at the end of April 1927, 'where I told him that I was exasperated by this [Sauvage's] suicidal neurasthenia, both for herself and for the children'. He also noted that Sauvage lived for the 'last six years of her life in a room that was never aired, never lit, never cleaned'.[60] Before her death, Sauvage wrote *Aimer après la mort* (1925–6), a lyric drama in 1,750 verses concerning 'angel musicians, whose marvellous melodies were the expression of divine happiness', perhaps as a panacea to her ailing relationship with her husband as much as a premonition of her own declining health. It also acts as evidence of a writing where eroticism is allied to mysticism in the wake of her failed relationship with Jean de Gourmont, who married Suzanne Baltasar (1890–1941) in February 1920 and who died barely six months after Cécile on 19 February 1928.[61]

Pierre Messiaen married Marguerite Élie in 1929, and she became, in Pierre's words, 'a second mother' to the children. They moved, with Alain, to 44 quai Henri IV, near the Île Saint-Louis.[62] Their first child, Charles-Marie, was named after Pierre's parents and became an agronomist and author. He was born on 8 February 1930 and died on 9 November 2020. Marguerite's presence rectified what Pierre saw as a house 'in grand disarray' after Cécile's death, bringing into it 'a second springtime'.[63] They then had another child, Jacques, who died in infancy on 21 July 1934.[64]

Messiaen rarely wrote about – and never spoke of – his half-brothers, but Pierre makes it clear that, although adolescence had its difficulties for the older boys, the new family regime was a happy one. Messiaen paid tribute to his mother in *Le Banquet céleste* (1927), *La Mort du nombre* (1930) and *Le Tombeau resplendissant* (1931), all works that exercise a faith in reconciliation after death.[65] Messiaen only discovered Sauvage's poems, written under the influence of her relationship with Jean, in September 1972 (her sister, Germaine Tatin-Sauvage, had kept them a secret until the year of her death in 1972).[66] He later referred to his mother's mental state, describing her as carrying 'a sort of hidden despair within her . . . she was unhappy'.[67] In 1925 Sauvage wrote: 'The beloved flees, not through fear, but to suddenly estimate in solitude the weight of his joy . . . The true heart speaks a language more grey than tears. Tenderness is more enveloping than love.'[68] Pierre made it clear that he should have done more to vanquish his wife's sense of 'melancholy' and her 'solitary and mute hopelessness that my children have kept as a very heavy memory when they speak rarely of their mother'. He stated: 'Each

Messiaen's extended family: Pierre Messiaen, holding Pascal, Marguerite Élie and Charles-Marie Messiaen.

Classe de Georges Falkenberg, 1919
(Messiaen in middle row, second from the right).

man must carry his cross. My great sadness is that, for the being that I loved and admired the most, I did not know what inevitable fate crushed her.'[69] Yet, in 1927, just before her death in Paris, Sauvage spoke of her husband with great affection: 'Pierre has always been for me goodness itself, because of my small gift of poetry. He was my companion ... At the moment of his death, he shall have much sunlight. It is necessary to leave believing in love that is like light.'[70]

In 1919 Messiaen began at the Conservatoire de Paris (then on the rue de Madrid, not where it is today at Porte de Pantin) as an *auditeur* before registering as a student in October 1920.[71] The composer Gabriel Fauré (1845–1924) was the director at this time, but retired in 1920. At the Conservatoire Messiaen learned his métier with Georges Falkenberg (1854–1940) (piano) and Jean Gallon (1878–1959) (harmony), the latter of whom was described by Messiaen's friend the composer Henri Dutilleux (1916–2013) as 'one of the most eminent pedagogues ever called to the Conservatoire'.[72] Messiaen also privately studied with Noël Gallon (1891–1966) (counterpoint and fugue), who had a quasi-filial relationship to the composer.[73]

Messiaen was schooled in nineteenth-century and *fin-de-siècle* French music theory. He owned theory books, including those by Théodore Dubois (1837–1924), Charles Lenepveu (1840–1910), Auguste Chapuis (1858–1933), Paul Fauchet (1881–1937), Henri Reber (1807–1880) and the Gallon brothers.[74] His other teachers at the Conservatoire were Georges Caussade (1873–1936) (fugue), César Abel Estyle (1877–1961) (piano accompaniment) and Marcel Dupré (1886–1971), with whom he studied organ repertoire, plainchant, improvisation and registration from 1927. He studied the timpani (Joseph Baggers, 1858–1938), history of music and Greek metrics (Maurice Emmanuel, 1862–1938) and composition, initially with Charles-Marie Widor (1844–1937) in 1926–7 and then with Paul Dukas (1865–1935) from 1927 to 1930.[75] This was a rich, varied and rigorous musical education.

Messiaen later described Dupré as the 'Liszt of the organ'.[76] Dupré played the complete organ works of Bach in ten concerts (from memory) at the Conservatoire de Paris in 1920 and then at the Trocadéro in 1921, and gave over 2,000 recitals worldwide in his lifetime. Dupré's music went beyond César Franck (1822–1890) and Widor in rejuvenating counterpoint and virtuoso pedal technique in French organ music. His compositions, of a refined yet extreme chromaticism, remained tonal and were dominated by the organ.

Dupré was a famous exponent of improvisation, and he specialized in symphonic and contrapuntal forms. His 1925 treatise on improvisation

Messiaen, detail from p. 26.

was well known to Messiaen and included discussions of the acciaccatura technique of harmonization – chords that vertically inculcate neighbouring pitches into the main functional pitches.[77] It also included seven-note Carnatic or Hindu modes and interversions – musical cells or 'closed circuits', as the composer Jean Barraqué (1928–1973) called them, in which a discrete musical cell could be varied.[78] Even before Dupré's tuition, Messiaen had a particularly good understanding of fugue. His exam fugue from 1926 was written on a subject created by the director of the Conservatoire, Henri Rabaud (1873–1949), in a closed room between 6 a.m. and 11.30 p.m., 'without access to an instrument or any didactic work'.[79] His fugue shows a thorough understanding of fugal form and counterpoint: the subject is employed in contrary motion, in fragmentation, stretto, canon, augmentation and a pedal point is employed at the end.[80]

Messiaen began to play the organ in 1927, committing Bach's Fantasia in C minor (possibly BWV 562) to memory in eight days, to Dupré's surprise.[81] Dupré stated in 1941 that 'in sixteen years, two of my students should have had their First prize in the first year: Messiaen and that one [pointing to Jeanne Demessieux (1921–1968)].'[82] Dupré's comments about Messiaen were not always so laudatory. In Demessieux's diary for 16 April 1943, she noted that Dupré stated: 'I've taught a few capable of managing at Paris's grand churches, nothing more. No, I'm telling you; and I put Messiaen in the same category. He tricks people with false ideas.'[83] At the Conservatoire, Dupré encouraged Messiaen to improvise on Greek

Marcel Dupré's Classe d'Orgue in 1929. Seated (left to right): Joseph Gilles, Gaston Litaize and Messiaen; behind (left to right): Léon Levif, Tommy Desserre, Jean Langlais, Henri Cabié, Rachel Brunschwig; Henriette Roget (seated at the organ); seated on the right: Marcel Dupré.

rhythms and to study plainchant. In 1959 he reflected that Messiaen's 'musical language was already completely formed', but Messiaen believed that after his conservatoire education, with the exception of Emmanuel's teaching, he knew very little about rhythm, and it was at this time that he discovered the Hindu rhythms, including the 120 *deśītālas* of the thirteenth-century Indian musicologist Śārṅgadeva (1175–1247), through an unnamed Hindu friend.[84] Despite his privately expressed reservations about Messiaen's work, Dupré also stated (in 1959) that he had 'the interior pride to be the first to give Messiaen confidence in himself as a composer'.[85] It should also be noted that, like Dupré, when Messiaen improvised there was no extraneous or flamboyant movement. Even in strident or violent improvisations, his hands and body were calm and rigorously controlled, directed by the mind.[86]

Messiaen developed a keen interest in modes and 'kept little scraps of paper in his pocket on which he wrote harmonic formulas, modal characteristics and progressions, some of which he collected from the works of Debussy'.[87] From Dupré also perhaps came Messiaen's practice of staying silent about his music until it was completely finished.[88] Dupré described his métier in a missive to his student Rolande Falcinelli (1920–2006), an organist, improviser and pedagogue:

> Principles of my vocation:
> Work:
> Carry your work everywhere.
> In a few minutes, one can advance several steps.
> All realizations of projects to be taken to the end: one at a time.
> . . .
> Think through writing, all ideas immediately noted and ordered.
> . . .
> Write large drafts.
> Take time to order your work.
> Never ask to borrow.
> Work in solitude.
> Destroy all unnecessary papers, drafts, duplicates.
> Never let a piece of information, any information, or idea be lost.
> . . .
> Read by annotating, and clearly summarize the essence.

He later wrote other pieces of sage advice : 'Never give away a manuscript. To publishers, copies. Nothing to libraries. Keep and file all manuscripts. Respond to mail promptly, briefly . . . All great work is born of necessity,' and as an 'aim' of music he advocated for 'Eloquence: (it is to have the conviction that one proclaims a truth). In music: combine inner emotion with the discipline of rhythm.'[89]

Messiaen shared this meticulous approach to composition. When travelling, he took other composers' scores with him alongside his own work; he worked in solitude, wrote drafts and ordered and classified his thoughts through teaching and pedagogical treatises. He did not ask to borrow material from other composers for his music but took material freely from others for his own creative development, and was therefore 'affected by the phenomenon of mimeticism' in his own way, as the French composer Henri Dutilleux politely observed.[90] From 1949, he kept his final manuscripts in a bank vault, but he did not destroy all his sketch material or 'work by accident'.[91] Messiaen made several drafts of his compositions, systematically marking their progress; he marked final drafts 'relu – bien' (reread – good). Like Dupré's scores (from his *Sept pièces* for organ, op. 27 (1931), onwards) Messiaen included performance indications, fingerings, pedallings (although most often not in the same detail as Dupré) and, for some pieces, metronome marks.[92]

At the Conservatoire, Dupré's organ class lasted for two hours (1.30 to 3.30 p.m.), three times a week: Monday would cover improvised fugue; Wednesday, improvisation on a free theme; and Friday, performance of repertoire.[93] Messiaen later deputized for Dupré's class on occasion, and his organ music was written with Dupré's 'rules' on articulation and 'absolute legato' in mind. His fellow students in Dupré's class included two blind organist-composers, Gaston Litaize (1909–1991) and Jean Langlais (1907–1991), the latter of whom would be a guest at Messiaen's wedding to his first wife, Claire Delbos, on 22 June 1932 (just as Messiaen would be a guest at Langlais' first wedding on 3 December 1931). Messiaen regularly shared coffee with cream or hot chocolates and croissants with them after class at the café 'les Capitales', and they remained lifelong friends.[94] Langlais described Messiaen as being 'like a brother, a very dear Brother', and Messiaen helped him with orchestration for many years, reading scores to him every Wednesday from 5 to 9 p.m.[95]

Messiaen's history teacher was Maurice Emmanuel, a composer and historian who had worked as a choral director with Charles Tournemire (1870–1939) and who had written an extensive scholarly chapter on Greek music.[96] He was well known for incorporating Greek rhythms and Hindu modes into his music, and these compositions, alongside his *Histoire de la langue musical* (1911), were admired by Messiaen. Emmanuel's teaching on modal theory 'sharpened' Messiaen's awareness of the potential of mode.[97] Messiaen particularly appreciated Emmanuel's *Trente chansons bourguignonnes du pays de Beaune* (1913), whose modal 'eternal freshness' he heard in 1932.[98] In a letter to the physician, writer and historian Pierre Balme (1882–1963) of 10 January 1932, Emmanuel revealed how highly he thought of Messiaen:

> Messiaen? Parbleu! A young musician of the *first order*! Seven *premier prix* at the Conservatoire (one of my best students) [piano (keyboard harmony) – 1924, fugue – 1926, accompaniment – 1927, organ and improvisation – 1928, history of music – 1929, composition – 1930].[99] With this, he has an elite soul – the manner of a saint. Organist at La Trinité. Make him come and give a recital at the cathedral. It will be amazing.[100]

Messiaen and Jehan Alain (1911–1940), described by Messiaen's brother as 'two visionaries' who 'connected east and west',[101] along with Maurice Duruflé (1902–1986) and Langlais all studied composition with Paul Dukas, a highly cultured man who wrote fluently on other composers, but who was highly critical of his own classicist music and published relatively few works. Messiaen admired Dukas' colourful Symbolist opera *Ariane et Barbe-bleue* (1907).[102] Dupré, Emmanuel and Dukas were modernist, classicist composers (not to be confused with neo-classicism) for whom formal clarity, transparency, purposefulness and the renovation of tradition were paramount. These figures were among Messiaen's formative mentors, but his contemporary environment was also important.

France was – and still is – politically, administratively, commercially and artistically centred on Paris, 'the capital of the Nineteenth century', as the literary critic Walter Benjamin put it. The Paris that Messiaen knew as a student was transformed between 1853 and 1870 through grand central boulevards and architecture, much of which was created by Baron Haussmann (1809–1891), who also constructed new public spaces, railway terminuses (the Gare du Nord and the Gare de l'Est), churches (including Messiaen's church, the Église de la Sainte-Trinité), theatres, sewers, fountains, kiosks and aqueducts, and reshaped the city into twenty arrondissements (from the previous twelve), increasing its central population.[103]

Paul Dukas (left) with Claude Arrieu and Messiaen (seated), and Maurice Duruflé standing (between them).

The last wing of the Louvre was completed in 1857, the Opéra Garnier was opened in 1875 (including a two-manual organ by the great French builder Aristide Cavaillé-Coll (1811–1899)), and two major Paris Métro lines launched in 1910 and 1911, with stations designed by Hector Guimard in his famous *style moderne*, with others under construction. Paris was an emerging modernist metropolis, with a consciousness of itself as a world capital.

Paris embodied a sense of possibility; it was a place where old and new could coexist, where new ideas could find audiences and acceptance, and where foreign traditions and thought could be absorbed into French culture, partly through the legacy of French colonialism. These features attracted many artists to the city, especially between the two world wars – the time of Messiaen's education. The avant-garde flourished in the stability and permissiveness of post-First World War culture, a period known as *Les années folles* (following *La belle époque* from 1871 to 1914).[104]

This was the Paris where émigrés such as Igor Stravinsky, Sergei Prokofiev, Bohuslav Martinů, George Enescu, Aleksander Tansman, Amedeo Modigliani, Marc Chagall, Artur Rubinstein, Cole Porter and Sidney Bechet worked and lived, along with American writers such as Ernest Hemingway, F. Scott Fitzgerald and Gertrude Stein and the Irish writers Samuel Beckett and James Joyce. It embraced new fashion, a thriving jazz scene (including Josephine Baker and 'La Revue Nègre'), a flourishing café culture and vibrant nightclubs. European artists such as Salvador Dalí, Joan Miró and Piet Mondrian also lived there. It was an age of 'isms': notably Cubism (Georges Braque and Pablo Picasso), Dadaism (Tristan Tzara and Marcel Duchamp) and Surrealism (Guillaume Apollinaire and André Breton). The Ballets Russes and Ballets Suédois flourished, and the age was marked by the birth of radio and a burgeoning mass-print media.

Paris was the location of world fairs and exhibitions in 1878, 1889 (when the Eiffel Tower was inaugurated and Debussy heard gamelan music) and 1900. At the 1931 Paris exhibition Messiaen heard Balinese music,[105] and for the 1937 Exposition Internationale des Arts et Techniques dans la Vie Moderne he wrote *Fêtes des belles eaux* for six ondes Martenots (premiered on 25 July 1937 and choreographed with displays of water and light) for the *son et lumière* spectacles. Paris was a hub of gastronomy, shopping, philosophy, poetry, painting, science, decorative arts, cinema and silent film music (by 1920 there were more than two hundred cinemas in Paris).[106] It was a crucible for new forms of literature, from the exploits of Fantômas and Gaston Leroux's *Le Fantôme de l'Opéra* (1908–10), which mixed journalism, fact and fiction, to Marcel Proust's *À la recherche du temps perdu* (1913–27) and the philosophy of 'durée', or introspective personal time, of Henri Bergson, one of the philosophers in Messiaen's intellectual pantheon.[107] Paris was also a place where social and artistic hedonism manifested through controlled anarchy, iconoclasm and refinement could coexist.

This environment offered the young Messiaen access to a panoply of artistic and musical styles, including those of Stravinsky and Les Six (a group of six composers briefly associated with neo-classicism but who sometimes collaborated and forged their own musical pathways), but also gave him exposure to different generations of composers. An older guard was present: Camille Saint-Saëns, Widor and Fauré (all organists), Vincent d'Indy (at the Schola Cantorum, founded in 1892, with its regeneration of Palestrina, Monteverdi, Rameau and Gregorian chant), Louis Vierne and Charles Koechlin, and the legacy of Wagner in various French operas (including Debussy's *Pelléas et Mélisande*), as well as Jean Cocteau's call to regenerate and emancipate French music from Germanic influences in *Le Coq et l'arlequin* (1918). The generation of Debussy and Ravel included other fascinating composers such as André Caplet, J.J.A. Roger-Ducasse, Florent Schmitt and Tournemire, and there were more radical voices to be found in Erik Satie, Edgard Varèse and the American pianist-composer George Antheil, the self-styled 'bad boy of music'.[108]

This was a fertile cultural landscape. Messiaen's fellow student Elsa Barraine (1910–1999) noted his single-minded determination and his capacity for hard work, as well as his religious fervour.[109] As a young organist-composer of the 1930s, he might be thought of as another iconoclast, belonging above all to a kind of subculture centred around the organ in Paris. But he can also be understood as a product of religious, political and modernist tectonic plates that had already shifted in France, who yet transcended this organ cult, for instance, and enriched it by revalorizing and enriching the ideology of mysticism in art.[110]

The polarization of the progressive left and the nationalist Catholic right flavoured *belle époque* France in the wake of the French defeat in the Franco-Prussian War (1870–71), rising tides of nationalism and the Dreyfus affair (1894–1906), and it led to the legal separation of Church and State enacted on 9 December 1905, which instituted new aspects of secularism affecting churches and society (*la laïcité* has had a long history in France).[111] This period was also noted for Symbolism, decadence (and occultism) and the Catholic literature of writers such as Jules Barbey-d'Aurevilly and Joris-Karl Huysmans. Joséphin Péladan's Rose + Croix salons, held from 1892 to 1897, sought to provide cathartic images of a supra-Catholic religious idealism, elevating his ideal of beauty and promoting a form of redemption through art. For Péladan, Bayreuth (associated with Wagner's music) provided one artistic 'mecca', but another was the monastery of Solesmes (about 240 kilometres (150 mi.) southwest of Paris). The monks of Solesmes had gained the papal right from Pope Leo XIII to print plainchant, and Dom Guéranger (1805–1875), among others, undertook the task of researching, restoring and interpreting Gregorian chant from manuscripts. This palaeographic work was supported by a 'Motu proprio' from Pope Pius X on church music on 22 November 1903, in which Gregorian chant was instituted as 'the Chant proper to the Roman church'. As the 'supreme model for sacred music', Pius recommended that it 'be cultivated by all with diligence and love'.[112]

The monks of Solesmes restored their monastery in the nineteenth century and adjusted plainchant so that it could impart a sense of timelessness through its metrical fluidity.[113] Plainchant became an aesthetic device that spoke of the anonymous patristic artisans of the Church, while providing material for modernist compositional deformation.

The first wife of Charles Tournemire, Alice Georgina Taylor (1870–1919), was Péladan's wife's sister. He described Péladan in 1930 as 'one of the most passionate and heroic spirits I have known'.[114] Tournemire sought out Péladan prior to composing his opera *Nittetis* (1907): 'It was in this époque', Tournemire stated, 'that my mind was truly furnished with a mystical ideal enveloping the next thirty years of my production that began to develop in a continual ascension in my brain and heart.'[115] In an interview from 7 April 1999, Maurice Duruflé's second wife, Marie-Madeleine Duruflé-Chevalier (1921–1999), testified that her husband 'truly had a Gregorian soul'. She attributed this to the 'spirit of Tournemire', whose 'improvisations were the most celebrated of his time' and which had imbibed the 'traditions of Solesmes'.[116] Duruflé described Tournemire's liturgical improvisations as 'poetic, picturesque, capricious but passionate, tumultuous, unchained then restrained, mystical, ecstatic',[117] and he noted that 'the Gregorian book was always on the music desk before his eyes. He used exclusively liturgical themes as the source of his improvisations, which are always impregnated with profound religious sentiment.'[118]

Catholic culture and Tournemire's art had a profound influence upon Messiaen. It is unclear how Messiaen came to meet Tournemire; it is likely that he had simply heard of his reputation as an improviser and made a pilgrimage to Sainte-Clotilde, in the 7th arrondissement. This is a common thing for organists to do even today, and in the 1920s one could also hear Widor at Saint-Sulpice, Eugène Gigout at Saint-Augustin, Henri Mulet at Saint-Phillippe-du-Roule, Vierne at Notre-Dame and Henri Dallier at La Madeleine. Messiaen did not have formal lessons with Tournemire, but he and his lifelong friend Jean-Yves Daniel-Lesur (1908–2002), who also set some of Sauvage's poems to music in the 1930s, sat on either side of the composer at Sainte-Clotilde, pulling stops for Tournemire on Sundays and in concert.[119] This image of two of the musical and spiritual sons of Tournemire is striking.

Messiaen was intimately familiar with Tournemire's musical style and religious-modernist aesthetic. He deputized for Tournemire, meaning that

Tournemire trusted Messiaen with his organ and with the Catholic liturgical tradition of organ playing that he practised.[120] Tournemire finished his *L'Orgue Mystique* (51 books containing 253 pieces based on the plainchant for Sundays and feasts) on 5 February 1932. His friend Félix Raugel described it in words that pre-date Messiaen's aesthetics: it contained 'All of the liturgical year in sonic stained glass!' and was a 'renovation of the most pure Christian ideal' through the 'modern art of the organ'.[121]

In his letter of recommendation for Messiaen's candidature for the post of organist at the Église de la Sainte-Trinité (a position he took up in September 1931), Tournemire testified:

> I am very particularly interested in a young and magnificent Christian Artist – pure Christian, of a *sound* 'mysticism': Olivier Messiaen . . . Olivier Messiaen is only twenty-three years old, his future is splendid – and what is even better, much better, he prays and conceives his musical works to the glory of Christ [*Xrist*].[122]

Through Tournemire and Dupré, Messiaen, along with his entire generation – Alain, Jean-Jacques Grunenwald (1911–1982), Duruflé, André Fleury (1903–1995), Langlais and Litaize (these last four organist-composers were students of Tournemire) – discovered the profound relationship between Catholic spirituality, mysticism (a concept of which Dupré was especially critical where Messiaen was concerned) and the organ.[123] For Falcinelli, Messiaen was 'the great Christian, the great Catholic who, despite his great literary, philosophical and musical culture, expanded mysticism towards a cosmic universality'.[124]

The 'mysteries' in Catholic doctrine are connected to the life of Christ; they are devotional tools that point towards spiritual goals for the faithful.[125] The Church's liturgy celebrates these mysteries, and they are reflected in Tournemire's and Messiaen's catechistic outputs.[126] They concern things that are hidden and revealed, not merely ineffable; Tournemire's and Messiaen's works attempt to manifest these mysteries through a 'living' (*la vivante*) spiritual tradition essential to their modernism.[127] Mysticism also signals the mystical union between the body of Christ and humanity.[128] Music therefore becomes a symbolic means of making present this union for the believer. Listening functions as a form of participation.

Although Messiaen sought to distance himself from mysticism on a number of occasions, in 1939 he placed himself in this tradition and confirmed Tournemire unequivocally as the composer of sacred art par excellence:

> In *L'Orgue Mystique*, Charles Tournemire shows how . . . to modernize plainchant, and to adapt Debussyan harmonies, polytonality and the polytonality of the jubilant arabesques of alleluias through a supple and strikingly contemporary rhythm. Such a work is truly Catholic, liturgical and living. It is perhaps, at this time [*l'heure actuelle*] the masterpiece of sacred art.[129]

This is Messiaen writing three years after the manifesto declaration of La Jeune France, a collective comprising the composers Yves Baudrier (1906–1988), Daniel-Lesur, André Jolivet (1905–1974) and Messiaen, on 3 June 1936, which advocated a music of 'spiritual violence' and 'courageous reactions' as a counter-measure to the mechanization and depersonalization of life.[130]

Set in this context, Messiaen's advocacy for mysticism can be understood as part of a modernist emancipatory project, and as a form of religious re-enchantment that both extends and perverts the ideals of his contemporaries and that underpins the *jouissance* (pleasure and pain) of this music.[131] These connections with mysticism are essential to the aesthetic, construction and effect of this music. Mysticism should also be understood as part of an ascetic tradition in which a particular musical vision of the universal is manifested. Essential to this vision is an understanding of art as anti-normative, as sacred in terms of its inspiration, conception and semantic content and cultural placement.

Mysticism espouses a condition of separation from other contemporaneous art, but also an aspiration, yet inability, to constitute the religiously conceived, desired and imagined redemptive whole. It is not therefore a stable position or a point of agreement; rather, it reads the world against its own grain. In 1990 Messiaen described the purpose of his role as organist as creating a 'sensibility' that brings the listener closer to 'the mystery that we have yet to understand . . . to a spiritual truth'.[132] In its advocacy of mysticism, Messiaen's music and rhetoric finds its place within the broad church of radical modernism as a transgressive and even reactionary form of ideology. It attempts to search for God through a music appropriate to this traumatic project; it carries within it the composer's own sense of shock through the encounter with the impenetrability of the Other (conceived as the desire but inability to reach God). The ecstatic and excessive quality of this music moves beyond the memorialization and trauma that followed the First World War (in which more than 1.5 million French people died)[133] and aims to contribute positively to a modernist project of eschatological desire and fantasy. It therefore attempts to instantiate a faith in the hereafter in the 'now'. These investments are crucial to the meaning of mysticism for Tournemire and Messiaen, and they would help define Messiaen's music thereafter.

2
On Becoming 'Messiaen', 1927–39

Messiaen's emergence from the chrysalis of his student years was precipitous. He was *suppléant* (assistant organist) at the Église de la Sainte-Trinité from 1929 to 1931, to Charles Quef (1873–1931). It is not every parishioner arriving for Mass on Sunday morning who desires to be confronted by dissonant organ music expressing 'the shock of lights and colours', as Messiaen described the apocalypse, or making present the 'unheard violence' of psalm texts.[1] Messiaen was forced to write an obsequious letter of apology to Curé Hemmer for the musical-religious zeal of his improvisations, having scandalized the congregation, especially the 'old ladies'.[2] This early confrontation exposed an important issue – how personal belief, musical expression and public understanding could align. His texts and programme notes helped the public to understand his music, but they also sometimes inflamed debates about it.

Messiaen gave his first organ concert at La Trinité on 20 February 1930, playing Bach, Schütz, Händel, Langlais, Henriette Roget (1910–1992) (a fellow student at the Conservatoire) and his *Diptyque* (1930), a work that, like the *Prélude* for organ (*c.* 1928–30), shows the contrapuntal and formal influence of Dupré.[3] Messiaen became the *titulaire* organist of this church on 14 September 1931, playing for Mass at 9.15 a.m. and 11 a.m., and at vespers at 5 p.m., which involved interpreting repertoire (including Bach, Frescobaldi, Grigny, Daquin, Franck, Boëllmann, Guilmant, Widor, Vierne, Tournemire, Fleury, Langlais, Daniel-Lesur and Dupré) and some improvisations.[4] After the Second World War, Messiaen played two morning masses at 9 a.m. (classical music) and 11 a.m. (classical music and improvisation), with vespers at 5 p.m. (improvisations) and occasional celebrations (funerals and weddings).[5] From 1947, Chanoine Lanecron created a midday Mass, and Messiaen would improvise continually for around an hour. The function of the organ was concomitantly reduced at the 11 a.m. Mass.[6] Messiaen's assistant organist (and choirmaster) at La Trinité from 1901 to 1952 was his friend the composer André Coedès-Mongin (1871–1954).[7] From the mid-1960s, Messiaen played two masses (9.30 a.m. and 11.15 a.m).[8] His role as an organist was an essential part of his working, creative and devotional life.

The organ at La Trinité was built by Aristide Cavaillé-Coll in 1868, the same year that the organ of Notre-Dame de Paris was completed at his atelier on rue de Vaugirard.[9] It is set high up on the west wall of the church, suspended between earth and heaven. This organ loft was Messiaen's private laboratory, and the organ was his muse for the translation of improvisation into composition. The sound, touch and rich and refined tonal resources of this instrument were vital to Messiaen's

Messiaen at the organ of L'Église de la Sainte-Trinité in the 1930s.

creativity. Messiaen was not the only composer to use the organ as a medium for creative inspiration. The composer Jonathan Harvey (1939–2012) also described his own 'strange improvisations' on the organ: they invoked 'childish excitement' in him and enabled him to participate in 'the glory of singing to nobody but God' as 'the sunlight [streamed] through the stained glass' in church.[10] For Messiaen the organ was a means of engaging with God and of speaking about the divine to his listeners in the church below.

The composer Edgard Varèse (1883–1965), whom Messiaen admired for the 'colour and intensities' of his 'prophetic . . . sonorities', noted that in the 1920s the problem for composers was working out 'how notes of chords can be properly distributed in space'.[11] Varèse, who had studied with d'Indy, Albert Roussel and Widor, regarded the organ as 'not suitable at all' for his ideals of musical sound, owing to its fixed registers 'that the organist cannot change', but for Messiaen it was a 'very modern' instrument whose registers facilitated an engagement with harmony and registral and physical space.[12] Messiaen changed the instrument in 1934–5 by adding seven stops, which kept the rich, orchestral Cavaillé-Coll sounds but added harmonic brilliance through mutation and mixture stops. Further additions of seven stops were made from 1962 to 1966.[13]

The organ was a medium of encounter and serendipity, an instrument for spontaneity, the assimilation and the refinement of musical material. Messiaen developed his rhythmic language and modes of limited transposition at the organ. His modernist, classicist organ music absorbed but radically redirected the symphonic heritage of Widor, Vierne and Alexandre Guilmant (1837–1911), Messiaen's predecessor but one at La Trinité. Messiaen belonged to a new generation of organist-composers: Alain, Daniel-Lesur, Duruflé, Fleury, Grunewald, Langlais (who had also applied for the post at La Trinité) and Litaize.[14] These composers used the organ as a means to express more explicitly religious praise, joy, glory, pathos and supplication. This 'renovation' of the spiritual possibilities of the organ would inspire later organist-composers such as Jacques Charpentier (1933–2017), Jeanne Demessieux, Rolande Falcinelli, Jean Guillou (1930–2019), Jean-Louis Florentz (1947–2004), Naji Hakim (b. 1955) – who, like Messiaen, also made a disc of improvisations with Sauvage's *L'Âme en bourgeon* at La Trinité in 2003 and was his immediate successor at this church (1993–2008) – Thierry Escaich (b. 1965), and Thomas Lacôte (b. 1982) with Loïc Mallié (b. 1947), who became *titulaires* at La Trinité in 2011 and 2014 respectively. Messiaen is the only major composer in the twentieth century to have written extensively for the organ.[15]

Messiaen's generation adopted Tournemire's interest in the chorale, which signified the religious sublime, as Tournemire put it, for a 'legion of Christian artists, so that they may purify contemporary art and carry in this knowledge and faith!'[16] For Messiaen, it was a vehicle for modernist harmonic deformation as a form of beauty and religious revelation. Crucially for Tournemire and for Messiaen, there is a sense of the organist/artist as both countering the secular modern world and transforming it through modernist means, providing the opportunity for a cathartic transformation of the listener. Music was therefore a form of proclamation that represented a desire to realize something of Christ's eternal kingdom *now*. This emancipatory thinking embodied a timely response to various forms of interest in apocalyptic prophesy, but it should also be understood as a form of modernist enchantment. Messiaen's music represents a vision of faith beyond institutional religion, arguably doing the work of the Church in its musical provision of wordless messages of hope, praise, supplication and redemption.

Messiaen's first significant work after the death of his mother in 1927 was *Le Banquet céleste* (1928), a quiet, ethereal seven-minute organ piece that assimilated the apocalyptic mysticism of Tournemire's music. It can be understood as cathartic and curative, its slow-moving, meditative sound world enacting a sense of oneness with Christ through the Mass, and, by analogy, a spiritual connection to his mother. It was also a response to a predominant religious interest in the work of St Thomas Aquinas. Aquinas had been declared patron of all Catholic educational institutions on 4 August 1880 (*Cum hoc sit*) by Pope Leo XIII; the 'angelic doctor' had become an authority figure for the Catholic right in France following the First World War. For a range of artists and intellectuals (including Jacques Maritain), Aquinas's theology embodied traditional Catholic values in the face of a perceived rising secularism.[17] Aquinas's opinion on time is sedimented in Messiaen's work: time is the property of man, eternity is God's time – a paradigm Messiaen considered apposite for his modernist music.[18] The *lenteur* of *Le Banquet céleste* belies the rhetoric of classicist musical architecture that Messiaen had partly learned from Vincent d'Indy's *Cours de composition musicale* (1909) and Dupré's pedagogy.[19]

Le Banquet céleste is prefaced by a scriptural epigraph: 'He who eats my flesh and drinks my blood will have eternal life.' This was new for organ music, although Tournemire's music had included Gregorian chant and, by implication, its texts in his music. The opening musical idea of this piece is derived from the second theme of a rejected orchestral work, *Le Banquet eucharistique*, which was performed on 22 January 1930 by a student orchestra from the Conservatoire de Paris, conducted by the director, Henri Rabaud.[20] The opening theme of *Le Banquet céleste* employs a subtle deformation of the plainchant antiphon *O sacrum convivium* for the Second Vespers of the Fête du Saint-Sacrement (Corpus Christi), which Messiaen may have noticed was published in d'Indy's *Cours de composition musicale*.[21] This melody is also reconfigured in his later motet *O sacrum convivium!* (1937). Plainchant would inspire works from all of Messiaen's contemporaries, but he used it with greater textural, harmonic and melodic complexity. The second idea in *Banquet*, perhaps suggestive of drops of blood from the communion chalice, crucially liberates the pedals from their usual function as a bass, something that is also present, but not to the same degree, in Tournemire's contemporaneous *L'Orgue Mystique*.[22]

Le Banquet céleste uses the octatonic scale, a scale of alternating semitones and tones that is found in the music of Liszt as well as Russian music, German Expressionist music and other French music, including Tournemire, Langlais and others. It is not used here with the characteristic harmonizations of Messiaen's modes of limited transposition that would later be formalized in *Technique de mon langage musical* (1944). These modes – scales with their own internal organization, but without the definitive hierarchies necessarily implied in such terms as 'tonic' and 'dominant', for example – can be transposed a certain number of times before returning to the same pitches. Messiaen's seven modes are each harmonized in different ways that allude to, but defer from, tonal hierarchies.[23] Yet they are flexible: they can be used within quasi-tonal circumstances or self-referentially. These modes were a source of inspiration for Messiaen's improvisation and composition.[24] Writing to Langlais on 17 September 1931, he comments on the relationship between the two:

> I'm composing, I'm playing the organ. At the organ, the realization happens so fast that the concept doesn't have time to be idealized. But in composition, what a difference between the sublime heights of one and the lamentable platitudes of another! The more I work on music, the more I am indignant at my nothingness before that elusive ideal.[25]

Mode was a way of reaching towards Messiaen's 'elusive ideal'; it invoked the anonymous artisans of the Middle Ages (Gregorian chant), non-Western exoticism and the possibility for the modernist renewal of musical language, and it provided an alternative to tonality and atonality.

Le Banquet céleste is written in F# major – a favourite key of Messiaen's, associated in his music with religious transcendence. This key (with minimal sense of the polarity necessary for tonality itself) provides an anchor here for the modal discourse to reshape tension and resolution. The circular rather than teleological quality of mode embeds a sense of atemporality in this music perfectly suited to Neoplatonic and Thomistic thought, in which clock-bound time is understood as a property of humanity and God's time is regarded as undivided, unchanging and eternal. Crucially, mode was essential to the project of aesthetic, religious fantasy that informs Messiaen's output. In *Le Banquet céleste* it helps to impart a surreal sense of being in the real presence of Christ in the Mass. Messiaen's music therefore has a performative function: it enrols the religious and secular listener in his project.

Messiaen's modal language becomes synonymous with religious intentions; even works that lack such religious titles come to participate in his religious-modernist project. In an interview with José Bruyr in 1931, Messiaen described the piano *Préludes* as 'a collection of successive states of the soul and of personal sensations'.[26] They were premiered privately on 28 January 1930 by the composer at the publisher Durand's salon and then publicly by Henriette Roget (nos 2–6 and no. 8) at a Société Nationale concert on 1 March 1930, as well as publicly (complete) by Bernadette Alexandre-Georges at the École Normale on 15 June 1937. Messiaen's 1937 description of Tournemire's music as employing 'audacious harmonies, shimmering rhythms, sumptuous modes and the timbres of the rainbow!' applies to his own music.[27] Alain Messiaen described the *Préludes* as works in which Messiaen's style was 'already all there', noting the influence of Debussy and Ravel, the 'coloured modal sadness' of the sixth movement, 'Cloches d'angoisse et larmes d'adieu', and the 'eucharistic triumph over this sadness' in 'Chante d'extase dans un paysage triste' (no. 2).[28] In 1968 Messiaen observed of these pieces:

> I was already a 'sound-colour' musician. By means of the harmonic modes, transposable only a certain number of times, and drawing their own particular colours, I had come to oppose discs of colour, to interlace rainbows, and to find a music of complementary

> colours. The titles of the *Préludes* hide studies of colours [*études de couleurs*].[29]

Messiaen's discussion of 'opposing discs of colour' and 'complementary colours' perhaps implies a reference (retrospectively) to the influence of Robert and Sonia Delaunay's paintings, which he came to admire for their use of what they called 'simultaneous contrast' of colours, something he observed in his own music.[30] Messiaen later stated that he believed in the 'resonance of sounding bodies and complementary colours'.[31] For him, these phenomena were 'connected to the sacred, and the musical dazzling [*l'éblouissement*], like stained-glass windows, which generates reverence, adoration, and praise'.[32] For Messiaen such colours were attached to physical images (rainbows, stained glass), and connected to his synaesthesia as a form of internal revelation and, like Tournemire, to an interest in the colours and stones of the apocalypse as images of both divine revelation through music and possible human emancipation.[33]

This 'interlacing' of colours is evident in 'Les sons impalpables du rêve' (*Préludes*, no. 5), later reworked as the opening of 'Les Bergers' (*La Nativité*, piece II), where the imbrication of musical cells or 'planes' is connected to the superimposition of two of Messiaen's modes.[34] Synaesthesia is a neurological condition, more acute in some than others, that results when a 'trigger (known as an *inducer*) . . . [generates] an experience in a different sensory modality (known as a *concurrent*)'.[35] The Swiss painter Charles Blanc-Gatti (1890–1966) had an acute form of synaesthesia whereby he physically saw colour as a response to sound; for him, 'sounds not only have a colour, but a form.'[36] Messiaen, by contrast, involuntarily saw colours in his mind that 'move' in a 'very fugitive' fashion that was 'impossible to write and fix in an absolute way'.[37] His 'musician's colours' reveal his search for a way to assimilate his musical language with classical notions of phrase extension and form (binary, ternary, rondo) in his *Préludes*.[38]

In a sketch by Messiaen from the early 1930s, possibly based in part on Dupré's thought in his improvisation treatise that Messiaen knew well, one can see Messiaen being 'Messiaen': superimposing two and three triads (sometimes using different transpositions), with respect to modes 2 and 3, and identifying the resulting colours.[39] He is also seen working out which non-harmonic notes might make the most impactful or preferred colouristic effects when added to a triad (in second inversion with an added sixth), a typical 'Messiaen' sound.[40] Messiaen was aware of his own synaesthesia early on, but it was reinforced when he met Blanc-Gatti, known as 'the painter of sounds', who created pictures of organ pipes with colours emerging from them (one of which Messiaen owned) and had painted a representation of Messiaen's *La Nativité du Seigneur* (1935) in 1936.[41] Colour is present at a simple level in the confluence of consonance and dissonance in Messiaen's harmonizations of his modes of limited transposition. The harmonization of mode 2^1 is replete with triads and appoggiaturas, or 'added notes', that lend a 'delicate gilding [*orfèvrerie*]'[42] when integrated into the chord, a thinking derived perhaps from Dupré's analysis of Ravel, for example.[43]

Messiaen's modal harmonizations internalize the notion of colour change implied in flat- and sharp-side notation (from common-practice tonality) and in the potential of enharmonicism. The composer and pianist Michaël Levinas (b. 1949) observed that the modes also have a 'spectral genealogy'.[44] They embody a superimposition that he associates with the 'shimmering' of colours in Messiaen's music.[45] The modes reinscribe the 'acoustic laws dictated by the internal structure of timbre', as Levinas explains spectralism, a movement in French music partly derived from Messiaen's class in 1969–70 (see p. 155), that was concerned with the elaboration of ramifications derived from the harmonic spectrum through time and the 'decomposition and the spectral recomposition of timbre' as musical narrative.[46] Messiaen's modal harmonizations created his sonic identity, and they provided a means of organizing form according to internal hierarchies, as evidenced in movement v from the *Quatuor pour la fin du Temps* (1940–41), for example.[47]

Tournemire had explicitly connected modal improvisation (Hindu and Gregorian modes) to the colours of the apocalypse, something that was important for Messiaen's later music especially.[48] Following Wagner's musical thought, colour can be created through small changes in voice leading (and timbre, density and texture) to achieve maximal aesthetic effects that are concerned with, as Levinas puts it, an 'acoustic logic and not merely with [the] structural combinations . . . [that] enormously influenced my generation'.[49] 'Complexes of sound' and 'complexes of colour' change with the transposition of each mode, as shown in the following table.[50]

MODE	COLOURS
2^1	Blue-violet rocks speckled with little grey cubes, cobalt blue, deep Prussian blue highlighted by a bit of violet-purple, gold, red, ruby and stars of mauve, black and white. Blue-violet is dominant.
2^2	Gold and silver spirals against a background of brown and ruby-red vertical bands. Gold and brown are dominant.
2^3	Light green and prairie-green foliage, with specks of blue, silver and reddish-orange. Green is dominant.

Messiaen's mode 2: transpositions and colours.

For Messiaen, different colours exist for other classified types of chords and transpositions, including 'chords of inversions transposed onto the same bass note', 'chords of contracted resonance', 'turning chords' (extrapolated from Jolivet's *Cinq danses rituelles* (1939/41) and used from *Visions de l'Amen* (1943) onwards) and 'chords of the total chromatic'.[51]

Messiaen's synaesthesia was an embodied experience of music essential to his creative process; it provided a physical presence but also confirmation of his own religious vision and vocation. It was a mental and kinaesthetic experience that he tried to convey to performers and listeners through information in scores and commentaries. The *Préludes* reveal a musical language in formation, including what Messiaen would later call the 'incantatory aspect' with reference to Jolivet's *Cinq danses rituelles*, and 'effects of resonance' (as Dukas put it).[52]

Messiaen published three of his five early orchestral tone poems.[53] *Les Offrandes oubliées* (1930) was first performed on 19 February 1931, and it was enthusiastically reviewed by Tournemire.[54] Messiaen described it in a letter to Emmanuel as concerning 'Christ's offering of his life on the cross of his body given to us through the host [the bread in the Mass]. To forget these two gifts of his love is [our] sin.'[55] It was the first of Messiaen's works to be performed in America (by Serge Koussevitzky on 16 October 1936).[56]

Offrandes was based on a short poetic text by Messiaen, and its three sections connect Christ's offering through 'the cross', human forgetfulness of this 'sin' and his eternal presence in 'the eucharist'. *Le Tombeau resplendissant* was composed in 1931 and first performed on 12 February 1933, but only published in 1997. It is superscribed with a text by Messiaen that cites Matthew 11:28 and the Beatitudes, perhaps eulogizing his mother and the end of his youth. Finally, *Hymne au Saint Sacrement* (1932), first performed on 23 March 1933, was lost and then reconstructed as *Hymne* by the composer, and performed on 13 March 1947 by Leopold Stokowski with the New York Philharmonic.

La Mort du nombre for soprano, tenor, violin and piano (1930) was first performed on 21 March 1931. It is a cantata in which two souls sing to each other, the female soul (perhaps a metaphor for Messiaen's mother) calming the male and reassuring him of the gloriousness of eternal life displayed in the radiant B-major coda of the work for violin and piano alone. Messiaen also had two shots at the prestigious Prix de Rome with the cantatas *Sainte-Bohème* (*extrait des Odes funambulesques*, 1930) and *L'Ensorceleuse: cantate à trois personnages* (1931, performed 4 July 1931), a work for orchestra, soprano, tenor and bass soloists that shows the influence of Debussy and especially Dukas.[57] Although unsuccessful on both occasions, Messiaen was in good company: Saint-Saëns, Dukas and Ravel never won the prize either; Falcinelli noted sanguinely that no Dupré student had won it.[58] By August 1931, Messiaen had renounced competing in this prize again. Living in Rome for four years (a requirement of the prizewinner) would have been injurious to his future employment at La Trinité in September 1931 (Messiaen was also playing the organ at two cinemas at Place Pigalle in 1930–31), and the time in Rome for the *prix* would have also interrupted his prospective marriage.[59]

La Mort du nombre and the three extant orchestral pieces contain burgeoning characteristics of Messiaen's originality (the ecstatic ending of *Offrandes* or *La Mort du nombre*, for example). However, their nascent religious ideology received mixed critical reviews, and they lack the stylistic homogeneity, purposefulness and sustained quality of ideas that would blossom in the cyclic works of the 1930s.

On 22 June 1932 in Saint-Louis-en-l'Île (also Pierre Messiaen's parish church), Messiaen married Claire Delbos, who was the daughter of Victor Delbos, a Sorbonne philosophy professor, and Lucie Devillez; Claire was the youngest of their three children, whose family home was at 46 quai Henri IV, in the 4th arrondissement.[60] She had been a violin and composition student at the Schola Cantorum, where Messiaen later taught an organ improvisation class from 1935 to 1939.[61] Their first home together was at 77 rue des Plantes, in the 14th arrondissement.[62]

At this time, Messiaen wrote one of his most iconoclastic organ works, the *Apparition de l'Église éternelle*.[63] The accompanying poem (crossed out in one version of the autograph[64]) speaks of suffering, exemplified by the grinding iambic rhythm in the pedals, which leads to a redemptive vision of the eternal Church of Christ and the colours of apocalypse. Messiaen wrote out nine verses of the plainchant hymn 'Urbs beata Jerusalem' in the sketches, but he does not show that the melody of the work is, in fact, a deformed version of this plainchant.[65] *Apparition* is a chorale-like piece that presents an enormous crescendo to C major on the organ tutti, accentuated by elision of material, and a diminuendo (beginning at the golden section in bar 39) that telescopes the musical material and uses chromatic completion in the bass. Over the course of around ten minutes (in Messiaen's own recording), the singular vision of *Apparition* is sculpted through the material ability of the organ to create continuous sound (there are few rests), with articulation supplied through agogics and the varied pulsations of the Greek rhythms.[66]

Inside a privately owned copy of the work is a dedication: 'To my master Charles Tournemire: homage, respect and sincere admiration, Olivier Messiaen,' a tribute that suggests Messiaen's profound debt to Tournemire.[67] Tournemire had dedicated works to many students and associates, including Dupré (despite their rivalry), Duruflé, Daniel-Lesur, Litaize and Langlais, but not to Messiaen. He had, at some point, inscribed the last volume of *L'Orgue Mystique* (no. 51), a work that Messiaen described as 'mi-gothique, mi-ultra moderne' (half gothic, half ultra-modern) with the words: 'À son ami Olivier Messiaen, Organiste du Gd Orgue de la Trinité, à Paris,' but he crossed them out.[68] Somewhat ironically, Messiaen played the last movement of this suite in a concert at Sainte-Clotilde on 24 April 1932.[69]

Tournemire's *L'Orgue Mystique* for organ was a 'cycle of works' that expressed a mystical sublime designed for, but which also spoke beyond, the liturgy. Tournemire's ideal of the organ mass, connected to the liturgy, was a model that would be used by Grunenwald, Langlais, Litaize and Messiaen in his *Messe de la Pentecôte* (1950–51). Tournemire's cycle surrounds the catechistic events of Christ's life. This focus is also present in Dupré's *Symphonie-Passion* (1924), which Messiaen later described to Falcinelli as 'perhaps the most original work of our master', and in *Le Chemin de la Croix* (1931). Messiaen attended the first performance of *Chemin* at the Trocadéro, and performed pieces x and ix in the concert reopening the organ at La Trinité on 28 May 1935, which was shared with Dupré.[70] While Messiaen's organ cycles adapt aspects of symphonic development, they come to function like a reredos of icons moving beyond the examples of Tournemire and Dupré in the complexity of their religious expression and musical language.

Messiaen began work on the cycle *L'Ascension* in summer 1932, just before beginning teaching piano sight-reading and musicianship skills at the École Normale de Musique (1932–9).[71] Messiaen worked on it at Delbos' parents' chateau at Neussargues in Cantal, Auvergne, in the summer of 1933, before beginning compulsory military service that autumn.[72] In a letter to Langlais in August, he stated that 'religious music is a difficult art. I feel myself hopelessly little and incapable. The decision not to compose any more came to me – then it left.'[73]

In 1934 he rewrote the work for organ with a more successful replacement third piece, the 'Transports de joie d'une âme devant la gloire du Christ qui est la sienne'. Messiaen premiered the organ cycle on 29 January 1935 in the Église Saint-Antoine-des-Quinze-Vingts. In a review of this concert, the critic (and friend of Tournemire) Félix Raugel described Messiaen as an 'impeccable virtuoso'. He noted his 'ardent

Messiaen as a soldier during his national service (1933).

religious soul' and praised *L'Ascension*, in language redolent of Tournemire, as a 'large and luminous symphonic paraphrase of the gospels, like the master stained-glass makers of our Cathedrals'.[74] Messiaen played it again at Sainte-Clotilde on 4 April 1935, and at the Trinité organ reopening on 28 May 1935.[75]

L'Ascension contains four pieces in rising keys (E, F, F# and G) that dramatize Christ's ascent for the believer/onlooker. Tournemire privately ridiculed the work (especially the melody of the last movement), and Messiaen himself as an 'accomplished poser' and as a 'little fool'.[76] Perhaps this was because Tournemire could sense Messiaen's burgeoning originality and the development of his own religious-modernist aesthetics, partly derived from Tournemire's work. Early reviewers recognized the innovative qualities of the work and its mystical portent. The composer and critic Suzanne Demarquez (1891–1965) noted:

> In *L'Ascension* Olivier Messiaen has sought, as in certain previous works, to fire up the spirit [*frapper l'esprit*] of his listeners, by all means . . . He has, simply, sincerely exposed the mystical ideal that it possesses, and it is in this that his work is stirring [*émouvante*].[77]

The work is the first proper organ cycle in French organ music, and the first to use scriptural epigraphs for all of the movements, something that Messiaen regarded as 'inseparable from the origins of my organ pieces' and the work's 'religious content'.[78] It was perhaps the first work in Messiaen's output to derive its inspiration from a specific theological source. Dom Columba Marmion's *Le Christ dans ses mystères* (1919) had been through many reprints by 1927, backed up by papal imprimatur for its orthodox and clear exegesis of Catholic doctrine. Its chapters move through the church year, providing a kind of blueprint for Messiaen's own output. Marmion didactically illustrates these events, using the biblical texts from the Missal that Messiaen borrows. Marmion's emphasis (as with Messiaen) is on a sense of vicarious journeying with Christ, of desiring to follow his trajectory.

Messiaen employed two chorales as the outer movements (I and IV), the legacy of which can be heard in *Signals from Heaven – Two Antiphonal Fanfares –* (1987) by the Japanese composer (and friend of Messiaen) Tōru Takemitsu (1930–1996). The outer movements of *L'Ascension* frame two central more developed pieces: the 'Alleluias sereins d'une âme qui désire le ciel', which is in verse-refrain form (II), which Messiaen originally wrote out in the key of G, and he described it in language redolent of Tournemire's *L'Orgue Mystique* as '*Thème alléluiatique* with complex rhythms (plainchant) in the brass . . . exposed 3 times in variations', specifying 'perpetual trills' in the fourth variation.[79] This is followed by 'Transports de joie d'une âme devant la gloire du Christ qui est la sienne' (III), described by Messiaen as a 'joyous and victorious toccata, alléluiatique, fff.'[80]

Messiaen's sketches for this work reveal the extraordinary connections his mind could make. In his 'Cahier vert' he cites bar 17 of Bach's Toccata in D minor (BWV 565) and a version of bar 4 of 'Transports de joie', described as 'in modes 2 and 4 and the new [unspecified] mode', and reveals, through use of appoggiaturas, part of the formation of his final score. He does not, however, disclose how one fragment of music became another – this creative jump remains mysterious.[81] Messiaen's 'Transports' gradually compresses two opposing ideas as its means of development. The composer Pierre Boulez's criticism that Messiaen 'does not compose – he juxtaposes', and that his music does not develop, is shown in this movement to be tendentious.[82] The colour of Messiaen's music is created here through tension and release, and techniques of musical development such as fragmentation, compression and extension. His rethinking of traditional classicist compositional techniques is a hallmark of his modernism.

Messiaen followed *L'Ascension* with *La Nativité du Seigneur* (1935), a nine-movement organ cycle first publicly performed by Messiaen's student comrades at La Trinité on 27 February 1936. Daniel-Lesur played movements I–III, Langlais, movements IV–VI and Grunenwald, movements VII–IX. Messiaen described Langlais' performance of 'Les Anges' as 'prestidigitous', and noted in a letter to Dupré inviting him to the concert that all were playing with 'love'.[83]

In a letter to Alain Messiaen of 4 August 1936, the Surrealist poet Max Jacob noted: 'I have seen with a strong emotion the enormous success of your brother the musician. This gave me great pleasure. I don't know why.'[84] The publisher Leduc released an 'Extraits de presse', an extensive four-page publicity leaflet revealing glowing reviews of *La Nativité* from distinguished musicians and commentators such as Georges Auric, Henri Sauguet, Bernard Gavoty, Daniel-Lesur and Jacques Ibert. Much later, Messiaen tacitly differentiated *La Nativité* from the work of the previous generation of composers, describing it as 'proof . . . that one can write organ music in a different way from a post-Franck aesthetic'.[85]

Messiaen's preface to *La Nativité* speaks of the 'emotion and sincerity of the musical composition, which will be at the service of the dogmas of Catholic theology . . . the abundance of technical means allows the heart to overflow freely.'[86] *La Nativité* is grounded in five theological themes and supported by a clear symbolic use of leitmotifs that connect musical means to theological ends. Messiaen's sketches for the work show superimposed motivic relationships between the beginning of the cornet theme (last section of piece IV) and the 'chute du Christ' idea (a loud, slow descending line in the organ pedals) used in pieces IV and IX, a theme which is also related, in Messiaen's thought, to the central canon of contrary-motion chords (marked 'Modéré') in piece IV.[87]

'Dieu parmi nous' (piece IX), perhaps the best known of all Messiaen's organ works, presents three initial themes that Messiaen refers to as a 'Debussyiste X Y Z procedure'.[88] This probably also refers to the beginning of *Pelléas*, of which Messiaen remarks, to his class of 1971–2, on the 'mobility of the rhythm' and the 'very long and very short values'.[89] This is exactly the contrast created at the beginning of 'Dieu parmi nous' in the asymmetrical 'mobility' of the Hindu rhythm rāgavardhana at the start (in short values) and the progressively longer values in the ensuing pedal motive. For Messiaen, structure, symbol and emotion were intimately connected. He also comments on the different colours of the themes in *Pelléas*, something that seems to have both enchanted and mystified his students, especially Levinas (as can be seen in the film *Olivier Messiaen et les oiseaux* (1973) – Levinas is seated directly to Messiaen's right).[90] The three themes in 'Dieu parmi nous' embody differences of rhythm, colour and character. They symbolize the Incarnation (bars 1–3, *chute du Christ*),[91] 'the love of God' (bars 4–7, *thème d'amour*) and the *style-oiseau* joy of the Christian soul upon receiving this love (bar 8, *thème d'allégresse* – the 'Magnificat'). This last theme was later given by Messiaen, harmonized, to André Marchal (1894–1980) as an improvisation theme.[92] In the body of the piece that follows, these themes are all developed and expanded in reverse order, making the 'chute du Christ' motif, representative of 'God among us' (theme 1), symbolically the Alpha and Omega in the piece.

La Nativité, like *L'Ascension*, is theologically grounded in Marmion's book,[93] but Messiaen reinvents its themes and ideas in startling ways. His organ music acts as a critique of prevailing conservative Church doctrines on music, showing how 'modern forms of music' give 'expression to the majesty of the edifice and [give breath to] the sacredness of the religious rites'.[94] Messiaen's music is therefore best thought of not merely as 'mystical' or 'theological' but as re-enchanting or transcending such contexts.

The transparency and originality of the musical language, and Messiaen's use of the organ, is striking in *La Nativité*. Asymmetrical rhythms, inspired by nature,[95] Hindu rhythms, the addition or subtraction of a smaller value added to a longer one (Messiaen would also find resonances of this in the music of Guillaume de Machaut (*c*. 1300–1377)), and the inexact diminution and augmentations of rhythms are ubiquitous in Messiaen's language here.[96] Messiaen's adaptation of Hindu, Greek and plainchant rhythms through asymmetry was a potent way by which he sought to refine and refresh the rhythmic language (dominated by the choral and traditional counterpoint) found in symphonic French organ music, such as the work of Franck, Widor, Vierne, Tournemire and Dupré.[97] Messiaen further connects what he calls 'non-retrogradable rhythms' (quaver, dotted quaver, quaver, for example – the same forwards as backwards) to his symmetrical modes through the 'charm of impossibilities', signifying a form of 'magical enchantment'.[98]

Messiaen uses interversions (in the pedal), his modes (left hand) and deformed plainchant (right hand) in what he refers to as the 'carillon' central section of piece I.[99] Following Tournemire (in *L'Orgue Mystique*) and his own practice in *Le Banquet céleste*, where the pedal motive (not as a bass) is prominent in the texture because of the register (using mutation stops and no 8' stops), the use of such stops (in *La Nativité*, piece I) here, by contrast, functions as an integrated line within an innovative contrapuntal texture in which three types of material are imbricated.[100] Messiaen used Greek rhythms in III, the interlacing of interversions in IV, the chorale (in almost all movements), again connected in Tournemire to mysticism and plainchant,[101] and the imitation of birdsong in IX. His melodic thinking was inspired by the architectural rise and fall in musical phrases (arsis and thesis) theorized by Dom Mocquereau (1849–1930), whose work at Solesmes inspired Tournemire's *L'Orgue Mystique*. Messiaen later applied this thought to his analysis of plainchant, alongside Mozart, Debussy and other composers.[102] His radical form of modernist classicism is therefore considerably distant from Marmion's conservative rhetoric, and the alterity of this music therefore provides a form of re-enchantment of this central Christological event.

In *La Nativité* one can also detect the avant-garde spirit of Messiaen's friend Jolivet, and parallels with his wife Claire Delbos' *Paraphrase* on the last judgement for organ, written in 1935 and later performed by

Messiaen at La Trinité on 14 March 1939 (including six movements from *La Nativité*).[103] Delbos' *Paraphrase* is in four movements (Messiaen transcribed, with modifications, the second for four ondes Martenots), and the third is similar in its registration and texture to Messiaen's third piece in *La Nativité*.[104] Delbos' work is marked by a similar mystical aesthetic, including the use of Gregorian chant. Like *La Nativité*, it reimagines the possibilities, opened up by Cavaillé-Coll's musical palette, that had been extended by Messiaen in 1934–5, following what Tournemire had done with the organ at Sainte-Clotilde in 1932–3. *La Nativité* also appears just after Tournemire's *Sept Chorals-Poèmes d'Orgue pour les sept paroles du Xrist*, op. 67 (premiered by Tournemire at Sainte-Clotilde on 6 June 1935), and Dupré's *Chemin* (1931) – all three works employ recurring musical ideas (like leitmotifs) that, in Messiaen and Dupré especially, reconfigure the baroque ideal of *Affektenlehre*, a form of theological teaching through the shape of musical ideas. It is therefore tempting to see Messiaen's work on the birth of Christ as a natural response to these other organ works on the subject of Christ's death. The final four descending pedal notes of *La Nativité* echo the final movement of Tournemire's work: 'Consummatum est' (It Is Finished) is reimagined as 'Dieu parmi nous'.

Messiaen's activities as a journalist and polemicist through the 1930s became increasingly fervent in his advocacy of mysticism and his rejection of imitation and neo-classicism, and what he perceived to be secular musical idioms. Despite his praise for Tournemire (in four articles on Tournemire's musical and pedagogical works), his claiming and advocacy of mysticism had caught his mentor's ire.[105] However, the alterity of his thought, countering contemporary secularism, contributed to the formation of La Jeune France.[106] The group was inaugurated officially on 3 June 1936, and its manifesto, written by the composer Yves Baudrier (1906–1988), partly as a rejection of Jean Cocteau's artistic manifesto *Le Coq et l'arlequin* (1918),[107] announced:

> The conditions of life have become harder and harder, mechanical and impersonal; music must relentlessly bring a spiritual violence and garner generous reactions from those who love it ... far from academicism and revolutionary cliché. The tendencies of the group are diverse: they unite to whisper and spread a living music with the same élan of sincerity, generosity and artistic conscience.[108]

The members of La Jeune France, left to right: André Jolivet, Jean-Yves Daniel-Lesur, Olivier Messiaen and Yves Baudrier, May 1937.

This left little doubt as to the political, spiritual, aesthetic and even nationalist vanguardism of the group, which included Daniel-Lesur and Jolivet. Certain shared interests – mode, rhythm, research, non-Western music and the defining of French music – allowed the group to form a loose association, but it was not to last, mostly because it comprised composers with strong individual aesthetics and artistic personalities.

In fact, the group formed part of a longer trail of political polemics in French music – defined against Wagner and German music, other continental influences and consonant with the proliferation of manifestos and -isms of the early twentieth century. The letters between the group members show aspects of complicity and also subtle rancour. Financed by Baudrier, Le Jeune France organized concerts of the members' and others' works, and formed a continuation of the earlier group La Spirale, founded in 1935 with Georges Migot as president, which overlapped aesthetically with the journal *La Nouvelle Saison* (1937–9).[109]

Jolivet had possibly known Messiaen's music since 1932 and had contact with him from 1933 – Messiaen had introduced himself with a note: 'You compose the music that I would like to compose.'[110] It is no surprise then that Jolivet's *Prélude apocalyptique* (1935) for organ was written for Messiaen. Daniel-Lesur (Tournemire's assistant organist from 1927 to 1937) had stood with Messiaen on either side of Tournemire's organ console, and Baudrier (also an organist, and a sailor who competed in the 1936 Olympics) appeared in their midst from 1935. In a letter to Daniel-Lesur of 6 January 1938, Baudrier appositely differentiated the four comrades: 'You [Daniel-Lesur] the renaissance, me Romanticism, Messiaen the Middle Ages and Hindustanism, and Jolivet the super-Impressionist modern.'[111] Under the auspices of the group, Messiaen's song cycle *Poèmes pour Mi* was premiered on 12 March 1938. 'Mi' was Messiaen's nickname for his wife, Claire Delbos, with whom he had bought an alpine house at Petichet in Isère in 1936, a lifelong summer haven of work and leisure. Early photos show a young couple very much in love, but Claire reportedly also had 'troubles with pregnancy' and regretted 'not having children'.[112]

Messiaen sometimes played in duo with Claire at La Trinité from November 1932 to January 1946.[113] He composed his *Thème et variations* for violin and piano for Delbos as a wedding present, and they performed it on 22 November 1932. He also composed *Fantaisie* for violin and piano (1933, published in 2007). Messiaen invited Langlais to the concert in 1932 'to make a lot of noise and make us repeat this work, which is one of my best, unless you prefer to boo, which would also make a lot of noise'.[114] Langlais later recalled: 'Of course I was noisy.'[115] This was a time in Messiaen's life where he was a performer on the piano (as soloist and accompanist), but more an organist and composer, appearing in concerts at the École Normale, the Société Nationale, the Schola Cantorum and at various Paris churches.

The nine songs of *Poèmes pour Mi* have texts by Messiaen and were first written for piano and then given one of Messiaen's most exquisite and colourful orchestrations in 1937. 'Mi' is addressed in various ways through imagery, and compared to the blue of the Grand lac de Laffrey, at Petichet (see p. 184), in song II. Throughout the cycle, the couple are united through love, suffering and adversity, finally relinquishing human companionship for the glory of the resurrection. The cycle extols the Catholic understanding of the sacramental bonds between humanity and the Church as a reflection of both divine and human love.

Messiaen's texts are marked by Paul Éluard's Surrealist poetry. Eyes are the vessels for love and desire, the spiritual connection between beings (also in *La Mort du nombre*, for instance), and there are images of light, sky, sea, stars, colours and birds. Messiaen's poetry uses the Surrealist device of *fil conducteur*, a lightning rod connecting distant ideas and concepts and transforming them, and also litanic verse structures.[116]

Messiaen's *O sacrum convivium!* (1937) for four-voice mixed choir (with organ *ad libitum*) was first performed on 17 February 1938 in a concert at La Trinité with Grunenwald accompanying the motet, replacing Daniel-Lesur. This concert included the premieres of Alain's *Danse funèbre pour honorer une mémoire héroïque* (which became 'Deuils', no. 2 of his *Trois Danses*), *Le Jardin suspendu* and *Litanies*.[117] In March 1938, Messiaen was invited to London through the efforts of Felix Aprahamian (then secretary for the Organ Music Society and later music critic for the *Sunday Times*). He played two movements of *La Nativité* at the BBC's Broadcasting House on 22 June and, partly through the advocacy of Arnold Richardson, organist of St Alban the Martyr in Holborn (and the first English organist to play the work, according to Aprahamian), played it in its entirety at that church on 25 June.[118] Tournemire had also played there earlier, on 22 February 1936.[119]

Aprahamian had first met Messiaen at the International Society for Contemporary Music festival in 1937 and was his guest at La Trinité on 27 June that year where he heard Messiaen play *La Nativité*. The 'high commendations' given to Fleury's performance of four movements of this work at the Organ Music Society on 9 December 1937 were not afforded to Messiaen in England. C. H. Trevor, a prominent English organist, left before the second page of the first piece, muttering 'Enough of that rubbish' to Aprahamian on the way out.[120] Yet some years later he was teaching this music to his students at the Royal Academy of Music, including Simon Preston (1938–2022). Preston was the first English organist to record Messiaen's *L'Ascension*, in 1962 at King's College, Cambridge, a year before Litaize made his recording in Paris, and later recorded *Les Corps Glorieux* and *Le Banquet céleste* in 1969 at St Alban's Abbey. In 1964 Allan Wicks (1923–2010) was the first English organist to record *La Nativité* at St Paul's Cathedral, a year before Preston's recording of this cycle from Westminster Abbey and a year after Litaize at the

Messiaen and Pascal Messiaen.

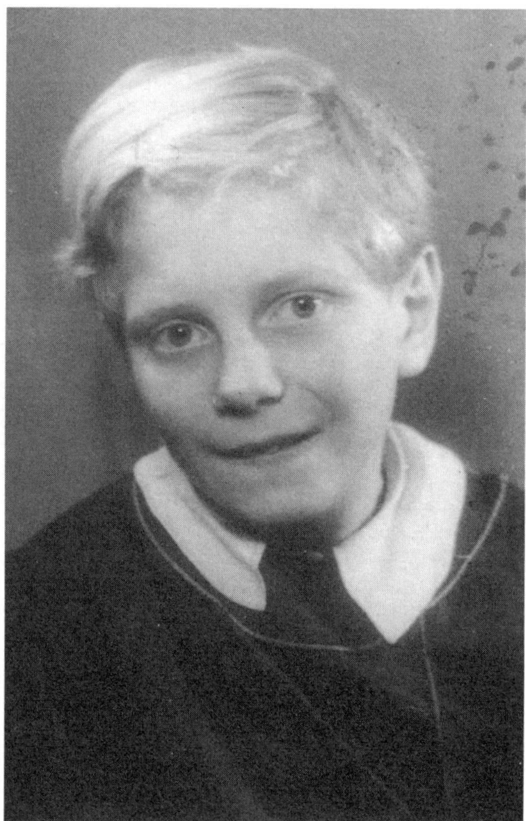

Pascal Messiaen.

Église Saint-François-Xavier in Paris. Such recordings gave access to this music and allowed it slowly to become standard organ repertoire.

The subsequent song cycle, *Chants de terre et de ciel* (1938), contains six songs, again with texts by the composer himself. It was premiered as *Prismes: six poèmes d'Olivier Messiaen* at the Concerts du Triton, held at the École Normale de Musique, on 23 January 1939 by the Wagnerian soprano Marcelle Bunlet, with Messiaen at the piano.[121] Messiaen later made a recording of his *Harawi* and Debussy's *Cinq poèmes de Charles Baudelaire* (1887–9) with Bunlet in 1954. *Chants de terre* reflects Messiaen's joy at the birth of his son, Pascal, on 14 July 1937 in Boulogne-Billancourt, Hauts-de Seine, addressed as 'Pilule' in song IV. Like the earlier cycle, *Chants de terre* adapted aspects of psalmody and plainchant vocalises to create the incantatory vocal lines.[122] Early photos show the intimacy of family life, but Messiaen's relationship with Pascal was not overtly close (he did not attend Pascal's wedding to Josette Bender on 2 August 1958, for example).[123] If it seems that Messiaen was repeating the pattern of being an absent father absorbed in his own work, career and vocation, an example set by his own father, such a view must be tempered by an understanding that there are many different ways of showing and manifesting love – Messiaen had bought the couple an apartment for instance, and they became reasonably regular holiday guests at Petichet.[124] Pascal Emmanuel Messiaen became a Russian teacher. He and his wife did not have children. Pascal died on 31 January 2020 in Pézenas, Hérault, in the same year as his half-brother, Charles-Marie Messiaen.

Messiaen's language and imagery is more complex in *Chants de terre* than *Poèmes pour Mi*. The piano writing is more sophisticated (such as the organ trio-sonata texture used in song II), there are long melismatic alleluias (II) and the use of made-up childlike language ('io, malonlanlaine, ma' in III), perhaps an affectionate portrait of the way small children imitate, but mispronounce, adult words. Song III also imagines the jumble of images of his son's internal world (through wonder and play), the 'exuberant and overflowing enchantment [*féerie*] of childhood', as Messiaen put it in his defence of the work.[125] *Chants de terre* represents Messiaen's joyous perceptions of the child ('All the light birds fly from your hands') and is also part regression and part Surrealist, a transcendent intellectualization of childhood, but reveals the profound bonds of love inscribed in 'the rainbows of innocence that have fallen from your eyes' (song IV). The carillons of the last movement of *Poèmes* return in songs III and IV (especially on the word 'pascal', alluding to both Easter and to his son) and in song VI of *Chants de terre*. The tenderness and the violence of love are mixed; Pascal's birth is linked to his death just as Christ's birth is linked to his crucifixion, but Christ remains as a panacea to mortal death through powerful musical imagery.

Messiaen returns to the image of the sleeping child, a trope of writing about the infant Christ. The final song is a vocalise 'Alleluia', an idea Messiaen had used at the end of the first song of *Poèmes*, with apocalyptic images of stars, colours and angels that sing of resurrection beyond death, encapsulated in the liminal timbral saturation of the final piano chord – the 'effect of a stained-glass window'[126] – and in the textual superego injunction at the end ('wash yourself in the truth'). As at the end of *Le Banquet céleste*, this piece (and cycle) concludes on the 'dominant' of F# major, which functions as a modal 'tonic' without needing to resolve.

Messiaen's final work before the Second World War was the organ cycle *Les Corps Glorieux*, completed on 29 August 1939 and subtitled 'seven brief visions of the resurrected life'.[127] The work addresses how sacred mysteries can be represented in modern music as a complementary liturgy refiguring Catholic theology. Later Messiaen was to reflect on the meaning of this dramatic work, with reference to both Aquinas's categories of the body's resurrected capabilities and Surrealism:

> I have always had a taste for the marvellous . . . my love of the marvellous is found in the choice of the qualities of the *Corps Glorieux*, agility, force, brilliance and subtlety to which I dedicated one of my most important organ works . . . How marvellous it would be, in effect, to pass through walls, to be transported in an instant across incommensurable distances, and to be one's own light. The truths of faith contain a certain Surrealist poetry.[128]

He would also reflect that this work (specifically the idea of the 'subtlety' of the resurrected body) was fruit born of his imagination, which had been informed in childhood by the fantastical characters (such as phantoms, sorcerers, fairies) in Shakespeare.[129]

Unlike *La Nativité*, there is no didactic preface for *Les Corps Glorieux*, but Messiaen defended the work in an article, noting that it 'seeks to charm more than surprise'. He acknowledged the 'innovative registrations' in *La Nativité* and endorsed the new language of *Les Corps Glorieux* as appropriate for expressing the alterity of its subject-matter.[130] Messiaen's musical language uses many technical acquisitions from earlier works, including the deformation of plainchant, such as the solemn-tone Gregorian 'Salve Regina' in piece I and the Easter hymn 'Victimae paschali laudes' in 'Combat de la Mort et de la Vie' (piece IV). There is also the refiguration of Hindu melodies (*jātis*) in piece III.[131] Messiaen's own analysis of 'Combat', unwittingly perhaps, opens up a modernist aporia between a didactic explanation of clear developmental and tonal traditional thought and its violent and abrasive musical expression.[132] Certainly, there is reinvestment in mysticism and human inadequacy, as well as ideals of 'ressourcement' theology, a conservative movement (*c.* 1935–60) that advocated for a rejuvenation of Catholic thought through a return to traditional sources and texts,[133] but this work moves beyond invoking or repeating religious ideologies or dogma. Instead, it attempts to redescribe our sense of being-in-the-world through what we might understand of the next. Beauty and mystery are informed by violence – by 'death punctuating all moments of life', as Falcinelli commented on 'Combat'[134] – by a confrontation with the aporias in human knowledge, and by a rupture and leaving of one phenomenal reality for an unknown spiritual domain. Truth – Messiaen's truth – becomes a necessary matter of vision and faith.

What is particularly revolutionary about the pieces in *Les Corps Glorieux* is the way in which the phraseology of plainchant is adapted and deformed. Like Duruflé and Tournemire, Messiaen had 'a Gregorian soul', and kept Gregorian books on his organ stand.[135] He played and taught what Tournemire called the 'inexhaustible source of mysterious and splendid lines – plainchant, the triumph of modal art'.[136] Messiaen went beyond Tournemire's 'interludes, fantasies, paraphrases, chorales, etc.'[137] in *Les Corps* to internalize the musical developmental changes found in a plainchant tract or alleluia, for example. In the second piece, 'Les eaux de la Grâce', for instance, the listener can perceive similar phrases in the right hand repeated, changed and recontextualized, and certain motifs that undergo creative changes that counter Boulez's later critique of non-development and 'staticism' in Messiaen's music.

In both *La Nativité* and *Les Corps Glorieux*, Messiaen created an iconography that is not merely a means of contemplating God for the viewer. These icons are meant, as the theologian Rowan Williams has pointed out, as a form of 'divine presence and action' through which we are opened up 'to the action of God . . . to be acted upon'.[138] Icons therefore are not only, as the psychoanalytic philosopher Jacques Lacan states, 'intended to please God', who is also looking at the icon, but to be understood as a two-way telescope through which God meets the viewer's gaze. Both participate in making meaning and belief.[139] According to Williams, the icon, in the way in which it is made, directs and suggests how we are to act.[140] Such works speak of Messiaen's contribution to humanity through exemplars, or images, but they also act as a form of redirection of our gaze, asking us to examine our place in a religious ecology with God: who we are and, in an apocalyptical vein, where we might like to be.

3
On Messiaen and the Second World War, 1939–45

Messiaen's organ cycle *Les Corps Glorieux* was completed only weeks before the outbreak of the Second World War. The work can be understood as a creative reconfiguration of Aquinian theological categories through a gestural, burgeoning avant-garde language that would start to dominate Messiaen's music from the 1940s. *Les Corps* looks beyond worldly turmoil as an act of Christian faith and as an eschatological fantasy projection of humanity's destiny through art. In a more psychoanalytic way, it can also be understood as a form of repression of Messiaen's surroundings, and as a regression into the sanctuary of religious imagery and imagination.

Such music attempts to reframe personal trauma through religious-modernist expression. It can be understood as a profession of faith animated through liminal expressions of joy, love, violence, death and hedonism. This infusion is technically manifested through a form of avant-garde artistic research. For Messiaen, the organ at the Église de la Saint-Trinité was a catalyst in this ecology. Although it might be considered a rather conservative medium, Messiaen's church organ loft acted as a locus for experimentation and synthesis that resulted in music that advocated for a form of worldly emancipation.[1] The listener to Messiaen's music is asked to participate in this vision that understands humanity as being in need not merely of redemption through art, as Wagner would have it – to achieve a higher vision of our own lives, purpose and relation to others – but of a Christian experience of salvation.

This vision of art was made more poignant through Messiaen's wartime experiences. On 10 May 1940, Germany invaded France; Paris fell on 14 June to the Germans, and an armistice was signed on 22 June. Messiaen had been mobilized on 4 September 1939 and worked as a

Messiaen as a soldier at Metz, winter 1939–40.

private in Sarreguemines in eastern France, near the border with Germany.[2] In a letter to Jean Langlais on 2 November 1939, he described his 'scratched and blackened hands': 'the handling of the pickaxe, the flies, the carrying of heavy and more unlikely weights (from tree trunks to lithographic stones) [prevented] me from maintaining a very intimate relationship with music.'[3] He played the organ for various services, including at Christmas 1939, improvising in an 'avant-garde style, with a certain solo on a 16' bourdon and tierce with a harmonic background that would make Schoenberg shudder'; Messiaen was surprised that, unlike his parishioners, 'the soldiers were not scandalized.'[4]

Messiaen then worked as a nurse 'with a long white coat' at nearby Sarralbe before helping to create events as a musician for the Centre Musical et Théatral of the 2nd Army (CMTA), based in Verdun, where he got to know the cellist Étienne Pasquier (1905–1997) and Henri Akoka (1912–1976), an Algerian Jewish clarinetist who by 26 January 1942 had returned from captivity and was 'en zone libre'.[5] The Centre Musical et Théatral was presided over by Charles Huntziger, the Vichy government war minister, and two others, and it was here that Messiaen met the Egyptologist and composer Guy Bernard-Delapierre (1907–1979; the eventual dedicatee of *Technique de mon langage musical*). By 29 November 1943, Delapierre had offered his house (formerly Racine's home) as a place for Messiaen to teach alongside his Conservatoire class.[6] This private tutoring included Boulez – who met Messiaen at Delapierre's apartment on 28 June 1944 and attended his class from 8 December 1944 – Serge Nigg (harmony class of 1941–4) and Yvonne Loriod (harmony class of 1942–3).[7] This class was known as 'Les Flèches' (The Arrows). It was here that Boulez heard Messiaen analyse Bartók, Berg's *Lyrische Suite* (1925–6) and Stravinsky's *Le Sacre du printemps* (1913) – an analysis 'with a virgin eye', as Messiaen described it.[8] Stravinsky and Berg were forbidden by the Nazis from the Conservatoire curriculum. Messiaen's thinking shaped Boulez's later analysis of *Le Sacre* and also his interest in the music of the Second Viennese School, which would be a lifelong touchstone of his writings.

The eight-movement *Quatuor pour la fin du Temps* for piano, clarinet, violin and violoncello had a complex genesis. Messiaen composed movement III, 'Abîme des oiseaux' for solo clarinet, at Verdun in June 1940 for Henri Akoka.[9] Messiaen was captured by the Germans on 22 June 1940 near Toul, and walked to a field west of Nancy with Pasquier and Akoka, where they stayed for around three weeks (this is where Akoka had the chance to play Messiaen's piece).[10] They were then transferred to a camp at Brabois-Villiers for ten days. Messiaen had only his clothes and a bag of pocket scores by Bach, Beethoven, Berg, Debussy, Ravel, Stravinsky and Honegger. Messiaen was also able to draw on his memory of 'whole acts of *Pélleas*' while in captivity.[11] All three musicians were taken to Stalag VIIIA Görlitz in Silesia, a large site of around 30 hectares (74 ac) that formed one of the *Stammlager*, short for *Kriegsgefangenen-Mannschaftsstammlager*. Messiaen had to wear a uniform with the initials K. F. (*Kriegsgefangener*, that is, prisoner of war) on it.[12]

In 1944 Pierre Messiaen described the abject conditions of Olivier's capture and transportation, his dysentery and convalescence, and the premiere of the *Quatuor*.[13] The train to Stalag VIIIA, he recounted, took four days 'among the urine and shit, with nothing to drink, and nothing to eat'.[14] Amid the privations of camp life (hunger, cold, brutality) that gave him 'dreams and colourful visions', Messiaen's imagination was nourished by reading the book of Revelation and seeing the Northern Lights.[15] Messiaen was given leave from camp chores and encouraged to compose by Hauptmann Karl-Albert Brüll (1902–1999), a lawyer, interpreter and member of the Wehrmacht who was also a Catholic.[16] Messiaen would later be described by the Polish writer Zdzisław Nardelli (1913–2006), a fellow prisoner (and camp librarian), as appearing 'like a human torso with a head of stone on top'. Nardelli also gave this peculiar but distinctive description of Messiaen: 'he heard with his eyes and watched with his ears.'[17]

The first piece of the Quatuor in the camp to be written was the trio 'Intermède' (IV). Messiaen adapted, from memory, movement V of the *Quatuor* from *Fêtes des belles eaux* (1937) for six ondes Martenots (a work that would later inspire Levinas' *Contrepoints irréels – variations répercutées* (1975), for the same combination of instruments), and movement VIII from the second part of the *Diptyque* (1930), 'L'Éternité bienheureuse'. Messiaen composed in the latrines and in the living quarters of the barracks in Hut 19A.[18]

The quartet was rehearsed for four hours a day by Jean Le Boulaire (1913–1999) (violin), Akoka, Pasquier and Messiaen in a makeshift theatre (Hut 27B), with Messiaen acting as coach.[19] Messiaen later described to Antoine Goléa the 'cello with three strings' (in fact there were four, as Pasquier would later remind Messiaen) and the unregulated upright piano with keys that stuck.[20] A poster was created to advertise the premiere, which was to be held on 15 January 1941. The audience included 'farmworkers, labourers, intellectuals, career soldiers, doctors and priests'. 'Five thousand people' were not 'fed' this work in the open air, however, to borrow Messiaen's biblical metaphor, but rather a few hundred sheltering in a large hut.[21] Messiaen stated: 'Never have I been listened to with such attention and such understanding.'[22] On 1 April 1941, a review appeared in the French-language camp newspaper *Lumignon: bi-mensuel du Stalag VIIIA*, which revealed mixed responses among the ranks of listeners while commending the work's 'sovereign mastery'.[23]

The subject of the work returned to the composer's pre-war obsessions – time and the colours of the apocalypse. The quartet was composed 'to escape from the snow and the war, from captivity, and from myself'.[24] In ecstatic Surrealist language, Messiaen declared:

> In my dreams, I hear and see classified chords and melodies, known colours and forms; but after this transitory stage, I pass into the irreal and undergo with ecstasy a whirling; a gyratory insufflation of super-human sounds and colours. These swords

> of fire, these flows of blue-orange lava, and these brusque stars: here is the jumble, here is the rainbow![25]

The *Quatuor pour la fin du Temps* was dedicated to the angel that announces that there would be 'no more time' (Revelation 10:6).[26] Messiaen would maintain that this idea should be taken literally.[27] Yet Messiaen radically misread this verse and took it out of context. The New Revised Standard Version of the Bible translates this verse as 'there shall be no more delay.' The angel in St John's narrative does not therefore announce the end of time, but that there will be no more time left before God completes his purposes; time and humanity will be changed in a way that remains unclear.[28] The promise of the transformation of the world into God's kingdom will occur in the future. Messiaen's *Quatuor* can therefore be more properly understood as an act of faith that this transformation will happen, but also, through the course of its eight movements, as an improvisation with time and our own experience of it as a semblance of this future time. The theologian Philip Edgcumbe Hughes comments on Revelation 10:6:

> Time, however, far from being an entity in itself, is but a convention for understanding and recording the sequence of changes and happenings that belong to human experience and that constitute history as a whole. As depicted in this book of Revelation, eternity is certainly not an uneventful, static, and quasi-frozen state, for the new heaven and the new earth are full of activity.[29]

Time only appears to be 'static', a trope that Messiaen uses to connect himself to Neoplatonic theology. Yet here and elsewhere in his music, Messiaen creates an ongoing tension and dialogue between stabilizing and centripetal musical elements and destabilizing and centrifugal elements. This is not 'staticism' but rather a music in which different types of dynamic systems interact at different levels and intensities to engender a variety of temporal paradigms and experiences.

The composer Harrison Birtwistle (1934–2022) regarded the *Quatuor pour la fin du Temps* as foundational for all Messiaen's work. He described some of his own music as being 'in a permanent state of exposition' and stated that Messiaen's *Quatuor* is 'music without transition'.[30] Yet the first movement of the *Quatuor* could be considered as being in a state of continual transition. The first movement contains a series of 29 chords with seventeen rhythmic values in the piano, made from three Hindu rhythms.[31] These function as a template for juxtaposed birdsong (a blackbird and nightingale), symbolizing 'freedom' and 'liberty' for the composer, and other improvisatory material.[32] The Hindu rhythms, 'independent of the metre', continually appear with different chords.[33] The modernist complexity of Messiaen's music entails engagement between background systems – which can perhaps be discerned, but not quantified, by the listener – and a foreground sense of continual temporal evolution that is dynamic and emergent without the necessity of a goal, such as cadence.

In the middle of the second movement, a unison strings melody (two octaves apart in its own modal and temporal paradigm) floats over modal and other chords in the piano. The limitation of the types of material and their repetition through superimposition and imbrication (without any metrical accentuation) structures this improvisation with time (rather than timelessness). The rhythmic elasticity of the melody is created through a delicate balance of centrifugal and centripetal forces focused around the pitch of D. The gentle disjunction between the melody and piano accompaniment can be understood as an evolving timbral and harmonic colourization of the melody that contributes to a narrative flux of densities and intensities in this music. In the mostly unison sixth movement, there are very clear phrase structures and a sense of 'antecedent-consequent' structures, fragmentation, variation and other traditional means of musical and temporal development. In the two 'louange' movements (v and viii), traditional phrase constructions are disguised by the slow tempo. While the poetic meaning of the work is clear for the composer, the images these movements provide are not of 'the end of time' but of its creative reformation.

Messiaen described the *Quatuor pour la fin du Temps* as a 'summit', but it was a work that also looked forward to many of his compositional preoccupations of the 1940s.[34] The *Quatuor* became one of the most celebrated chamber works of the twentieth century. It inspired Tōru Takemitsu's *Quatrain* (1974–5) for this group of instruments (piano, violin, cello and clarinet) as soloists and orchestra, and also his *Quatrain ii* (1977), for the same quartet of instruments. Takemitsu went to Messiaen for advice on these works. He described Messiaen while playing the piano and discussing his instrumentation of the *Quatuor*: 'It sounded like an orchestra. Each of his fingers made a different instrumental sound.'[35] Messiaen's former student Tristan Murail (b. 1947) also wrote *Stalag viiia* (2018) for the same instrumental combination as the *Quatuor*, a work commissioned by the Festival Messiaen au Pays de la Meije. It uses various clearly recognizable textures, rhythms, chords and ideas from Messiaen's *Quatuor* as points of creative departure, and can lead directly onwards (in performance) to Messiaen's work. The *Quatuor* has also inspired a version of the work as a ballet.[36]

Had Messiaen died in Stalag VIIIA, his contribution and originality would still be significant, yet this work helped to refine and amplify his musical mission. At this same time, Messiaen's brother, Alain, was a prisoner (no. 81.342) in Stalag VIIB in Memmingen, Swabia. Alain wrote a poem on 26 August 1941, the fourteenth anniversary of his mother's death, which concludes with an invocation of the last verse of Olivier's description (in the score) of the second part of 'Combat de la mort et de la vie' (*Les Corps*), and also cites Cécile Sauvage's last major work, the lyric drama *Aimer après la mort*. Like his older brother, Alain clearly sensed his mother's sadness, but likely did not know the reason for it until much later. The conclusion of the poem reads:

> Mother! Mother who sacrificed for us
> Her young life, died loved, don't leave us! . . .
>
> The Father holds you back: his moving voice
> Recalls the joys and tribulations
> Of my brother musician and of the poet
> Who invokes you here – evening of your beautiful song
>
> In the sunlight, of your silent sadness.
> O Mother, you who knew *love after death*,
> Ask the blessed Virgin for him
> To be liberated soon from his fate![37]

During Olivier's incarceration, his wife Claire Delbos was busy with their son, Pascal, and the composition of *L'Offrande faite à Marie* for organ. Messiaen would later perform this work on 17 November 1943, between the first public performance of *Les Corps Glorieux* on 15 November – he had played it privately to his students on 22 July 1941 – and *La Nativité* on 19 November.[38] The manuscript (with Messiaen's fingerings, pedal indications and registrations) records Delbos' movements.[39] The first piece, 'Voici la servante du Seigneur' (one page), was written at Neussargues between October 1940 and January 1941 and uses a modal monody over chords, a texture similar to that used in 'Le Sourire' (from Sauvage's *Primevère*) the second of Messiaen's *Trois mélodies* (1930) and his only song to employ a text by his mother. The other pieces of *L'Offrande faite à Marie* are:

- II 'Vierge digne de louanges', five pages (Neussargues, May–August 1941)
- III 'Mère des pauvres', two pages (Paris, October 1938–March 1939)
- IV 'Mère toute-joyeuse', three and a half pages (Neussargues, July–August 1941)
- V 'Debout, la mère des douleurs . . .', one and a half pages (Paris, March–July 1939)
- VI 'Secours des Chrétiens, Reine de la Paix', eleven pages (Petichet, August 1939, and Neussargues, September 1939–27 May 1940)

Delbos' writing has a classicist, modernist asceticism and a completely distinct musical voice. Her melodies often deform plainchant, with dissonance frequently arising from contrapuntal and canonic writing. The last movement uses triple-pedalling and includes a section to be played on all three manuals at once in the final fugue, and a chorale, marked *ff*, with another two *ff*s added in Messiaen's hand in the autograph.[40] The work appeared in a catalogue of the publisher Combre but was not published, possibly owing to Delbos' declining health.

Messiaen was liberated on 10 February 1941 through Marcel Dupré's petition to Sonderführer Z Dr Fritz Piersig (1900–1978), a musicologist responsible for controlling French musical life who also worked in the Nazi propaganda department in Paris.[41] Upon release, Messiaen passed through a quarantine camp at Sathonay, near Lyon, arriving there on 16 February 1941.[42] He then went to Neussargues before moving on to Vichy on 12 March, where he was welcomed by Daniel-Lesur and Maurice Martenot (1898–1980), the cellist who invented the ondes Martenot in 1928.[43] In Vichy, the 'Association Jeune France', a reformation of La Jeune France (including Baudrier and Daniel-Lesur), was created (Jolivet was in Paris) and continued until 10 July 1942, when the group was dissolved.[44] Messiaen wrote some incidental choral music for *Portique pour une fille de France* on the subject of Joan of Arc (*Jeanne d'Arc*) – a paragon of French patrimony. It was written as a pageant by Pierre Schaeffer and Pierre Barbier as a propaganda work for the Vichy regime and was performed in stadiums in Lyon and Marseille and many other small towns and villages on the feast of St Joan of Arc on 11 May 1941; Joan had been appropriated as a liberating spiritual and nationalist figure by many different regimes in French history and was well known as a subject in film (notably in Georges Méliès' *Jeanne d'Arc* (1900) and C. T. Dreyer's *La Passion de Jeanne d'Arc* (1928), for example) and oratorio (Honegger's *Jeanne d'Arc au bûcher* (1938)). Two of the choruses, written by Messiaen (a 'Te Deum', using Gregorian melodies, and 'Impropères'), have survived.[45] Perhaps understandably, Messiaen almost omitted these events from his biography.

Upon his return to Paris in 1941, Messiaen began teaching privately at the home of Nelly Eminger-Sivade at 53 rue Blanche, near La Trinité, who was Yvonne Loriod's godmother. It was here that Messiaen first encountered Loriod – in fact, through her playing of his piano *Préludes*.[46] Eminger-Sivade provided a space to rehearse and perform Messiaen's works, notably *Visions de l'Amen* on 9 May 1943.[47] From March 1941, Messiaen sought an appointment at the Conservatoire de Paris, and on 25 March, after some wrangling on account of his reputation as an avant-gardist, he became a professor of harmony – a decision made under Henri Rabaud's directorship of the Conservatoire.

Messiaen gave his first class at the Conservatoire on Debussy's *Prélude à l'après-midi d'un faune* on 7 May 1941, just after Claude Delvincourt (1888–1954) was appointed as director on 15 April.[48] Messiaen's 'harmony class' was one of five that existed at the school.[49] His lessons were presented three times a week, and each would last for four hours.[50] Loriod was in this class, and she was later joined by Boulez, who enrolled on 23 January 1945 and finished on 11 June.[51] Loriod would later become a piano professor at the Conservatoire from 1967 to 1989.[52] Messiaen had replaced the Jewish musician André Bloch (1873–1960), and in order to obtain the position he had to sign a letter attesting: 'I am not Jewish, my four grandparents are not Jewish, and there is absolutely no Jewish blood in my family.'[53] Such declarations formed part of the larger sphere of German control of concert life, repertoire and performance in occupied Paris.

Signing this document made Messiaen an unwilling participant in the Nazi regime, but this was a necessary part of rebuilding his life after captivity. It enabled him to work in a prestigious institution in Paris and

Messiaen at the piano in 1945, class of 1945–6, with Jean-Christophe Benoît (seated to his left).

provided the basis for financial and professional security. Messiaen's music had continued to be performed in his absence, and upon his return to Paris he attempted to forge his career as pianist, organist, concert organizer and impresario under the constraints of occupied Paris, including work for the Association de Musique Contemporaine.[54]

In summer 1942, Messiaen was already at work on his *Technique de mon langage musical* (TMLM) in Neussargues.[55] According to Langlais, Messiaen discovered his system of composing through analysis of his own music, 'and that is his artistic personality'.[56] TMLM is a stocktaking of Messiaen's work: it demonstrates his fertile imagination through musical examples, sometimes with little explanation, which invite the reader to engage with their own creative 'capacity for adaptation'.[57]

The *Quatuor pour la fin du Temps* received its Paris premiere on 24 June 1941, with mixed reviews; it was published on 21 May 1942 and was later recorded by Messiaen with Jean and Étienne Pasquier (violin and cello) and André Vacellier (clarinet) in 1956.[58] In 1941 Messiaen also composed a piece for solo ondes Martenot: *Musique de Scène pour un Oedipe* (intended for a play called *Dieu est innocent*).[59] Messiaen was offered a commission by the film editor and sound technician Denise Tual

(1906–2000), also known as Denise Batcheff, who had been impressed by hearing Messiaen's organ improvisations in La Trinité for the Concerts de la Pléiade in October 1942.[60] The piece for Tual would be the *Visions de l'Amen*, which, according to Loriod, reused the themes from *Musique de Scène*.[61] For Messiaen, the Concerts de la Pléiade 'represented an extraordinary heroic effort of a protestation of the French intellect against the physical, physiological and material occupation of the Germans'.[62] The *Visions de l'Amen* was also partly his response to the German edict that prohibited large-scale performances of French music. Messiaen had already begun work on *Visions de l'Amen* in or before October 1942, and he finished it on 17 March 1943.[63] This seven-movement work is another cyclic piece that self-consciously used a main leitmotif, the 'thème de la creation', and other musical motifs identified in the score's preface. It was premiered on 10 May 1943 before a distinguished audience including such figures as Jean Cocteau, Christian Dior, Francis Poulenc and Paul Valéry.[64] Honegger attended the premiere and stated that this was one of 'the most important works he had heard in years'.[65] Messiaen and Loriod first recorded the work on 18 June 1949, with Loriod playing piano one and the composer playing piano two.[66]

Messiaen's *Visions* are grounded in theology and mystical literature, in particular the writings of Léon Bloy (1846–1917), whose interest in ascetic, worldly suffering and expiation as paths to faith were important to both Tournemire and Alain Messiaen.[67] The *Visions* were also inspired by Marmion's theology and *Paroles de Dieu* (1899) by Ernest Hello (1828–1885), an author referred to by Tournemire as 'the Franck of literature'.[68] It is also possible to see this work partly as a response to Tournemire's *Douze Préludes-Poèmes*, op. 58, for piano (1932), which charts the ascent of humanity from birth through various life stages, 'preparation for death', mediations on the Father, Son and Holy Spirit, and then finally a 'glorification of the Trinity'. Messiaen's *Visions* likewise move from the dawn of Creation (by God), cosmic creation to human consummation in God after death.

Much later, Boulez reflected that in the early 1940s, Messiaen was regarded as an 'eccentric' and 'marginal', not the 'grand maître' of today.[69] In the programme note for the premiere of *Visions de l'Amen*, Messiaen summed up his life and observed that his work

> utilized a particular language without any attachment to a school . . . The procedures of this language . . . and the bizarre terminology used to describe them, have often been criticized

> – perhaps wrongly! Because the author did not know the workings of this language until recently, he exploited them unwittingly throughout these years.
>
> Olivier Messiaen is above all a Catholic musician. Religious or not, his works carry the mark of the Christian faith, and implicitly sing of the mystery of Christ.[70]

The subjects of the work – both eschatological and cosmic – would seem perhaps too big for the sound of two almost identical pianos. Yet Messiaen attempted to surpass such constraints, especially in the majesterial A-major resonances of the two pianos produced at the conclusion of the work. The understanding of liminality is an obsession of modern thought, and both the *Quatuor* and *Visions* can be understood as works concerned with finitude.

Messiaen outlines several meanings of 'Amen' in his preface – creation, the acceptance of God's will, desire for reciprocity with God and the sempiternal, and consummation in Paradise.[71] His music engages the human capacity to imagine beyond finitude. This concept can be understood as being towards an ending, but also 'the inescapability of limit or destruction'.[72] In this thinking, we are bound by God's creation. But this concept can also mean an inability to achieve finitude or completion – a state of dwelling for the community of believers. Messiaen's music addresses this contingent state, but it crucially invests in a resistance to finitude, to the necessity of an ending, exemplified in the resurrected Christ, and this provides for a form of traumatic enjoyment – a 'filling out the gap' – that is essential to the experience of his music.[73]

There is much ritualistic, repetitive and almost hallucinatory music in *Visions*, especially in movement II; its quasi-magical mien, in the form of stars and planets dancing, can also be detected in Jolivet's later *Hopi Snake Dance* for two pianos (1948). This type of music is likewise present in movement V, in which the possibility of radical human alterity after death is figured through liminal beings: angels, saints and birds. In a psychoanalytic vein, this excessive music might be associated with hysteria 'characterized by the function of an unsatiated desire', the inability to achieve wholeness, and the attempt to overcome such issues.[74] This knowledge causes both pleasure and pain (*jouissance*), which can be detected in the reception through the so-called 'cas Messiaen', discussed below. The gestural language and tempi in the work are important to this sense of overcoming. This sense is manifested in an attempt to defeat time through slow music, and in the ecstatic crescendos in movements I and VII that build towards images of fulfilment and reinscribe the inevitable progress of time towards an ending.

The third movement, 'Amen de l'agonie', recalls Dupré's *Le Chemin de la Croix* XI and the first movement of Messiaen's *La Nativité*, effectively conjoining the death of Christ with his birth – both understood as forms of 'agony'. Through their dissonance, these melodies develop Christ's abject and willing suffering as an image of human finitude against the backdrop of creation. Messiaen had considered orchestrating this piece as *Chant du paradis*, but he had actually thought of writing a piece with this name some years earlier while sketching 'Les Bergers' (*La Nativité*).[75] This is but one of many prospective works mentioned by Messiaen in his sketches that never came to pass, such as *Paradis* for orchestra, piano and ondes Martenot (adapted from the last two chapters of the Apocalypse); *Poème symphonique sur la Noël*; *La Souffle de l'esprit* for ondes Martenot and orchestra; and a *Litanies du Saint Nom de Jésus* for two pianos.[76]

The largest central movement of *Visions* (added in winter 1942–3) is the 'Amen du désir' in F# major. In psychoanalytic thought, desire is understood as already being within the onlooker; it is unconscious, indestructible, something that both forms and organizes fantasy and is constructed to be unfulfilled.[77] Messiaen's trope of static eternity as a zone of *jouissance* is reconfigured here as divine longing and human libidinal desire, and a desire for knowledge of what lies beyond finitude.

The ideals of ritual, liturgy and desire are amplified in Messiaen's *Trois petites Liturgies de la Présence Divine* for piano, ondes, female choir and small orchestra, again commissioned by Tual and originally intended, like *Visions*, for two pianos. Messiaen wrote his *Liturgies* between November 1943 and 14 March 1944. It was premiered in the Concerts de la Pléiade on 21 April 1945.[78]

Messiaen had written the accompanying text (in the score), what Stephen Schloesser calls an 'ecstatic extended meditation on divine immanence': God within me (inspired by plainchant tracts and the Song of Songs); the ascended God in himself (a set of increasing bacchanalian variations alternating with varied refrain and couplets also varied, and punctuated by a choral in the middle and a short reminiscence at the end); to God in all things.[79] The work continued a scandal in the press, the 'cas Messiaen', which had broken out after the premiere of *Visions de l'Amen*.

Messiaen later described the effect of his commentaries at the premiere of his *Vingt Regards sur l'Enfant-Jésus* (1944) as a 'bomb' that created more of an effect than the music, because he had expressed himself in a Surrealist language and because he was a 'believer'.[80] His commentaries for the premiere of the *Visions de l'Amen* as much as the music provoked the young Jeanne Demessieux, who noted this in her diary for 22 June 1943:

> Concert of works by Messiaen, Salle Gaveau. The *Poèmes pour Mi*, the grand [*Visions de l'*] *Amen*, [and] an excerpt from the *Quartet for the End of Time*. An introductory lecture. Commentaries on the works almost as lengthy as the works themselves. I was very tired when I left the concert.
>
> I've refrained from taking sides, being disgusted with the polemics. (My non-involvement in the 'Messiaen case' scandalizes all the hotheads.) I can't help doubting the sincerity of this music, which is more philosophy than music. And this [kind of] philosophy irritates me; I have my century's horror of mysticism, which seems false and smacks of paganism.
>
> As I see it, use of an abstract language to preach moral laws or religious dogma is either an outrage or heresy. Anything is possible with abstraction. That's the totality of Messiaen. As a result, those who would follow him cannot end up with anything other than nothingness. His music? There were two times in this concert in which I thought I perceived musical momentum, beauty, moderation. The large ensemble seemed all the same to me, formulaic (Messiaen's formulas). The dense, vertical writing absolutely suffocated me; by this, I'm not speaking of his endless melancholy melodies, which have nothing to do anymore with counterpoint. In the last Amen, the high-pitched counterpoint was a relief.
>
> Detail: Messiaen appeared on the stage to play (and this was in the evening) in unusually colourful attire, with a blue shirt with turned down collar(!). They gave him sustained applause.
>
> In summary: too many notes; I miss Mozart.[81]

Demessieux's teacher, Marcel Dupré, commented privately to her in 1945, concerning the same concert: 'Do you know why Messiaen is wrong? Because he publishes texts of his own devising, and only priests have the right to do this.'[82]

The 'cas Messiaen' was later described by Antoine Goléa as *comme d'un cas pathologique* (like a pathological case).[83] One critic described the

Trois petites Liturgies as 'a work of tinsel, false magnificence and pseudo-mysticism . . . looking about anxiously like an angel wearing lipstick'.[84] But Poulenc, who was at the premiere, described it aptly as a 'a marvellous work', yet also noted the 'unfortunate influence of Dukas' in the piece.[85] Honegger described it as 'a magnificent work . . . created by a great musician' and observed that a 'cas' appears each time 'a notable personality appears in music'.[86] The American composer and critic Virgil Thomson observed that, despite the 'obvious' 'faults of his taste' attributed to mysticism, it fulfilled his earlier judgement of Messiaen's 'religio-musical style as the determination to produce somewhere in every piece an apotheosis destined at once to open up the heavens and to bring down the house'.[87] Stockhausen was touched by *Liturgies* and later described it as 'very interior' and 'oneiric', but Boulez described the 'annoyance when we heard A major in the *petites Liturgies*!'[88]

In 1962 Messiaen described the work as 'glittering [*chatoyant*]' and stated that it was attacked because his critics 'found it too coloured . . . too melodic . . . too well harmonised . . . too well heard [by the composer]'.[89] For Messiaen, looking back with rose-tinted glasses in 1978, the premiere of *Liturgies* was an 'immense and immediate' success; he noted that 'the public' at the premiere, which included Georges Braque, Paul Éluard, Pierre Reverdy, Pierre Boulez, Pierre Henry, Georges Auric, Henri Sauguet and Claude Delvincourt, was 'especially brilliant and cultured'.[90] He provides some unhelpful apologetics, referring to the 'attack above all aimed at the poem', which, because the work was 'doctrinal', he observes, 'seems unattackable'. He then advises the listener to forget the words, the music and the scandal and to take the work in from a unitary perception, like looking at a stained-glass window.[91]

At the heart of this 'tempête' was a perceived conflict between revolution and tradition, public testament and private faith, between religion and sensuality, even of 'torrid eroticism' and an irritation at the mawkish 'mystical-poetic' texts 'with which he surrounds his works', as Poulenc put it.[92] Invective conflated Messiaen's work with Messiaen the man, yet it also recognized the powerful sensual and affective quality of his art, which embodied the Surrealist ideal of *dépaysement*, or aesthetic disorientation.[93] Messiaen's involvement with La Jeune France and the 'cas' enabled him both to espouse a public ideological position, stronger than that of his fellow student organ composers Jean Langlais and Gaston Litaize, and partially to escape the cult of the organ (*Visions*, *Liturgies* and *Vingt Regards* were not organ works).

Some notable critics after the 'cas', such as Bernard Gavoty and Claude Rostand, would later become apologists and advocates for Messiaen. Others, such as Suzanne Demarquez and the composers Daniel-Lesur, Baudrier and Honegger, were unfailingly supportive and underlined Messiaen's originality. Darius Milhaud noted sanguinely that Messiaen's works 'enjoyed an enormous vogue after the liberation'.[94] Poulenc's responses, however, in public and in private, were more critical. He opined: 'One either loves or detests this music,' and noted that Messiaen had inspired a 'fanatical sect' (students who had booed Stravinsky's neo-classical works) around him 'despite an impossible literary jargon'.[95] More generously, Poulenc noted: 'Evidently Messiaen and I do not kneel in the same fashion, but this is of little importance if we make the public participate in our fervour.'[96]

In *Trois petites Liturgies*, Messiaen's 'cultured' public heard a conflation of liturgy, Catholic theology, hallucinatory repetition (perhaps owing something in its sound world to the Balinese music Messiaen first heard in 1931), and a form of Surrealist alterity and beauty that they (rightly) associated with eroticism and desire, but also with a form of public witness, ardour and zeal.[97] What they also heard (*pace* Messiaen) was doctrinal, didactic and even oppressive, not merely symbolic, and provided a form of superego injunction through music ('you will, you must' believe or feel these things). The *Liturgies* are empowered by a Surrealist dialecticism; the intentionally pseudo-psychotic or magical-incantatory quality of the music that embodies the Freudian compulsion to repeat (*Wiederholungszwang*): immanence is expressed not through restraint but through a form of release of repression. In this work there is a sense of displacement, of the Freudian *Unheimlich* (uncanny), in which the familiar – chanting, for example – is returned as unfamiliar, surrounded by counterpoint.[98] In this light, the quasi-grotesque elements of the work can be understood as creating a form of defamiliarization, even alienation (realized and released in the invective against Messiaen) that is essential to its didacticism.

The texts were problematic for some of Messiaen's audience, especially 'Posez vous comme un sceau de mon coeur' (Set me as a seal upon thine heart), reworded from the Song of Songs (8:6) – later used by Daniel-Lesur in 'Épithalame', the seventh and final movement of his twelve-part a capella choral work *Le Cantique des cantiques* (1952) – and 'Imprimez votre nom dans mon sang' (Imprint your name in my blood).[99] The saturation of 'shining brightness' in *Liturgies* (through the celesta, vibraphones, cymbals and an extremely virtuosic piano part), glittering trills and naive chromatic rising passages (in II) give the work a slightly mawkish, narcissistic quality, reinterpreted by Messiaen as 'sincerity', that yet informs what is one of his most original and memorable pieces.[100] In short, the *Liturgies* raised controversy about the degree to which personal religious belief should intrude into public life, but it also demonstrated how profoundly music could communicate belief, even though these 'truths', as Messiaen understood them, were difficult or even unpalatable for much of his audience.

In 1962 Messiaen described 1944 as 'the most fecund year of my existence' in terms of musical creation.[101] The *Trois petities Liturgies* was followed by a cycle of twenty piano pieces: *Vingt Regards sur l'Enfant-Jésus*. It likely owed its actualization to Maurice Toesca's request for music to accompany his *Les Douze regards* – twelve poems on the Nativity for a series of radio broadcasts, commissioned by Pierre Schaeffer – but its inception again stemmed from Messiaen's reading of Marmion and other theological writings.[102] Messiaen wrote his *Vingt Regards* with the virtuoso capacities of Loriod in mind; he completed it in under six months, from 23 March to 8 September 1944, but earlier sketchbooks demonstrate extensive preparatory research for the work, and the first set of sketches in fact show Messiaen working on the cycle with a title but no final order.[103] Messiaen also referred to this work with a different title in a note in his sketches, the 'Cahier vert' (1932–44): 'Pour Regards sur la crèche – faire 12 pièces –' which also includes an early sketch for the 'Première communion de la Vierge' (XI) that was not included in the initial set of twelve pieces.[104] This suggests that Messiaen may have been considering a piano work about the Nativity to complement his nine-movement *La Nativité du Seigneur* (1935) for organ, well before Toesca's request in 1944.

Messiaen's initial ordering of the pieces (crossed out) in one of his sketchbooks was: I, II, a third piece to be entitled 'Regard des bergers et des mages' (which partly relates to the title of XVI), then IV, XVIII, V, XIV, X, IX, VII, XVII and XX.[105] This bears some similarity to the final work in that each group of three pieces here contains the leitmotif for God, whereas in the final ordering of the cycle, this 'theme' occurs in pieces I, V, VI, X, XI, XV, XIX and XX, and it acts as a refrain (a little like a rondo) for four interpolated sets of three other pieces.[106] Messiaen also regarded the cycle distributed around 'marker' pieces for God the Father (I), the Son (V), Holy Spirit (X), the Incarnation (XV) and finally for the Church (XX), because the 'church is the body of Christ and it continues Christ's [life]'.[107]

The *Vingt Regards* were completed just after the liberation of Paris on 25 August 1944.[108] The cycle lasts around two hours and is usually programmed as the only work in a concert. This is a landmark piece in twentieth-century piano repertory. It uses a 'theme of chords' and a set of leitmotifs for God, the cross and the star, and it forms a constellation of stained-glass windows around the infant Jesus. *Vingt Regards* traverse a series of symbolic and theological personages, immaterial concepts (time, the word, unction), the kiss of the infant and love (of God, Christ, the Virgin, the Church) through an unseen, but perceived, vision that implies a form of divine benevolence. There are many extraordinary things in this cycle, but it is worth calling attention to the portrayal of intimacy and interiority; the refiguring of the relationship between form and content (formal classicism challenged through pianistic gestures); the use of resonance (instrumental, harmonic, rhythmic resonances); and the internal coherence through leitmotifs across the largest of Messiaen's works to date.

Messiaen marks the first piece 'Extrêmement lent – mystérieux, avec amour', and throughout the listener is invited to participate in this feeling of not merely looking but feeling an immersive adoration for Christ. The tenderness is present in the Virgin's gaze (piece IV), the gaze between the Father and the Son (V), the lightness of the angels (VIII and XIV), Christ as the implacable central point of time (IX), the first communion of the Virgin (XI), the kiss of the infant Jesus (XV), silence (XVII) and the sleeping Jesus (XIX). Messiaen's music moves beyond functioning as a screen of icons (iconostasis), to instead present a radical animation of this central Christological event. It figures something of the shock, mystery and love that informs the encounter between God and humanity through Christ's birth.

Much research and experimentation went into *Vingt Regards*. For the fugue, 'Par Lui tout a été fait' (VI), Messiaen used the seventh fugue (in E♭ major, BWV 852 or 876) of Bach's *Das wohltemperierte Klavier* (Book I (1722) or II (1739–42) as a model; Messiaen does not specify which one exactly) and the fugue (the final movement) from Beethoven's 'Hammerklavier' piano sonata, op. 106 (1818), a work that he later taught in his Paris Conservatoire class in 1955–6, 1956–7 and 1964–5.[109] In the Bach fugue (Book I), and in Beethoven particularly, the balance of stability and instability that would dominate the form is implicit already in the subject, a feature that was evidently useful to Messiaen. 'Par Lui tout a été fait' was not part of the original twelve-piece plan of the cycle. As 'a fugue absolutely contrary to the "school" fugue',[110] it contributed, in an unexpected way, to Dupré's regeneration of fugue, which was a strong element of his improvisational practice and teaching. Unlike Dupré's fugues, Messiaen's piece creatively refigured and fractured the relationship between the vertical (harmony) and the horizontal (counterpoint). It also adapts the correspondences that normally exist within contrapuntal forms (canonic relations, for example), through rhythmic and registral deformation, as a form of narrative development. The subject-episode or verse-refrain ideal is also rethought. The fugue's subject functions as an increasingly unstable quilting point, while the connective 'episodes' become increasingly violent as a form of further radical destabilization, acting as both development and destruction. This type of creative and formal strategy was a precursor of Boulez's thought in his *Piano Sonata* No. 2 (1947–8), and this form of compositional thinking is considerably intensified in Iannis Xenakis's organ fugue – although it is not marked as such – *Gmeeoorh* (1974), of which Messiaen stated, 'properly speaking, this isn't an organ work, but it's a sensational piece.'[111]

Controlled violence is a feature of the cycle. It occurs in 'Regard de l'Esprit de joie' (x), which begins with the deformation of the Easter plainchant melody 'Haec dies', in 'Noël' (xv) and 'Regard de l'Onction terrible' (xviii), and in the repeated chords that attempt to generate more power from the piano than it is capable of in 'Regard de l'Église d'amour' (xx). In a later text, Loriod noted many of the innovations of Messiaen's piano writing, including the use of the extreme registers together, the 'individuality of registers, geometrical movements including contrary movements of the hands over one another, chord clusters', and 'exacerbated relentless strepitosos, intransigent violence, the kneading of the keyboard in all its registers simultaneously', and the inflection of the orchestra into the piano.[112]

The phantasmatic virtuosity of 'Regard de l'Esprit de joie' includes the quasi-serial 'agrandissements asymétriques', a device already experimented with by Messiaen in the 'Cahier vert', where Messiaen calls it 'Spirales contraires' to be used 'pour l'échange terrible', which became 'L'échange' (*Vingt Regards*, iii), and that was also used in the fugue (vi) as a development and intensification of the fugal subject.[113] In 'Regard de l'Esprit de joie', the hands mirror each other when this device is employed. Each note of the five notes in the left hand moves up or down in a regular pattern from one iteration to the next (up, down, up, down) until all five sets of the twelve possible pitches have been heard, and a thirteenth iteration of the pattern repeats the first set. The last note of each left-hand set remains the same and therefore functions as a form of pedal point. The right hand complements the left as a form of diminution but with expanded registers. Here, a twelve-note set is employed without serialism. Each note is changed by a semitone in a pattern according to prescribed rule (down, up and so on) on each iteration of the set. Again, the last note (a thirteenth, and therefore repeated, pitch) remains the same and thus functions as a sort of pedal. The overall effect of the passage, created by the asymmetrical registers, is of an expanding fan. It functions as a quasi-magical formalist device placed seemingly randomly into the structure of the work that acts as a form of Surrealist *objet trouvé*.

In 'Première communion de la Vierge' (XI), again not part of the original plan for the work, the listener or onlooker hears and sees Mary adore Christ within herself, embracing him interiorly. Near the end, a low repeated F on the piano illustrates the beating of Christ's heart. For Messiaen, this is not merely a naive depiction, but, in a Symbolist sense, it comes to *be* the beating heart of Jesus. Through this diorama the listener comes to participate in the intra-uterine world of the mother of Christ. This is an extraordinarily audacious work that comes close to a form of idolatry and is redolent of many forms of Catholic devotional material, such as depictions of the bleeding sacred heart of Jesus. Understood in this tradition of imagery, here Messiaen's music asks the listener mimetically not just to use their own stethoscope but to feel empathetically this sound and presence within themselves.

Vingt Regards forms a harvest home of Messiaen's techniques placed at the service of theological depiction. At the instigation of friends (Jolivet especially), Messiaen had already taken stock of his influences and his techniques in *TMLM*, but much of the work in this volume remains unexplained. Responding to Pierre Bernac's gentle mockery of *TMLM*, Poulenc noted drolly that Messiaen was 'unstoppable . . . Dukas and Dupré are very responsible for this pedagogical state exacerbated by the mysticism of this Monsieur,' but later more astringently chides: 'for the majority of the time it is just simply silly.'[114] Yet *TMLM* was produced by a 33-year-old composer; it reveals the originality of Messiaen's thought and how he had passed other music through the 'deforming prism of our language' as a means of what I would prefer to call creative refiguration and craft, rather than 'borrowing'.[115] This strategy could be thought of, following Boulez, as a 'furious resistance' to his original models: the constitution, plasticity and potential of Messiaen's thought reigns.[116] *TMLM* revealed his vocation for research and pedagogy, and was a first sustained attempt to explain his religious-modernist aesthetics.

4
On Surrealism and Experimentation, 1945–51

Messiaen's experience of the war and of the 'cas Messiaen' had confirmed the prescience of his artistic mission to speak of God and the Christian ideal of eternal life after death through music. Yet in an article from 1946 he made the following extraordinary statement:

> I have tried to be a Christian musician and proclaim my faith through song, but without ever succeeding. Without doubt this is because I am unworthy of doing so (and I say this without any sense of false humility!). Pure music, secular [*profane*] music and, above all theological music (not mystical as my listeners believe) alternate in my production. I really do not know if I have an 'aesthetic', but I can say that I prefer a music that is iridescent, subtle, even voluptuous (but not sensual, of course!). Music that is tender or violent, full of love and vehemence. A music which soothes and sings, which honours melody and the melodic phrase. Music that is like new blood, a signed gesture, an unknown perfume, an unsleeping bird. Music like a stained-glass window, a whirl of complementary colours. Music that expresses the end of time, ubiquity, glorified bodies and the divine and supernatural mysteries: a 'theological rainbow'.[1]

There is little sense of compromise here after the 'cas Messiaen', but rather a refining of his iconoclasm. There is also another disingenuous disavowal of mysticism,[2] and the statement about not having 'an aesthetic' is somewhat specious from a man who had just written a textbook (*TMLM*) about his own musical language. The secular and profane in fact accentuate the potency of the sacred; they are not subsumed but celebrated. The 'cas' demonstrated that the violent, erotic, disturbing and Surrealist nature of Messiaen's religious-modernist aesthetics *was* being effectively communicated to his audience. It therefore provided a form of 'breakthrough' to the present as much as an intimation of a 'breakthrough towards the beyond'.[3] It also demonstrated the power of sensuality in Messiaen's music, despite his consistent denial of this and attribution of it to 'the prudes'.[4] Honegger decried this trait, while also admiring 'the voluptuous' in Messiaen's melodies.[5] Confrontation was therefore vital to Messiaen's emancipatory aesthetics – it preceded the possibility of transformation.

Messiaen's language in the statement above affirmed Surrealism's ascendancy in his aesthetics. His songs from the 1930s were already filled with Surrealist imagery, devices and structures.[6] Surrealism was founded by André Breton (1896–1966) after the First World War. Breton had trained as a doctor, and through his exposure to the traumatic effects of war, the philosophy of Kant and Hegel (the concepts of the sublime, dialecticism and the transformation of worldly ontology are sedimented in Surrealism) and Freud's writings on psychoanalysis, he became interested in the source of poetic creativity, dreams and how art could be a 'solution to the principal problems of life'.[7] Breton was an atheist with little regard for music. His quasi-gnostic thought concerned the modernist reconfiguration of beauty, love and what the Surrealists called the 'marvellous': violent, liminal, ecstatic expression and experience. Surrealism was enmeshed with ethnographic imagery and research; it was a secular modernist ideology ripe for Messiaen's religious refiguration.

Messiaen was already enchanted by fairy tales, his mother's poetry and Catholicism. In an interview in 1953, he stated: 'I am not a mystical musician, but a Surrealist musician who exceeds his desire for the Surreal by the supernatural.'[8] In 1961 Messiaen explained that his music of the late 1940s was 'plus ou moins surréaliste' and that he had attempted to pastiche the Surrealist writings of Breton and Paul Éluard (1895–1952), and the proto-Surrealist writings of Pierre Reverdy (1889–1960), in the *textes explicatifs* that accompanied his works.[9] By the late 1940s, Messiaen counted himself a 'grand lecteur' of these writers.[10] He made his own form of Surrealism through the controlled volatility of his music, and research into non-Western music that Poulenc described as 'the false Hindu language'.[11] This was something that the Italian composer Luigi Dallapiccola (1904–1975) also later expressed reserve about in a review of the *Quatuor pour la fin du Temps* on 10 August 1946, where he commented on the transferability of 'refined and voluptuous atmospheres of certain music from the Orient'.[12] Such concerns with non-Western music, however, were consonant with Surrealist interests, for instance in their 1929 map of the world.[13]

Love was a central Surrealist preoccupation for Messiaen, sometimes through the spiritualization of woman, as in Éluard's and Messiaen's poetry. In his novella *L'Amour fou* (1937), Breton makes clear to his daughter that love should be violent, explosive and transformative.[14] This image is taken up by Messiaen, who evokes Reverdy's poem 'La Jetée' from *Les Ardoises du toit* (1918):

> There is so much that is dry and inhuman in contemporary music! Will our innovator be revolutionary only in his language? It seems almost certain that he will also bring love. And not these blocks of despair, these uninhabited planets, but Love with a capital L, Love in all its forms: of nature, of woman, of Childhood, and above all Divine Love . . . pray with me to the years, the days and the minutes that they may make haste to bring before us that innovator, that liberator who is so patiently awaited: the composer of Love.[15]

This love was communicated through Messiaen's so-called 'Tristan trilogy'. The first work was *Harawi: chant d'amour et de mort* (1945), a cycle of twelve songs for 'grand dramatic soprano' and piano. Messiaen's *Harawi* was followed by Yvonne Loriod's *Grains de cendre* (composed July–October 1946, but likely first publically performed on 30 March 2023), eight short songs (to her own texts) written for soprano, piano and flutes or ondes Martenot.[16] The second work in Messiaen's cycle was the ten-movement orchestral *Turangalîla-Symphonie* (1946–8, revised 1990). This final title of Messiaen's only symphony is a composite word from Sanskrit: *Turanga* means the 'flow of rhythm', and *lîla*, the 'play of construction and destruction' of 'life and death, [human] struggles, the cosmos, the world,' symbolic of life, death and love;[17] the title also invokes rhythm no. 33 in Śārṅgadeva's table of 120 rhythmic *deśītālas* or rhythmic formulas.[18] The work is therefore a 'song of love, a study of rhythm, and a hymn of joy, all at once'.[19] The final work in the trilogy is the *Cinq rechants* (1948) for a capella choir.

Messiaen's trilogy promoted a Catholic 'universal' agenda of spiritual emancipation after the 'zero hour'.[20] The composer Jean Barraqué – who studied with Langlais from 1947 to 1948 and was an *auditeur* in Messiaen's class (1947–52) and was described by him as 'a rebel of the Boulez variety although in a different sense' – considered these to be 'transitional works, in the sense that they embellish or exasperate the procedures' that 'announce, in a sporadic and embryonic manner . . . the current preoccupations of this musician'.[21] But they can also be understood, with regard to previous music, as the apogee of a music that embodies the psychoanalytic concept of drive (*Trieb*).

Eros (erotic love) and Thanatos (death) are considered by Freud to be innate, constitutive forms of energy that are always conflicted in the id (the unconscious). Lacan connects the death drive to repetition and argues, in contrast to Freud, that drives are manifested by desire, an attempt to go beyond 'the pleasure principle' discussed by Freud in 1920 to attain *jouissance*, a supreme enjoyment in and through transgression.[22] The desired 'shock' experienced by Messiaen's critics was part of the gift not merely prescribed by *agapē* – an existential, transcendent, benevolent love reciprocated between God and humanity – but imparted through transgression made manifest through Messiaen's musical language.[23] Here the erotic is figured not as a taboo suppressed by Christianity but as fully compatible with godly and carnal desire.[24] In the 'Tristan trilogy', love and death, as in Wagner's opera *Tristan und Isolde* (1865), and classicism and violence are mixed, functioning as instruments of desire that remain unfulfilled.[25] The sacred and the erotic are necessarily coextensive. The Wagnerian fulfilment through death, or *Verklärung* (enlightenment or transfiguration), as he referred to it, is given an eschatological and erotic turn in Messiaen.[26] Transgression is repositioned as emancipation and celebration. Fulfilment in God in the afterlife is always *to come*, but this is predicated on not only the subjection and destruction of subjectivity but a remaking of this subjectivity. This intrinsically violent and cathartic process, figured in the musical language of Messiaen's 'Tristan trilogy', can be therefore understood as complementary and consonant with the dialectics of Surrealism in which liminal love emerges through opposition to the mundane.

Messiaen's *Harawi* was partly inspired by Joseph Bédier's *Roman de Tristan et Yseult* (1900), and it used some melodies from Raoul d'Harcourt (1879–1970) and the work of the composer Marguerite Béclard d'Harcourt (1884–1964) on Peruvian song.[27] But Messiaen's music transcends their folkloric descriptions of 'Yarawi' and the sound world of their transcriptions.[28] *Harawi* was also inspired partly by the painting *Seeing Is Believing* by the English Surrealist painter Roland Penrose (1900–1984), in which a woman's inverted severed head (likely the painter's partner and eventually

Roland Penrose, *Seeing Is Believing* (*L'Île Invisible*), 1937.

his wife, the model, photographer and photojournalist Lee Miller (1907–1977), whom Penrose had met in Paris in 1937) extends into the stars above, while below two male hands (one opaque) reach towards her.[29]

Messiaen has also spoken of the painter Marc Chagall's images of flying lovers,[30] which provide an apposite 'resurrected' image of the couple in *Harawi*. The work was premiered by Messiaen (piano) privately with the soprano Marcelle Bunlet on 26 June 1946, and publicly on 20 January

1947.[31] In his own description of *Harawi*, a Quechua word used in Peruvian folklore that signifies 'an irresistible and profoundly passionate love, which leads towards the death of the two lovers',[32] Messiaen indicates:

> There is above all in this work a great rhythmic research (added values, non-retrogradable rhythms, rhythmic canons, 'irrational' values and short notes linked to longer ones, inexact augmentations, *personnages rythmiques*, etc.); a great quantity of non-classifiable chords and sonorities (notably the chords of inferior contracted resonance); the pursuit of a melodic line that is vocal, simple, singing, with its own melodic cadences; birdsong; counterpoints of water drops; [and] atmospheric vibrations. It is finally, *and this is the only thing of import, a great cry of love.*[33]

Messiaen's 'cry' of desire and love is enunciated through an allegorical love story between Piroutcha and her unnamed male lover, a love pursued unto death and beyond. This has been understood partly as an autobiographical statement about Messiaen's burgeoning love for Loriod while his wife's condition deteriorated.[34] Despite operations (including a hysterectomy in January 1949), rest, psychiatric interventions and stays in psychiatric hospitals, Claire Delbos died on 22 April 1959, following her son's marriage on 2 August 1958.[35] Jacques Charpentier arrived at Messiaen's house,

Claire Delbos, Olivier and Pascal Messiaen, 1948.

Messiaen and Jacques Charpentier at Messiaen's wedding to Yvonne Loriod, 1961.

at 13 Villa du Danube in the 19th arrondissement, after Claire's death to find Messiaen 'in his pyjamas in the middle of a mountain of dirty washing . . . but wearing the légion d'honneur on his vest'.[36]

Messiaen's life in the 1940s and '50s continued unabated with teaching, performing and the organization of performances, his church duties, the collection of birdsong (involving travel and notation in the 1950s), childcare (he was effectively a sole parent) and composition. He would eventually marry Loriod on 1 July 1961 (with Charpentier and his wife, Danièle, as guests) in a civil ceremony at the town hall in the 18th arrondissement, with the religious blessing at Sainte-Geneviève-des-Grandes-Carrières, near her apartment at 230 rue Marcadet, also in the 18th. This was expanded with the purchase of other apartments in the building so that the Messiaens could work and live together; Olivier moved in with her definitively in 1964.[37] During their wedding a blackbird sang on the roof of the church, taken by the couple as a form of benediction, but it is perhaps unlikely to have been the same blackbird that Messiaen had noted at 4.15 a.m. on the morning of 1 July.[38]

In a letter of 25 June 1945, Serge Koussevitzky (1874–1951) invited Messiaen to write a work for his foundation, which was based in America; Messiaen later said that he had been dreaming of the work for six years, while his diaries show he was thinking about it from at least 1944.[39] Messiaen's association with America was significant. On 5 March 1936, he gave the world premiere of some of Charles Ives's iconically modernist songs for La Spirale,[40] and Koussevitzky had premiered *Les Offrandes oubliées*. Messiaen responded on 20 August estimating that the composition would take between six months and a year.[41] It would, in fact, take much longer.

The seven books of sketches for the work bear the title *Symphonie-Tâla*; they are mostly on a reduced number of staves (2–4) with orchestral indications that clearly show Messiaen's thinking for the orchestra through the piano.[42] He was also thinking of a four-movement *Symphonie de la joie*, conceived as 'Jardin du sommeil' (he then changes his mind and makes this movement 2), '2ième chant d'amour', '1ère Tâla' and 'Joie du sang', but he also considered the title *Symphonie du chant d'amour* for the whole piece.[43] The order of the movements is not finalized in the sketches. Messiaen's idea for the work at the end of the sketches, with his estimated timings, can be seen in the table overleaf. Here we find the movement order, with Messiaen's timings as noted in his sketches and timings taken from the recordings of the European premiere on 25 July 1950 of the *Turangalîla-Symphonie*, the 1961 supervised recording, and the composer's revised version of the work (1990). These recordings reveal a marked disparity in speed for many of the movements, and between Messiaen's imagined length of the work and their realizations.[44]

Different titles from those given above are present in his diaries from the end of 1947, which also included a nine-movement version of the work with movement titles such as 'Chant de rêve', 'Chant de tendresse', 'Chant de passion' and 'Kheyâla-Mâruta'.[45] Messiaen noted at Petichet on 26 July 1948 that the 'Symphony was finished today', but he continued to revise it.

Referring to the final titles, Messiaen later clarified that he 'wrote movements I, IV, VI and X. Then the three rhythmic studies called "Turangalîla" 1, 2 and 3 – these were originally the *Trois Tâlas* performed in Paris on 14 and 15 February 1948 under André Cluytens. Then No. II. Then the large development which is No. VIII. And I finished with No. V.'[46] This is different again from the order of work in the sketches, here given using the final numbering: VIII, IV, III, II, V, I, VI, X, IX, VII, VI again, VII again.

When the piece was finished, Messiaen went to the annual Tanglewood music festival in Massachusetts to teach. Leonard Bernstein (1918–1990), who had a taste for excess, premiered the *Turangalîla-Symphonie* on 2 December 1949 at the festival (repeated the next day), and then in Carnegie Hall, New York, on 10 December 1949, Messiaen's fortieth birthday. In a letter to Bernstein of 5 October 1949, Messiaen stated that he had

TIME (sketches)	TIMINGS	FINAL ORDER AND TITLES	1950	1961	1990
Symphonie-Tâla		*Turangalîla-Symphonie*			
I. Introduction	6.15	1. Introduction	5.45	6.13	6.25
II. Premier Tâla	4.10	2. Chant d'amour 1 (formerly movement 3)	6.41	8.06	8.13
III. Premier chant d'amour	10.10	3. Turangalîla 1 (formerly movement 2)	4.30	5.33	5.26
IV. Deuxième Tâla	4.50	4. Chant d'amour 2 (formerly movement 7)	7.59	11.26	11.02
V. Jardin du sommeil d'amour	7.10	5. Joie du sang des étoiles (formerly movement 6)	8.01 (followed by an interval)	6.19	6.41
VI. Joie du sang des étoiles	13.40	6. Jardin du sommeil d'amour (formerly movement 5)	7.46	10.04	12.39
VII. Deuxième chant d'amour	11.10	7. Turangalîla 2 (formerly movement 4)	3.30	4.05	4.10
VIII. Turangalîla	10.30	8. Développement d'amour	9.05	11.39	11.40
IX. Troisième Tâla	5.30	9. Turangalîla 3	4.11	4.42	4.27
X. Final	13.30	10. Final	6.11	7.02	7.44
Total timings	86.55		63.39	75.09	78.27

Messiaen's *Turangalîla-Symphonie*: prospective and final order of movements.

'put into my symphony all my powers of love, of hope and of research'.[47] A surviving recording of a rehearsal demonstrates that Bernstein rehearsed the work meticulously, but he never conducted it again.[48]

Turangalîla-Symphonie received mixed responses in America, as it also did in France when it was premiered at the Aix-en-Provence festival on 25 July 1950. Here it provoked furious debate between Georges Auric and Honegger (who was for the work and who had used the ondes in his *Jeanne d'Arc au bûcher* (1935) and other works) and Poulenc,[49] who found it 'atrocious', 'dishonest' and mixing the 'bidet and the baptismal font'.[50] Later, upon rehearing the work, Poulenc wrote that it was 'full of magnificent music' and praised Messiaen as being from 'a great race that I admire profoundly', and a 'leader' in French music.[51] Boulez told Messiaen on 14 February 1948 that the work made him want to vomit; he later called *Turangalîla* 'brothel music', but while he never conducted the whole work, he did include 'Turangalîlas' I, II and III in a BBC promenade concert on 17 August 1973.[52]

Felix Aprahamian, who attended the French premiere, noted that while Messiaen's French colleagues had 'contented themselves with modern pre-fabs, Messiaen has built a skyscraper which is in danger of being mistaken for a Tower of Babel'.[53] Aprahamian facilitated the first London performances conducted by Walter Goehr, father of Alexander Goehr (b. 1932), and the London Symphony Orchestra on 26 and 27 June 1953.[54] Peter Maxwell Davies (1934–2016), who had been an *auditeur* in Messiaen's class in 1954–5,[55] admired its originality as 'totally uninhibited, which was deliriously vulgar'. He noted that it could be offensive if one were not aware of Messiaen's naivety in the 'soppy tunes' and the way he uses themes as 'signals'.[56] The critic Massimo Mila opined that it was 'extremely simple', 'an openly confessed banality', and described it as a 'Broadway Carnival'.[57] Stravinsky was also scathing, describing it as 'more embarrassment than riches'. He criticized the technical language, and Messiaen's creative refiguration of ideas from his own music: 'I am flattered by the attention, of course, but I would prefer to receive royalties.'[58] He noted the way that Messiaen here crossed the 'barrier of taste ... [through] a mixture of gamelans, Léhar, and some quite superior film music ... Little more can be required to write such things than a plentiful supply of ink.'[59] Stravinsky also denigrated Messiaen's work as 'improvisation which is the slag heap of art', and critiqued it as 'too loud ... piling up decibels as though he were jealous of the sonic boom'.[60] His epithet for Messiaen was 'naïf'.[61]

Naivety is a recurring theme of Messiaen criticism, but it can also be understood as a form of artistic and religious sincerity and authenticity.[62] Messiaen stated that he had a 'horror of politics'.[63] Yet the *Turangalîla-Symphonie* (and the works that caused the 'cas') created an artistic and political controversy that Messiaen did not shy away from. *Turangalîla* was first recorded commercially in 1961. During the sessions, Claude Samuel asked Messiaen what advice he would give to an enthusiast coming to hear one of his works that would be difficult at first hearing. Messiaen said that the public must come with no 'a priorisms' and with a sort of 'aural virginity' (*virginité d'oreille*). Samuel then asks: 'He must hear a shock?' Messiaen responded emphatically: 'Yes! A Shock!'[64]

The work's appeal outlasted any controversy. The *Turangalîla-Symphonie* was later performed as a ballet to critical acclaim (and to Messiaen's delight) on 21 June 1968, with set designs by the Surrealist Max Ernst – one of the few Surrealists who spoke highly of music – and Roland Petit as choreographer.[65] *Turangalîla* became a modern 'classic' and a signature piece that accompanied Messiaen around the world. When he went to Australia in 1988, it was the main featured work in Melbourne (21 May 1988). It was also the centrepiece of a Messiaen festival in 1989 in the Duke's Hall at the Royal Academy of Music, London.

Desire and the fatality of love until death are figured and overcome in this work. Messiaen described it in terms of love and 'joy' that is 'superhuman, overflowing, blind and unbounded' – ideas that are consonant with the emancipatory ethics of Surrealism and with Messiaen's religious-modernist aesthetics.[66] The liminal aspirations of *Turangalîla* are served well through the excessive gestures and superimposed orchestral textures that Stravinsky diagnosed as 'inane'.[67] Alain Messiaen called it a 'disproportionate concerto', but its auditory excess evidently caught André Jolivet's ear, as evidenced in his *Piano concerto* (1950), which also caused a scandal at its premiere on 19 June 1951.[68]

The overwhelming effects of the *Turangalîla-Symphonie* are created through noise and repetition, as in 'Joie du sang des étoiles'. Here, the volatile content pulls away from the stability of the form. Michaël Levinas noted that this movement taught him that one could have in 'living music emotional relations to which one is not given immediate keys', and he marvelled at Messiaen writing in D♭ major 'in the middle of the crisis of Darmstadt'.[69]

Excess is also figured in the long, sustained, ecstatic chorale lines of the ensuing movement. 'Jardin du sommeil d'amour' represents the 'cristal bubble of Jerome Bosch [Hieronymus], in the prison of air of Vivian and Merlin, in the glasshouse of Tristan and Isolde'.[70] F# major is coloured – or temporally 'hovers, stretched', as Levinas puts it – by delicate bird roulades that, as in *Réveil des oiseaux* and the *Catalogue d'oiseaux*, present birdsong as 'stylised, surrealised, and sublimated'.[71]

In *Turangalîla-Symphonie*, there is a difference between what one hears immediately (effect) and its technical substance; Honegger expressed scepticism about Messiaen's 'rhythmic refinements', which are perceivable on paper but 'remain imperceptible to the ear', but this was an aspect of the work that entranced the ear of Jean-Louis Florentz (1947–2004) when he studied it in Messiaen's class of 1971–2.[72] For example, just before rehearsal fig. 4 in 'Jardin du sommeil d'amour', a duo of temple blocks (doubled by triangle and small Turkish cymbal) commence a dialogue (noted separately in the sketches, on two staves, and later superimposed).[73] The second temple block plays values from 7 to 38 semiquavers while the first starts from 48 and regresses to 32.

Messiaen had already prepared a sketch for something like this in his 'Cahier vert', in which he created two lines with near identical phrases, marked 'rhythm progressively and uniformly slowing down' and 'rhythm progressively and uniformly accelerating'.[74] Around this (barely noticeable) asymmetrical internal system in 'Jardin du sommeil d'amour' flows birdsong in the piano, plainchantesque vocalises, the main string melody and other material, creating 'rhythmic and melodic counterpoints'.[75] Systems are laid upon systems, but with a refined sense of balance and transparent expression.

This section is an example of the way, for Barraqué, 'the organization of the rhythmic domain is clear of [*dégagée*] the purely musical,'[76] something already notable in the first movement of the *Quatuor pour la fin du Temps*. Such a 'conscious dissociation' facilitated the magical devices in this music, which function like Surrealist *objets trouvés* – non-retrogradable rhythms, pedals and rhythmic canons.[77] Boulez calls these canons 'amorphous' precisely because of what he perceives as a lack of responsibility between the structure and these objects, but it is their mechanical, alienated and therefore magical Surrealist qualities that were important to Messiaen.[78]

None of the 'Tristan' works mention Christianity explicitly – gone are the scriptural epigraphs and the naked conflation of musical techniques with religious or theological meaning, but these aspects remain sedimented in Messiaen's language. For some composers, the level of invective in the 'cas' might have given them pause for thought. Messiaen was in a delicate position in both his career and his personal life. His 'analysis class', conducted from the piano, described by Poulenc as giving 'the young a taste for risk',[79] had just begun in 1947, and his family situation was demanding. Messiaen's 'aesthetics and musical analysis class', which ran between 1947 and 1954, became obligatory for composers in 1949.[80] Tony Aubin (1907–1981), who taught composition at the Conservatoire, considered Messiaen a 'dangerous man', a term also used by Marcel Dupré of Messiaen in 1941, and in 1951 Aubin advised Michel Fano to avoid Messiaen's class, but Fano was unable to resist.[81]

The composer Claude Ballif (1924–2004), like Messiaen an ardent Catholic,[82] confirmed that the students that surrounded Messiaen 'looked at their great master with the eyes of dazzled rabbits'. He also noted that going to this class was 'courageous . . . already an anti-conformist act'.[83] Although Ballif preferred his rapport with Aubin, whom he found more provocative, he also observed: 'Messiaen at the piano, it was magic.'[84]

Ballif's friend the organist and composer Jean-Pierre Leguay (b. 1939), a member of Messiaen's class from 1967 to 1970, admired 'the immense culture of Messiaen, his feline pianistic touch, his prodigious ease as a lecturer, and his infallible and voluptuous auditive acuity', which 'stimulated my own production' for the organ and 'opened perspectives that [encouraged me] to plough [the field of] my own curiosity'.[85] For Ballif, Messiaen created a 'new rhythmic liberty, new formal liberty' (in the *Quatre Études* and the *Livre d'orgue*) that assimilated diverse, 'exotic' sources, and the sense of renewed agency and choice for the composer in the way materials could be employed and articulated.[86]

These features are found in the *Cinq rechants*, premiered on 15 June 1950, which continued Messiaen's taste for excess through virtuoso vocal polyphony (see the twelve-part canon in *Rechant*, III), Surrealist language, vocalization and hallucinatory imagery, and their evocation of courtly love. Messiaen used Hindu rhythms and the melodic shapes of Peruvian folk music, from the work of Marguerite and Raoul d'Harcourt, and invented words that emphasize the different timbres, attacks and percussive qualities of the voice.[87] The *Rechants* reinvent one of Messiaen's favourite pieces, *Le Printemps* (1603), a work in 39 sections by Claude Le Jeune (1528/30–1600) that employs *musique mésurés à l'antique*, a system in which syllables are given rhythmic values that correspond to their phonetic content, making a declamatory style evocative of Greek rhythms.[88] Messiaen borrowed the word *rechant* (refrain) from Le Jeune.[89] Barraqué, invoking Messiaen's personal canon of composers, moves fluently in his writings between the rhythmic thinking of Machaut, Le Jeune, Stravinsky and thence to Messiaen and Boulez.[90] Poulenc, perhaps surprisingly given his candid dislike (stated to Messiaen) of the *Turangalîla-Symphonie*, a work that caused him a 'profound shock' in its conception, had been 'delighted' by the *Rechants*. Dutilleux listed the *Cinq rechants* as among the finest of all twentieth-century musical pieces, and their legacy can be heard in Xenakis's *Nuits* (1967–8), also an a capella work in twelve vocal parts.[91]

The *Cinq rechants*, like *Harawi*, evoke Peru, and use a made-up Surrealist language to figure the unconscious that was indicative of a deeper reality and truth in a Surrealist sense. Messiaen's text evokes the Tristan myth, Chagall's flying lovers, Arthurian myth (Merlin and Vivian), Hieronymus Bosch, Éluard's love poetry and troubadour composers. Messiaen's *Rechants* reflect his holistic research, and their uncompromising avant-garde mien indicates that the 'cas' was both formative and generative. It had acted as a type of confirmation that religious-modernist enchantment, premised on rigour, refinement and a delicate violence, could be cathartic and emancipatory. This infusion helped to cement Messiaen's place at the 'head of his generation'.[92]

The *Cinq rechants* can also be understood as a transitional piece in which Messiaen perhaps came to understand that he had done all he could with the language of the 1940s. The works immediately after the 'Tristan trilogy' represent a renewed commitment to transformation. Boulez termed this period 'experimental . . . in the best sense of the term', owing to the relationship between research and music and an attempt to '"radicalise" his language' through hermetic systems, changes or processes that expose and engage with internal principles or are the result of specific techniques or materials, and a greater use of counterpoint freed from strictly harmonic considerations. 'Discipline' therefore was no constraint, but an engine of creativity.[93]

Messiaen's students Serge Nigg (1924–2008), in his *Variations for Piano and 10 Instruments* (1946), and Boulez in his *Piano Sonata* No. 2 (1947–8), had already engaged with serialism. Both had also been students of the composer and pedagogue René Leibowitz (1913–1972), who had sought to critique Messiaen's *TMLM* on its own terms.[94] Messiaen engaged briefly with his own adaptation of serial thought as modal thought. *Cantéyodjayâ* for piano, completed 15 August 1949 and first performed

Messiaen, Yvonne Loriod and Pierre Boulez at Darmstadt in 1952 looking at Messiaen's *Quatre Études de rythme*. Messiaen is holding 'Île de feu 1'.

23 February 1954, uses a mode of durations, pitches and intensities,[95] and this thinking is also present in *Le Merle noir* (March 1952), a Conservatoire test piece for flute and piano. *Cantéyodjayâ* demonstrates the way in which a traditional formal structuring (refrain-couplet) can be a stable vessel for volatile material. It was partly inspired by John Cage's thinking and his visit to Messiaen's class to demonstrate the prepared piano on 7 June 1949. Messiaen described this, according to the Belgian composer (and his student) Karel Goeyvaerts (1923–1993), as his 'most riveting musical experience since he first discovered Śārṅgadeva's Deśītālas'.[96]

Serialism was also adapted in Messiaen's *Quatre Études de rythme* for piano. This work comprises 'Neumes rythmiques' (1949), which translates plainchant neumes (groups of notes with a defined shape) into Messiaen's language, 'Mode de valeurs et d'intensités', 'Île de feu I' and 'Île de feu II', these last two études written with themes from Papua New Guinea.[97] 'Île de feu II' develops, through interversions and episodes, the theme of the first, and its coda clearly develops Hindu melodies, or 'jātis'.[98] 'Mode de valeurs' was composed in June 1949 (possibly begun during three days of teaching at the Darmstädter Ferienkurse), but the idea of creating a series from other musical dimensions dates from teaching Berg's *Lyrische Suite* in 1942.[99] Messiaen's sketches for the *Quatre Études* include extensive analyses of Berg's rows, Webern's piano *Variations*, op. 27, and tables of his *permutations symétriques* that would be used extensively in *Chronochromie* (1959–60).[100] There is also a focus on categories for the materiality of sound (a written-out technical plan on what he calls 'cinematic order [rhythmic movement], quantitative order [long and short durations], phonetic order [timbres and attacks], dynamic order [intensities and densities]') and a diagram of sixteen rhythmic formations labelled 'simple, scissors, statue, the oars, breathing, tensions, the hands, the back, the chairs, reversed chair (or gallows?), by the mouth, the side, the rings, view from a plane, in water, the luge', corresponding diegetically to mental images.[101]

In 1949 Messiaen began the *Traité de rythme, de couleur, et d'ornithologie*, in seven tomes (eight books), a collection of essays, self-analyses and teaching notes published posthumously. He premiered the *Quatre Études* on 6 November 1950 in Tunis. Messiaen recorded them on 30 May 1951 (unedited) on a piano without a middle pedal – which would, as Peter Hill has demonstrated, have created clarity for 'Mode de valeurs' – and performed them fifteen times between 1950 and 1955.[102] Loriod gave the French premiere on 7 June 1951. 'Mode de valeurs' was described by Barraqué as 'very important' because of its 'conscious dissociation' of elements to create a musical narrative, something that Boulez notes had been done by Berg in the concepts of *Hauptrhythmus* (*Lyrische Suite*) and *Monoritmica* (*Lulu* Act I).[103] Levinas noted that 'the divorce between the musical phrase and the horizontal succession of notes' and the '*statistical* evaluation of duration' in this piece was important for Boulez and Stockhausen.[104]

This 'dissociation' marks a concern with structuring the materiality of sound. In a sketch from the early 1930s, Messiaen describes 'Rhythms (seen melodically)' and he lists up to 34 values and then interversions using this table.[105] Messiaen's diary entry from 22 July 1945, 'Faire des séries de tempo . . .', also points to the creation of a neutral form of pre-compositional material without characteristics.[106] This was later theorized by Boulez, with reference to intervals, as an 'infratheme' that became subject to 'envelopes' – specific 'features of application, placement and implementation' to musical parameters external but imposed onto the material (evidenced, for example, in the organizing principles imposed upon each of the three staves of Messiaen's score) – which Boulez identified in his flute *Sonatine* (1946).[107]

Messiaen later distanced himself from the 'Mode de valeurs', saying that it was 'next to nothing'.[108] He had already experimented with *Klangfarbenmelodie* in 'Turangalîla' II and the connection between duration and timbre in 'Turangalîla' I, II and III (that is, *Turangalîla-Symphonie*, III, VII and IX).[109] In 'Mode de valeurs' Messiaen went further, and organized this work through the infusion of 'modes' of 24 durations divided into 3 × 12 pitches (on three staves) making three 'rhythmic registers',[110] four modes of attacks (timbre), 3 × 12 durations and seven dynamics, maintained for the whole piece. Silence is absent, but what remains unsaid in Messiaen's discourse is that his work creates a dialogue of different types of decay that partly result from the pre-compositional parameters. There are no chords in each line, but vertical aggregates do arise through the counterpoint (even what could be inferred as tonal chords).

The work absorbed Messiaen's understanding of Indian ragas and Machaut's *Messe de Notre-Dame* (important to Barraqué, Boulez, Stockhausen and Goeyvaerts) into sets of imbricated descending waves of material. What Boulez thought of as an 'absence of profile' that 'cannot generate a strong and convincing form' in 'Mode de valeurs' can also be understood as a radical transformation of the Wagnerian shaping of musical time, like the overlapping structural waves in the prelude to *Tristan und Isolde*, but presented differently and through the most anti-Wagnerian content.[111] The infusion of different musical parameters and the permutations of the rhythmic series create 'the quantitative [long and short durations], phonetic [timbres], and dynamic soundscape [intensities and densities of attack]', categories described with relation to 'Les Augures printaniers' at rehearsal fig. 13 of Stravinsky's *Le Sacre du printemps*, that operate within the sonic capabilities of the piano.[112] A combination of different instruments would undoubtedly have created greater differentiation between Messiaen's material parameters.

The work is modal, not serial: registers are fixed for each pitch and there is no sense of transposition, inversion, retrograde or retrograde inversion that would imply serial manipulation. Messiaen thought of the piece in terms of 'variations of colour', deferring from his equation of serial music with 'fear, terror, the night' and 'greyness'.[113] He also thought of the series as being like blood in its interior and having an organic potential in its structure through its comportment and insinuation into a musical work. This sense of 'responsibility' of the material to itself was a lesson taken up by Boulez.[114]

'Mode de valeurs' inspired sonatas for two pianos by both Goeyvaerts (1951) and Michel Fano (1950–51), Stockhausen's pointillistic *Kreuzspiel* (1951) for conductor, oboe, bass clarinet, piano and three percussionists (with extensive notes and directions about the staging of the ensemble), and Boulez's *Structures 1a* for two pianos (1951–2), premiered with Messiaen on 4 May 1952 and performed again on 7 May (attended by Stravinsky).[115] In *Structures 1a*, the first division (top stave) of Messiaen's pitches is made into a series.[116] In 2011, Boulez dismissed his own work, with hindsight, as a piece where the 'responsibility of the composer is practically absent . . . It was a demonstration through the absurd.'[117]

Messiaen also experimented with *musique concrète* (the use of natural sounds in a composition that was electronically manipulated) in *Timbres-durées* (1952), a collaboration with Pierre Henry (performed on 21 and 25 May 1952) lasting a little over fifteen minutes, which relates rhythm and manipulated timbres through five timbral groups (compiled by Henry): 'water sounds, rubbed membranophones, the homogenous white sound from a Chinese cymbal, metallic percussion and wooden percussion'.[118] Messiaen then created four sets of rhythms (some using Hindu rhythms), or *personnages rythmiques*, which undergo symmetrical permutation to make 24 sequences of the four *personnages* (that is, 4! i.e. 4 × 3 × 2 × 1). Personnage A, for instance, connects '11 rhythmic values to a series of 11 timbres'.[119] Yet Messiaen's idea of a 'rhythmic work with no musical sounds' is somewhat specious;[120] timbres are linked to durations in the work (whose differences are less exposed than obfuscated by timbre). The sounds he chose have harmonic and inharmonic qualities, and they create a rather repetitive, if amorphous, melody of timbres with very little silence, despite different attacks, decays and densities of sound that in fact engender a rather anodyne listening experience.[121]

These 'experimental' works were nourished by Messiaen's reading of Gaston Bachelard's *Dialectique de la durée* (1936), in turn partly inspired by Bachelard's reading of Emmanuel's *Histoire de la langue musicale* (1911), a formative work for Messiaen. Messiaen theorized fourteen categories of the materiality of sound (the way the properties of sound intermingle experientially and the way they can be combined), including quantitative, phonetic and dynamic registers, a version of which is found in the sketches for the *Quatre Études* and the *Messe de la Pentecôte*.[122] He also created what he called the 'Law of the rapport between attack and duration' – when a long sound is followed by a short sound, the mind cannot distinguish (quantitatively) the length of the sounds. This connection between the material and phenomenal qualities of sound and perception would be formative for the avant-garde.[123]

Messiaen's 'law' was employed at the start of 'Les Mains d'abîme' (*Livre d'orgue*, III), a title derived from the book of Habakkuk (in the Old Testament) and discussed by the theologian Ernest Hello, who had a particular interest in ascetic suffering for spiritual improvement. A long chord on the organ *tutti* is juxtaposed with a short one and pedal interjections, for Messiaen a cry of human suffering from the abyss of the soul (connected in his mind with the Romanche gorge in Hautes-Alpes) towards God, followed by a section using the organ's highest and lowest sounds to depict 'that wonderfully gentle thing: God's reply and consolation'.[124] 'Les Mains d'abîme' translates Messiaen's reading of the Neoplatonic philosophy of Aquinas, which figures the difference between earthly divided time and eternal non-divided time. Messiaen employs philosophers that agree with his worldview to explain his music, including Henri Bergson and his ideal of *la durée*, in which interior, experiential private time is contrasted with clock-bound time.

Messiaen's 'experimental' period was a consolidation and redirection of earlier acquisitions. Messiaen's notes for his improvisations at La Trinité exist from 1932 in the Bibliothèque nationale de France. These usually detail liturgical texts from the particular day, together with notes for substitute organists, including care of the organ and what to play for different types of services such as weddings and funerals.[125] Two major works were germinated from improvisation and experiment with timbre, rhythm and duration especially – the *Messe de la Pentecôte* (1950, completed 21 January 1951, with at least two movements performed at La Trinité on Pentecost 13 May 1951),[126] and the *Livre d'orgue* (1951–2).

Messiaen had first thought of the *Messe de la Pentecôte* as a work in six movements ('Prélude', 'Interlude I', 'Offertoire et consécration', 'Interlude II', 'Communion', 'Postlude'), and also as six *Études rythmiques* for organ.[127] His sketches include much material and detailed working that is not in the final score, which is clearly a refined condensation of this thought. There are references to the materiality of sound and experiments with figurations, and the way in which the organ interacts with the acoustics of the church, for instance. In the sketches, Messiaen creates a striking passage (alas unused in the final score) that refigures the climax of the first piece of Dupré's *Le Chemin de la Croix*. In Messiaen's example, descending semiquavers emerge from the echo created by efflorescent *fff* chords. They are then reversed to return to these chords (stated twice), before the procedure is repeated to return again to the same chord, heard three times.[128]

The *Messe de la Pentecôte* (in its final five-movement form) is searing in its brevity and intensity.[129] It is notable for its experimentation with the organ's timbres (especially mutation stops), the level of textural differentiation and its significant technical demands of the player. The composer Jean-Louis Florentz considered it Messiaen's 'most important work for organ, infinitely prophetic for the present, and the future of the organ repertoire'.[130] The first movement, 'Entrée (les langues de feu)', evokes the Pentecostal 'tongues of fire' and uses a formula in the pedal that Messiaen had thought of for settings of poems from *Le Vallon* by Sauvage (Messiaen was unaware that these poems were dedicated to Jean de Gourmont).[131] It juxtaposes four different timbres (corresponding to the three different keyboards and the pedals at La Trinité). 'Irrational values' refigure Greek rhythms through what Messiaen called *le monnayage* (minting) – longer regular rhythms are 'filled in' by shorter irregular ones.[132] The rhythms are subject to continual variation, which Barraqué called an 'open circuit'.[133]

The 'Offertoire (les choses visibles et invisibles)' uses a monodic theme in the second section, created from Jolivet's *Cinq incantations* for solo flute (1936), which Messiaen used in many other works, such as 'Turangalîla' I.[134] This idea was given as a theme for an 'improvised symphony' to Dupré (created around 1950), and it was used for the 1977 improvisations on his mother's poetry referred to as the 'Thème de l'ombre' in his sketches.[135] It juxtaposes the growling 'beast of the apocalypse' (Messiaen's beloved 16' 'Basson' stop on the positive organ at La Trinité) with interversions.[136] The central section of the 'Offertoire' is formed through interversions, registral expansion, the addition of stops and, eventually, rhythmic and cadential compression. In the sketches, there are detailed notes for liturgical improvisations for the third and fourth Sundays of Advent 1950, with registrations and a musical theme (for the fourth Sunday). For the third Sunday, Messiaen gives eight combinations of registrations, and the fifth is:

> R: *voix célestes* – held dissonant chords *pp*
> Pos.: flute 4, piccolo, tierce – (staccato *goutte d'eau*) this makes a melody . . . arpeggiated in 4th, the augmented 4th ambitus 2/8ve
>
> Péd: Vcl. 8 – in unison (legato) with Pos.
>
> Alternate with birdsong E, D♯, E, D♯, A♮
> on Grand Orgue: bourdon 8 (in 2 pricked) [the two is underlined three times][137]

The exact music Messiaen improvised on 17 December 1950 is not recorded, but these written prescriptions correspond closely to the music (from the Jolivet-derived theme) at bars 103–4 of the 'Offertoire' (with the birdsong transposed up a tritone in the written piece). Messiaen here created a short, metallic percussive sound (redolent of a metallophone percussion instrument) against a smooth, undulating background (strings). Timbre, duration and intensity are fused. Referring to this passage, Messiaen described it as '"my thing", it is typical of the Messiaen organ style'.[138] It was a sound world that would later be imitated by Florentz in the coda to his unpublished first *Improvisation sur le Te Deum* for organ (1967–8).[139]

'Consécration (le don de Sagesse)' (no. III) explores Hindu rhythms across different keyboards and timbres and the deformation of plainchant. Messiaen describes this moment of the Mass as more important than the organ or stained-glass windows – the moment when the priest speaks the words 'this is my flesh, this is my blood . . . this is the moment that counts.'[140] The fourth piece contains Messiaen's first virtuosic dialogue of birds, and a juxtaposition of the highest and lowest sounds of the organ at the end (32' and 1' stops) using the 'total chromatic'.[141] The final movement, the toccata 'Sortie (le vent d'esprit)', contains a central birdsong section 'like a chorus of larks as a symbol of joy', notated near his aunts' (Marthe and Agnès) farm near Fuligny, with the right-hand birdsong 'minting' the interversions in the left hand (moving from 23 to 1 semiquavers) and the pedal (from 4 semiquavers to 25) creating compression and tension.[142] This is complemented through a dramatic implosion and explosion of sound at the end (engendered largely monophonically), with material perhaps derived from Webern's piano *Variations*, op. 27.[143]

The *Messe de la Pentecôte* was a form of litmus test for the malleability of his previous techniques, and a refinement and validation of his research through the organ. It showed, within a relatively small space, how variety of material could create a rich and fascinating narrative experience. Crucially, it revealed to Messiaen how his techniques could coalesce, complement or even oppose each other. This therefore provided a model for works in the 1950s such as the *Catalogue d'oiseaux* (1956–8) and *Chronochromie* (1959–60).

The experimental vein of the *Messe* was continued in the *Livre d'orgue*. Messiaen premiered the *Livre* at the Villa Berg in Stuttgart on 23 April 1953, and in Paris on 21 March 1955 for Boulez's 'Domaine Musical' concerts at La Trinité (such was the crowd that Messiaen struggled to get into the church himself).[144] As Messiaen had reimagined the organ mass (from Tournemire, Litaize and later Grunenwald and Charpentier), here he refigures the organ 'Suite' (already rethought by Tournemire, Alain, Duruflé, Grunenwald, Dupré, Langlais and later by Litaize).

Messiaen's *Livre* contains seven pieces, five of which use the 'total chromatic', beginning with 'Reprises par interversion' (I).[145] 'Pièce en trio I' (II) uses 'minting', expanding and deforming Hindu rhythms. He described it as 'dodecaphonic' – a musical image of seeing 'through a glass, darkly' (1 Corinthians 13:12).[146] 'Pièce en trio II' (V) and 'Les Yeux dans les roues' (VI), a title that would 'delight a Surrealist',[147] are also dodecaphonic. 'Les Yeux' was inspired by Messiaen's hearing of the images present in the religious text, written on the score, from Ezekiel 1:18 and 1:20: the noise of the storm, of water, the running beasts that lead the chariot, the raging fire and the 'living' eyes within the wheels.

This is Messiaen's most uncompromising organ toccata – a continual fortissimo. It uses three twelve-note series (one each for the hands and another in the pedal).[148] Both hands and feet continually and pointillistically range over the whole of both keyboards (manuals all coupled to the Great, and the pedal). The pedal, by contrast, is legato and uses a chromatic scale of twelve 'sound-durations' as an 'interversion' without fixed registers, an idea associated in *Couleurs de la Cité céleste* with colour, resonance and the apocalypse.

'Soixante-quatre durées' (VII) explores different registrations across the three keyboards and the pedal, and forms of density and intensity of material to inform the phrasing, rhetoric and narrative of the work. It uses a chromatic set of durations from a demisemiquaver through to a semibreve (exactly 64 demisemiquavers). Messiaen orders these durations as two sets of chromatic *permutations symétriques* (in groups of four durations), moving from the extremities of the piece to the centre in a retrograde canon, a technique like that used in 'Jardin du sommeil d'amour'. This acts as a rhythmic template for the piece that allows birdsong from Petichet (through 'minting') and properly serial material (using the four forms of the row) to colour and demarcate this temporal organization.[149] Messiaen associates such complexity with magic, enchantment and serendipity consonant with his religious adaptation of Surrealist thought.[150]

'Reprises par interversion' (I) employs three Hindu rhythms as *personnages rythmiques*, and employs the 'total chromatic' not as serial music but for its sense of ordered 'fantasy'.[151] Each rhythmic duration has its own timbre, created through the organ keyboards and pedal, connected to different forms of attack or articulation, register and very different types of registration. The piece is in four sections and is created in the following ways. The first section is played backwards note for note in the fourth section, while the second and third sections reprise the material from the first section but vary it through interversions. Messiaen refers to his technique of using these interversions as a 'closed fan' in section two, in which the duration (register, organ registration and attack) is reordered and durations appear (one at a time) by alternating each duration taken from the beginning and end of section one respectively. Section three, meanwhile, is an 'open fan' in which each duration (register, organ registration and attack) from the centre of the first section alternates outwards (in opposite directions) from the middle of the third section.[152] In addition, the third section is the retrograde of the second, so that the centre of the whole piece (the second and third sections) is a mirror construction. Messiaen therefore creates different internal temporal paradigms that are barely appreciable to the listener. Through such machinations, the internal clock-bound time of the listener, and their human capacity to remember the order of the sounds, is undermined to produce a semblance of eternal time (the time of God).

Messiaen and Yvonne Loriod, with Karlheinz Stockhausen (to Messiaen's right), 1 March 1952.

In 'Chants d'oiseaux' (IV), four clearly differentiated birds are played on the organ's three manuals (at La Trinité), including a nightingale notated at dusk, which Messiaen described as 'one of my most beautiful memories'.[153] It is the first monophonic bird writing in Messiaen's output. Like Messiaen's other birdsong writing, it requires the performer to touch the instrument in a particular way in order to achieve a verisimilitude and lightness that imitates the original creatures.

The length of 'Pièce en trio II' is caused by the durational substructures of the lines. Messiaen did not 'work by accident'.[154] Sketches have not survived for this piece, but this piece and 'Soixante-quatre durées' (VII) would have necessitated much compositional pre-planning (something that must have informed the strophes of *Chronochromie* too). The manuals' parts of 'Pièce en trio II' are dodecaphonic and the pedal *mélodie principale* is chromatic; the contrapuntal rapprochement between Hindu rhythms (manuals) and pedal interversions is admirable. Instability, improvisation and fantasy are couched within a rigorous, stable and finite structure. After hearing Messiaen play the work, Stockhausen wrote to the composer Karel Goeyvaerts on 3 March 1952 that the *Livre* was 'exceptionally good in parts: unfortunately, more than once, it comprises passages that are so stupid, and which he should be over: birdsong, overtly programmatic details, added sixths, etc. . . . the fourth étude [likely 'Mode de valeurs'] is still the best. This is also the opinion of Boulez.'[155] Messiaen's comments on the piece form a fitting riposte: 'Even if one finds this music long, stupid, and useless, it constitutes one of my greatest *rhythmic victories*.'[156]

Close listening reveals the 'arsis' (stronger) and 'thesis' (weaker) stresses, already explored in 'Neumes rythmiques' (*Quatre Études*), where, through his reconfiguration of plainchant, Messiaen (as he does here) concentrates on the independence of rhythm from pitch.[157] As in 'Mode de valeurs', Messiaen asks the listener to hear tension and release within paradigms of intensity and density, and register and timbre. The abstract, alienated beauty of 'Pièce en trio II' can be understood as a form of the sublime in music that complements his observations of the sun, rocks and snow before the glaciers of Râteau, La Meije and Tabuchet, themselves apposite images of rhythmic layers moving in different temporal paradigms. This piece can be thought of as exemplifying a revalorization of mysticism, despite Messiaen's comments in 1939 and 1946, and also a form of 'ascetic voluptuousness' proper to the *jouissance* of transgression and rigour in this and other pieces in the *Livre d'orgue*.[158] There is a sense of marvelling at God's creation implied in the scriptural epigraph in the score: 'For from him and through him and for him are all things' (Romans 11:36). This should be read with the rest of the verse: 'To him be the glory forever! Amen.'

Messiaen's representation of glory in these pieces is another aspect of continuity. Glory is no longer represented merely by loud, colourful (dissonant) chords, sometimes resolving to consonance, but rather in the divine manifestations of wisdom and intelligence, of abstraction as a realization of the humanly figured incommensurable and the invisible. This iconoclastic rethinking of glory marks the next stage in Messiaen's music: irrigating the ears of a secular world through birdsong.

5
On Birdsong, 1952–63

Messiaen had a long engagement with birdsong. When he was three, he was with his father, Pierre, in the countryside of the Puy-de-Dôme in the Auvergne, and at the sound of skylarks, he brusquely took his bread from his mouth and made a sign that he wanted to hear them.[1] Later, when he was eighteen, at his aunts' farm near Fuligny, he was 'bored minding the [three] cows' and 'became fascinated with birdsong'; it was here that he 'first began noting [it] down'.[2] He also acknowledged that it was at the hillside near Chassors that he 'first began serious notation' of a skylark (*alouette des champs* in French) in 1928, which he described as having a 'jubilant' song and as 'the bird of glory'.[3] This bird featured in Messiaen's 1977 improvisations to his mother's poetry using his own *Cahiers*.[4] He also mentions it explicitly in his 1987 preface to *L'Âme en bourgeon*, and it featured in his last piano piece, *Petites esquisses d'oiseaux*, VI (1985).[5] At the Conservatoire, Dukas directed him to 'Listen to the birds. They are great masters.'[6] For Messiaen, birds were harbingers of the unknown, phenomenal representations of divine beauty and an aesthetic ideal of 'naturalness' in God's creation. Birds are frequently invoked in his mother's Symbolist poetry, and in Surrealist poetry as images of freedom.

Messiaen's first song from the *Trois mélodies* (1930, with words by the composer), 'Pourquoi?', begins with the text 'Pourquoi les oiseaux de l'air?' and rhetorically questions the subject's place in the natural world, something that was a powerful theme of his mother's poetry. This question sets off a chain of other questions that form a Surrealist litany or *fil conducteur* – a form of literary lightning rod that repetitively threads its way through the poetry. The final piano outburst at bars 22–3 is perhaps representative of birdsong. It has the brittle, metallic and percussive quality typical of

Messiaen's later birdsong at speed.[7] Spectral and modally derived pitches resonate out of stable chords on the subdominant (IV) of F# major, also used for the climax in *Le Banquet céleste*.

Messiaen's understanding of birds was nourished by reading *Pourquoi les oiseaux chantent* (Why Birds Sing, 1928) by the ornithologist (and brandy maker) Jacques Delamain (1874–1953). Delamain was a figure in the 1930s on the fringe of the Surrealist movement who published in *Minotaure*, an unofficial Surrealist journal. He became Messiaen's friend in 1952 and referred to birds as 'artists', which Messiaen qualified: '[they are] in effect great artists, much greater than we humans.'[8] Messiaen worked with many different ornithologists and had a considerable library of books on the subject.[9]

For Messiaen, birds 'speak in song' – that is, they have a 'simple language' of meanings, such as 'I love you' or 'It's time to eat', and they make sounds of 'danger [or] alarm' so they can be understood by other birds and animals. Birdsong has different functions: 'a territorial [song]'; courtship and 'love songs', more beautiful for Messiaen than the first category; and finally the 'most elevated category', which is 'improvisations for pleasure', usually at the beginning and end of the day.[10]

Messiaen's *style oiseau* is heard in the 'thème d'allègresse' near the opening of 'Dieu parmi nous' (*La Nativité*). A more definable indication occurs at the end of 'Ta voix' (*Poèmes pour Mi*, VI), where a window is thrown open onto eternity and the 'bird of springtime' sings (Messiaen's text). Here the bird sings, unlike real birds, in Messiaen's mode 2^1, and, as in the song 'Pourquoi?', it creates a delicate extension and distortion of F# major.

Messiaen first started transcribing birds from 78 rpm recordings in the 1930s. These aural feats of transcription made him a better musician and allowed him to hone his own particular hearing of birds.[11] Birds therefore acted as a prosthesis: Messiaen changed them, and they changed him. The search for birdsong also required long voyages, early mornings and the sacrifice of personal comfort.

Birds sing too high and too fast for human instruments to play, so Messiaen lowered their pitch, maintaining the 'truthfulness' of the songs 'transposed for human ears'.[12] They also sing in microtones, not in equal-tempered tones and semitones. Birds are ethereal, untouchable and they move very fast (they also have short lives). They are colourful, and Messiaen was quick to make the link between birds and the colours of the apocalypse. He thought of birds as 'artists who, like me, are sensitive to colour', responsive to the time of day or night.[13] For Messiaen, they were a refuge and a panacea to the humanly-created world, a source of solace and refreshment. Birdsong required him to make differentiations between species, attuning his ear to the different voices, styles and the aesthetics of each bird.[14] He created complementary literary descriptions and imaginative musical features – harmony and counterpoint, texture, timbre, rhythm – apposite for each bird. Birdsong was a way of infusing his music with nature and framing modernist dissonance within a religious and ecological framework.

From the 1950s, Messiaen evolved a procedure for musically capturing birds 'live'. This was not a form of 'photography', as he put it, but a 'transposition' of the bird into a different context.[15] He would mostly make a quick sketch *sur place*, relying on his ear and on musical memory, and a retranscription from recordings (later done on a hand-held tape recorder, assisted by Loriod), before brushing them up – sometimes into finished versions of a particular chant, but more often, as with the blackbird, which he notated hundreds of times, he would make a syncretic, ideal or idealized 'bird'.[16] These sketches have survived in 203 *Cahiers d'esquisses* from May 1952 to summer 1991, and reveal beautiful descriptions of nature and the sounds of birds' habitats. Partly travel diaries and partly daily workbooks, they embody Messiaen's sense of his own ornithological vocation.

Robert Fallon has provided a list of Messiaen's birds from the *Quatuor pour la fin du Temps* onwards, a total of 357 species.[17] One of Messiaen's blackbirds appears in the violin and clarinet parts of the 'Liturgie de cristal' (*Quatuor*). Here, birds appear as transcendental images hovering above human concerns. Birds appear in sketches from the 1930s and '40s and in many works of the 1940s, juxtaposed with elements of his musical language. This familiarity gave him the confidence to experiment and extend, and to liberate birds from some of these moorings, notably the kind of harmonic template found in the 'Liturgie', in the early 1950s. This evolution was complemented by his rethinking of musical materiality; for Messiaen, this was a taxonomic approach to the properties of sound and instruments and the ways in which these could be manifested in music.[18]

Jacques Charpentier wryly observed that Messiaen escaped the 'intellectual disaster' of dodecaphonic music through birdsong, as he himself had escaped it through Hindu modes.[19] The spectralists followed this emancipatory trajectory through their investigation of the psychological narrative of timbre and colour. Tristan Murail also noted of his *Couleur de mer* (1969), written in his second year at the Conservatoire with Messiaen, that his 'research into colours, timbral alloys, [and] a beginning of the research into "processes"' were 'a refuge from serialism'.[20]

Messiaen commented in 1972 that 'for some twenty years [musicians] have attempted to abolish the barriers between noise and sound', giving 'homage in part to pioneers [such as the composer] Pierre Schaeffer, who created *musique concrète*, and in part to the musicians [who created] electronic music'.[21] From an avant-garde musical perspective, birdsong embodied different parameters of attack, decay, pitch, microtones and the relationship between harmonic and inharmonic sound, features that help differentiate one bird's song from another. Messiaen's engagement with birdsong placed him in the vanguard of this exploration. The translation of noise is recreated, to some extent, in the types of attack required of his interpreters, and it is a part of the knowledge and imagination required to play this music. Schaeffer observed Messiaen's integration of birdsong and draws an ideological distinction between nature and human theory:

> Before concrete music placed the emphasis on the concept of the object, Messiaen was aware of it. If he finds inspiration in birds, it is not out of sentimentality or a desire to imitate them: the bird's song is his concrete experiment [Schaeffer's *Musique concrète* used natural or recorded sources, differentiated from electronic music produced in the studio]. This song has the double advantage of providing him with an object that is at the same time a language. Because birds are not human, their modulations provide schemas . . . different from algebraic grids. The bird is a living being, part of the universe of muscles and nerves. Its algebra is organic, and so infinitely more complex than series of dry numbers, and yet it is simpler, and in any case more effective, because it is mysteriously linked to human sensibility.[22]

The first pure presentation of 'Messiaen birdsong' occurs in *Réveil des oiseaux* for piano, woodwind and three keyboard percussion instruments (1953, premiered in Donaueschingen on 11 October 1953, revised 1988), and then in *Oiseaux exotiques*, written between 5 October 1955 and 23 January 1956, for Boulez and Le Domaine Musical. These works realize what Dutilleux recognized in the music of 'Messiaen and Jolivet, after Milhaud' as a 'sense of the fresco', and, as the composer Elliott Carter (1908–2002) noted of *Oiseaux exotiques*, they 'depend on design as well as sound for their effect'.[23] Birds conjoined from different countries (India,

China and Malaysia) and different continents create a narrative that is 'not true' but 'truthful'.[24] For *Oiseaux exotiques* Messiaen used mostly recorded birdsong, but also birdsong heard in particular natural places (such as near Tanglewood), as well as caged birds; it was first performed on 10 March 1956.[25] Both works were written with Loriod's talents to the fore and include her fingerings for the piano part (usually done by Messiaen).[26]

Messiaen described *Réveil des oiseaux* as 'not a good work', but one that 'made it possible for me to change', to find a way of composing extensively with this [birdsong] material.[27] Messiaen advised the pianist in the score 'to get to know the birds themselves': they need to understand and imitate the sound of each one. Messiaen's sketches for this work show different levels of working, sometimes on three staves and sometimes fully worked out, like the section from rehearsal fig. 17 in *Réveil*, but they do not show why or how he chose to layer the different birds embodied by the instruments.[28]

From fig. 17, the violin solo begins with a blackbird, the piano solo (in octaves) plays a red-throated robin, the celesta plays a different red-throated robin, and finally the flute comes in with a different blackbird (similar to the one that opens the *Quatuor*). In the *Quatuor* (movement 1) there is a sense of the birds providing counterpoints to the chordal template. But here in *Réveil*, there is no single stable element. In both works, bar lines act as orientating markers. Birds sing in fictive ¾ and 4/8 time signatures (respectively), but they do not do this in nature. Messiaen's organization balances vocal independence and timbral individuation to determine his own idealized verisimilitude. The contrapuntal infusion is important, but it is essential that the listener becomes attuned to the birds' voices as melodies. Each bird's rhetoric, gestural profile and narrative is key to Messiaen's transformation of them from natural sound to musical expression.

Messiaen's birdsong is not demonstrative or didactic transcription; instead it can be understood as both reification and, somewhat paradoxically, as a form of sonic emancipation, allowing the particularity of each birdsong to be exposed to an audience. The musical fabric interested Messiaen (birds and their environment), not the way birds called or learned from one another – Messiaen was aware of this ecology.[29] This was something that his student Jean-Louis Florentz would develop, along with his idea of 'microformes' (from his analysis of *Oiseaux exotiques*), in which the 'developmental autonomy' of certain figures (such as the *Grive des bois d'Amérique*, or American woodthrush in that work) upon repetition and variation 'may not have direct consequences in the progression of the work', but create a form within a form.[30] Through his own hearing, Messiaen created an aviary of icons, a moving ornithological pageant in music. Messiaen does not copy nature, something he regarded as 'foolish', but rather makes his own syncretic image of nature.[31] *Oiseaux exotiques* refined his thought through greater variety and characterization of birds, through figuration and registral deployment, and through harmonizations that added further colours and concretized this material as 'Messiaen birdsong'.

Messiaen would pursue these ideals and techniques in his *Catalogue d'oiseaux* (6 October 1956–September 1958), a set of thirteen pieces for his 'favourite instrument', the piano. These pieces are (palindromically) ordered in seven books, and the cycle lasts a little over three hours in performance.[32] Messiaen also considered writing a second *Catalogue* of seventeen piano pieces using French birds as subjects (and even a third *Catalogue*), and he regarded his work on birdsong as 'unending'.[33] *La Fauvette passerinette* (1961) was completed by Peter Hill, who noted the developmental quality of the main protagonist's solos; this piece was not part of Messiaen's unrealized plans for a second *Catalogue*.[34]

The *Catalogue d'oiseaux* was premiered by Loriod on 15 April 1959. It is remarkable for many reasons. First, it only uses French birds garnered from his travels, often accompanied by Loriod.[35] France is a country of enormously different landscapes. In 1962 Messiaen stated that he was aware of 200–250 places for the study of birdsong in France but that he knew around 50 very well.[36] Second, each featured bird is presented as 'naturalistic', placed into a context of the time and colours of the day, geographical features and other neighbouring birds. The work is prefaced by a list of 77 birds that appear in the text, a testament to Messiaen's extensive research as much as the speed of his hearing and creative assimilation of this material. Third, there is an extraordinary variety of sound and material within a seemingly limited expressive frame. Each bird is not only clearly delineated from its neighbour but given a specific ecology. Fourth, the pieces are not explicitly programmatic but have a strong sense of narrative built around their principal avian protagonist. Finally, there is an additive-constructivist variety of forms in the work, using formal building blocks that can be added in different combinations to create differently shaped and sized pieces. There is therefore a modernist fracturing of form and content, but also a sense in which form is created by the ordering of the content. This dialectic between form and content is present in many works of the 1950s and '60s but especially in the formal concentration of *Couleurs de la Cité céleste* (1963). These processes are commensurate with both the Surrealist ideal of *dépaysement* (disorientation) and Messiaen's later ideal of *éblouissement* (sound-colour dazzlement), both of which, understood from Messiaen's religious perspective, imply a form of worldly emancipation.

The beginning of 'Le Chocard des Alpes' (Alpine chough, I) uses quasi-serial music as an image of the 'massive and implacable' glacier of La Meije, around 66 kilometres (41 mi.) east of Petichet, a landscape that Messiaen loved and identified with himself.[37] Messiaen's harmonizations of the bird inflect the austerity of this mountain, and the silences in the work allow the listener to sense the birdsong resonating in this space. Messiaen regarded serialism, and indeed some music of the Second Viennese School (Schoenberg's monodrama *Erwartung*, op. 17 (1909), for example),[38] to be a rather grey, colourless technique. Yet he employed it in his own way to create the colours of night at the beginning of 'La Chouette hulotte' (tawny owl, V), for example, and to impart the mystery of 'la transubstantiation' in his *Livre du Saint Sacrement* (1984) for organ. He regarded this bird as 'quite terrifying' in its appearance and 'very solemn', 'very mysterious', a 'magician', 'supernatural'; its cry, likened to 'a woman being slaughtered [*égorgé*] or the sound of a child being assassinated', heard at 3 a.m., creates a Surrealist 'drama' aided by the alterity of Messiaen's quasi-serial language.[39]

The *Catalogue d'oiseaux* is full of extraordinary images, such as the golden eagle magisterially ascending on a current of air in piece I, contrasted with a great crow immediately afterwards, demonstrating Messiaen's 'pre-occupations with acoustic orders'.[40] The colours of 'Le Loriot' (golden oriole, II) (the homology with Loriod's name was not lost on Messiaen) resonate out of the tonal chords below. There is the extraordinary virtuosity of the 'Fauvette des jardins' (garden warbler) heard after strings of austere tonal chords. There are the colours of the blue sea (using mode 2^1) in 'Le Merle bleu' (blue rock thrush, III). Messiaen employs a saturated chromatic collection as his hearing of the swirling echo of sound from rockfaces. Here, the long 'resonance' is complemented by an equally long silence that is not merely an 'absence of sound' but an '*integral* aspect' of rhythm as 'substance – that is sound',[41] as Boulez states. It forms an emptiness that is paradoxically abundant and metaphysical. Silence is part of the *Catalogue*'s ecology. It provides space between the protagonists, allows their songs to resonate in the mind and connects aspects of the musical narrative.

Messiaen makes links between birds and other instruments, such as the Chardonneret 'like a glockenspiel' in 'Le Traquet stapazin' (Western black-eared wheatear, IV), and he creates a beautiful colourful image of the sun emerging from the sea. The sun rises higher in the sky and then descends behind a mountain, changing the colour of the mountain – red, orange and violet.

Other wonders present in the cycle include the music of the swamps of the Sologne in 'La Rousserolle effarvatte' (Eurasian reed warbler, VII), which represents 27 hours (from midnight to 3 a.m. the following day) in the life of this bird. There are immense stone statues in the moonlight, a stone stegosaurus and a 'cortège of stone phantoms transporting a dead woman' in 'Le Merle de roche' (common rock thrush, X); the circling of the buzzard in 'La Buse variable' (common buzzard, XI); the wind on the sea in 'Le Traquet rieur' (black wheatear, XII); and finally, in 'Le Courlis cendré' (Eurasian curlew, XIII), the powerful and haunting sound of the lighthouse on the Île d'Ouessant, off the coast of Brittany (where Tournemire had a summer house and composed his major works), cutting through the night and fog. The sense of being with Messiaen observing these things is entrancing throughout.

The pianist's task is to evoke these different characters and images through an instrument that, unlike the organ, produces essentially one type of sound. The sound of the piano is always decaying, but the pianist must create the opposite illusion. This is partly why Messiaen includes so much information on the score – to fire the imagination of the pianist, and thence the listener. Different composers use their hands to touch the piano in different ways in order to create different sound worlds, and Messiaen's music makes demands on repeated notes, on stamina and on finding the right sounds for each bird. The speed of his birds creates a flickering of intensities, rhythms, durations, accents and dynamics that imitates the physicality of birds. Messiaen's birdsong is experimental and volatile, but it was essential to his burgeoning compositional maturity.[42]

From the vantage point of the *Catalogue d'oiseaux*, works such as *L'Ascension* and *La Nativité* seem almost to belong to a different composer. What distinguished Messiaen from many of his contemporary organist-composers was that the transformational curve in his output became significantly steeper. The images of musical beauty in Langlais and Litaize, for example, were essentially wedded to the mysticism of Tournemire. But through *Catalogue*, Messiaen demonstrated that mysticism, divine glory in nature and a 'theological music . . . like new blood, a signed gesture, an unknown perfume, an unsleeping bird', could impart a different experiential understanding of God.[43]

The vast canvas of the *Catalogue d'oiseaux* is well complemented by *Chronochromie* (1959–60) for full orchestra, which takes its place among some of the 'big beasts' of the orchestral avant-garde, including Xenakis's *Metastaseis* (1953–4) and *Pithoprakta* (1955–6); Stockhausen's *Gruppen* for three orchestras (1955–7), *Carré* for four orchestras (1959–60) and *Punkte* (1952, 1963–93); Boulez's *Pli selon pli* (1957–8, revised 1983 and 1989); György Ligeti's *Atmosphères* (1961) and Luciano Berio's *Sinfonia* (1968–9). These works are radically different, but they all have strong elements of reconfiguring spatial, temporal, linguistic and musical elements. Each work is an 'event', as the French philosopher Alain Badiou might put it: they are monoliths, unrepeatable, and they impart their own 'shock', just as the *Turangalîla-Symphonie* had done.[44] Their 'avant-gardeness' exceeded the horizon of expectations; they and other works by Mauricio Kagel (1931–2008), Luigi Nono (1924–1990) and Krzysztof Penderecki (1933–2020), for example, form a mid-century vanguard of European works in which modernist alienation is bound to their sense of emancipation. Messiaen's theological and avant-garde output is a radical complement to these composers' works.

Chronochromie was described by Messiaen as 'a sunny protest against dodecaphonism, an ode to liberty' and as a 'synthesis of all my research'.[45] It uses birdsong from France, Sweden, Japan and Mexico, and, typical of his practice, the names of the birds (and countries) are reprinted in the score, along with the musical translation of the noise of mountain streams from the French Alps, Messiaen's spiritual home. At the core of the work is the idea of what Messiaen calls *permutations symétriques*, a technique that he had already trialled in the *Vingt Regards* XVI and XVIII and 'Île de feu II', and which was present in a more primitive form in the 'Cahier vert' and in the sketches for the *Quatre Études*.[46]

For this idea, Messiaen began with a set of durations – from a demisemiquaver to a semibreve, making 32 durations – which can be reordered. The number of possible reorderings increases factorially as the number of terms increases, so Messiaen finds a way to order and limit the combinations. From the 32 durations, he chose an ordering based on internal symmetries, retrogrades, a 'fan' (in the middle) and alternation of durational values in demisemiquavers. In the following table, sectional procedures and internal patterns and relations are indicated, and Messiaen's first set is divided into three sections. A prime set of ordinal numbers 1–32 (O) is related (only in this prime set) to cardinal durations of demisemiquavers (C). Brackets identify small binary sets of demisemiquavers, and square brackets reveal larger internal patterns:

O	1	2	3	4	5	6	7	8	9	10	11	12	13	14
C	[(3	28)	(5	30)	(7	32)]	[(26	2)	(25	1)]	[(8	24)	(9	23)]

15	16	17	18	19	20
[(16	17	18)	(22	21	19)]

21	22	23	24	25	26	27	28	29	30	31	32
[(20	4)	(31	6)]	[(29	10)	(27	11)]	[(15	14	12	13)]

Messiaen's first set of *permutations symétriques*.

To make a second set, Messiaen takes the third ordinal set of durations (that is, 5 demisemiquavers), then the 28th set (that is, 11 demisemiquavers) in the table above and creates a new cardinal order and then renumbers them 1 to 32 (new ordinal set). The table below presents the beginning of set 2:

O	1	2	3	4	5	6	7	8
C	[(5	11)	(7	14)]	[(26	13)	(10	28)]

Messiaen's second set of *permutations symétriques* (beginning shown).

This procedure is not serial but emergent. Messiaen then created a table where the 36 sets of interversions are superimposed (three at a time) to create twelve tables (or super sets), which, for the composer, emerge as an extension of the musical and mathematical serendipity he termed the 'charm of impossibilities' in *TMLM*.[47] For Messiaen, his sets of superimposed rhythms have a 'magical' internal order but manifest an external asymmetrical counterpoint. How Messiaen worked these sets and their relationship is unclear from the ten *Cahiers* of sketches for *Chronochromie*, however.[48]

Messiaen uses these sets of three interversions as the backbone of 'Strophes' I and II of *Chronochromie*, in the central part of *Couleurs de la Cité céleste*, and in 'Les Élus marqués du sceau' from *Éclairs sur l'au-delà…* (IV).[49] The durations of Messiaen's *permutations symétriques* in *Chronochromie* are each harmonized in different ways; time is therefore coloured. In 'Strophe I', each set of values is connected to different types of chords: 1) turning chords (sets of three eight-note chords); 2) chords in inversions transposed onto the same bass; and 3) chords of contracted resonance.[50] This procedure also effectively mollifies the experience of tempo as that which 'gives a *chronometric* value to numerical relationships', as Boulez stated.[51] The superimposition of timbres (rhythms) are 'minted', or filled in, with birdsong. Colour, understood as timbre, has 'secret correspondences' with Messiaen's own synaesthesia and the colours of the apocalypse.[52]

Messiaen's spatial, durational and timbral dispositions have a theatrical quality, and the transparency of his orchestration allows clear discernment of the birdsong. In the 'Épôde' (movement VI), eighteen solo strings (birds) play contrapuntally in a syncretic imitation of nature and as a saturation of temporal colour that 'passes the limits of human perception'.[53] The sketches show that Messiaen wrote out the birds individually and used this as the basis for superimposition. There are, however, no sketches showing his decision-making process. This avian texture is arguably a hollow tour-de-force; the sound and characters of the birds are rather undifferentiated, and Messiaen went on to learn from this experiment in terms of transparency and verisimilitude. The final short 'Coda' (movement VII) of *Chronochromie* provides a form of balance to the 'Épôde' through the reassertion of vertical harmonies, glittering timbres and its monumental yet terse mien.

Chronochromie was premiered on 16 October 1960 at the Donaueschingen Festival (conducted by Hans Rosbaud), but it was the French premiere at Besançon on 13 September 1961, the third performance of the work, that reawakened scandal in connection with Messiaen. Fault lines were demarcated in the critical responses to the work between rigour and nature, concerning technique and material (birdsong) and between organization and effect.[54] The Paris premiere on 13 February 1962 (the fifth performance) also caused a commotion in the audience, inflamed by Messiaen appearing on stage afterwards; Messiaen ducked to avoid a punch to his head as he walked through the audience.[55] He later issued a characteristic defence of the work in an explanation that focused on the techniques that organized the rhythm, birdsong and colours, and a diatribe on 'rigour and freedom'.[56] Birtwistle particularly admired *Chronochromie* (along with *Et exspecto* and the late organ music) – works, he stated, that 'I'd [have] liked to have written'[57] – perhaps for their monumental and iconoclastic qualities, not necessarily the pre-planned aspects, which he identified as à la mode for many composers of this period (Stockhausen and his 'form-schemes', for example).[58] Boulez also criticized this form of working, but it was clearly useful to Messiaen.[59] In *Chronochromie*, Messiaen attempted to balance such autonomy with a deeply personal response to avant-garde iconoclasm.

Chronochromie and the reactions to it point to issues of public communication for contemporary music, of narrative and stability, and of how large structures can be created from systems, all fundamental issues for many modernist composers.[60] In *Catalogue*, the structuring of building blocks enabled the careful balance and differentiation of material. *Chronochromie* reimagines these blocks into a larger-scale structure inspired by Greek poetry, creating a carefully crafted narrative experience over its seven movements. Further refinements and experiments with the relationship between form and content, and with narrative experience, would occur in *Sept haïkaï: Esquisses Japonaises* (1962) for solo piano, eight violins, thirteen winds and six percussion, premiered by Boulez on 30 October 1963 as part of Le Domaine Musical, and in *Couleurs de la Cité céleste* (1963) for solo piano, three clarinets, ten brass and six percussion instruments.

Messiaen sent an eightieth birthday present of some birdsong with 'one voice only', consisting 'of about a dozen short figures, most of them repeated three, four, or five times', to Stravinsky, with the inscription 'Strophe of the "grive-musicienne [song thrush]", collected for Igor Stravinsky on 25 May 1962 at the edge of the forest, Olivier Messiaen'.[61] The Messiaens were also invited to Japan from 20 June to 27 July 1962 by 'the remarkable impresario' Fumi Yamaguchi.[62] Messiaen immersed himself in Japanese life, food, culture, customs and birdsong through records.[63] He loved the Japanese for their 'innate sense of the sacred'.[64] In the film *Olivier Messiaen et les oiseaux* (1973), he can be seen, with Loriod, admiring his souvenirs from this trip, showing pictures of Japanese birds and wearing a blue yukata. Loriod is shown wearing a red kimono with silver brocaded cuffs, performing parts of *Oiseaux exotiques*.[65]

On 12 July 1962, Messiaen wrote a page of birdsong sketches featuring a description of Lake Yamanaka at sunset with Mount Fuji rising out of the pines below, 'noble and majestic' with 'clouds at its feet'.[66] The shape of some of these birdsongs (see p. 121) clearly appears in the finished score: the *uguisu* (Japanese bush warber), which is featured three

Messiaen wearing a yukata in Petichet, 1966.

times on this page, is reshaped at the opening of movement VI and becomes a clear formal 'marker' (Boulez), and the *kibitaki* (Narcissus flycatcher), also in the sketch, has a prominent role (see rehearsal fig. 3–5 of the score).

Messiaen wrote this detailed letter to his student, the Armenian composer and organist Raffi Ourgandjian (b. 1937), on 14 July 1962 about his experiences in Japan:

> First of all, twelve days of rehearsals with orchestra, and recordings. Three days at Karnizawa for notating Japanese birdsong. The *Turangalîla-symphonie* was performed in the immense Heno Benkakui Kom auditorium in Tokyo with Seiji Ozawa . . . Loriod in dazzling form, a formidable success (six bouquets of flowers, a quarter-of-an-hour of applause . . . I had to make a thankyou speech). Both piano concerts (Loriod and myself), and the speeches [*conférences*] at Osaka and Tokyo went very well and

Messiaen's bird sketchbook, 12 July 1962, MS 22033, p. 11.

Olivier Messiaen notating birds at Karnizawa, Japan, 1962.

for the concert at Hiroshima, a ten-minute choral was sung for us on the railway platform . . . !

We attended two presentations of the Kabuki (theatre). Bunraku (sad and dramatic marionettes), Nō (danced theatre with the cries and strange meows of the Tsutjumi [*sic*, tsuzumi] players (drummers)), and on 23 July I heard the marvellous music of Yayaku at the Imperial palace. I made the acquaintance of new Japanese birds at Subashiri, and then at Lake Yamanaka, at the foot of Mount Fuji. I saw new countryside with rice growers and bamboo and tea plantations. I visited the magnificent Buddhist temples around Nara and the great Buddha of Kamakura, and the Japanese gardens of Kyoto. For me the two greatest things I admired were: 1) the alley of lanterns at Nara (Shinto temple, the cryptomeria pines, 3,000 stone lanterns, free roaming fawns and hinds), and 2) Miyajima island (Shinto temple in white, gold and orange, mountains covered in Japanese pines), and the great red Torii (portico) in the sea [at the Itsukushima Shrine, which appears on the front cover of the *Sept haïkaï* and also a Messiaen lecture, the *Conférence de Kyoto* (1988)].

I leave tomorrow for the United States and [on] 9 August [I am bound] for Canada. Another month of concerts!![67]

For the listener, the 'Japanese' aspects of the *Sept haïkaï* are internalized in the score – there is nothing obviously ethnological. Like *Chronochromie*, *Sept haïkaï* is in seven movements. It continues to develop the relationships between internal processes, pre-conceived juxtapositions of rhythmic counterpoints and textural balance and stability. The spatial layout of the ensemble, as defined by Messiaen, is important. The 'Introduction' (I) employs the idea of 'métaboles: rhythmic modulation or the *transformation of one rhythm into another*', in which the Hindu rhythm Simhavikrama (in the xylophone and xylorimba) becomes the rhythm Miśravarṇa.[68] This forms a developmental principle, and a layer of counterpoint against bells and cencerros (spatially requested by Messiaen to be on the far left and right of the stage) and metallic percussion (on the left and right). The timbre of these rhythms is augmented by the brass instruments, which emphasize the beginning (the attack) of each rhythmic value. Set against this are the piano, which provides the only real bass notes; the violins, in two ranks at the front have the only real 'melody', and the woodwind instruments, in different combinations, provide another layer of rhythm and timbre.

In the second movement, 'Le Parc de Nara el les lanternes de pierre' (II), the eight violins (doubled by crotales and bells) play a choral, using tables four and five of Messiaen's *permutations symétriques* against 'minted' and altered Greek rhythms, birdsong (marimba) and free piano material. The third movement, 'Yamanaka cadenza', alternates the volatility of contrapuntal birdsong material with a piano cadenza three times, which acts as a plateau of relative stability in the landscape. 'Gagaku' is the title of the fourth movement, alluding to a type of Japanese courtly music also important for Stockhausen's *Telemusik* (1966) and Jonathan Harvey's *The Tree* (1981).[69] Messiaen imagines his Western ensemble doubling the sounds of Eastern instruments – for example, a long trumpet solo doubled by cor anglais and two oboes imitate the *hichiriki*, a doubled reed Japanese flute – with the other instruments (without piano) providing rhythmic and timbral counterpoint. The violins play spectral chords imitating the mouth organ *shō*, an instrument that Boulez appreciated for the 'microtonal deviations' that occur between different instruments.[70]

Messiaen's note in the score to the conductor for 'Miyajima et le torii dans la mer' (V) not only explains the balance of the different instrumental blocks and the way they should be heard and conveyed to the listener, but reveals his compositional thinking through layered textures or what he calls 'plans sonores'.[71] Boulez (a dedicatee of this piece, alongside

Loriod) had criticized Messiaen in 1948 for writing 'accompanied melody';[72] this is essentially what happens here, but Messiaen transcends this texture to exploit different types of attack, densities, and qualities of sonic sustain and decay. The balance of different combinations in multi-voiced but monophonic writing is carefully controlled in 'Les oiseaux de Karuizawa' (VI) to produce clear events and a sense of controlled, quasi-cadential release of tension near the end. The final 'Coda' (VII) returns to the music and techniques of the 'Introduction', creating formal balance, development and a denouement.

The relationship between form and content is brought to the fore in *Couleurs de la Cité céleste*, a work written for Boulez, Loriod and the Donaueshingen Festival – the orchestra of Le Domaine Musical premiered it there on 17 October 1964. Messiaen states that 'the form of the work depends entirely on colours. The melodic or rhythmic themes, the complexes of sounds and timbres, evolve like colours.' He goes on to say, 'the work does not finish, having never really begun: it turns upon itself, interlacing its temporal blocks, like the flamboyant and invisible colours of a rose window in a cathedral.'[73]

Perhaps more than any work thus far, *Couleurs* comprises small blocks of material (each labelled by Messiaen), like stained glass. These blocks are diverse in their imagery: Messiaen presents birds in identifiable timbral formations, as well as the reappearance of plainchant themes – which had not appeared in his work since the *Messe de la Pentecôte* – as chorales and juxtaposed with other material. There are discrete blocks of material such as the seven brass instruments that symbolize the seven trumpet-blowing angels who announce different catastrophes before the end of the world in the book of Revelation. There is a block that represents the 'star that fell into the abyss' through a piano figuration that uses all twelve tones. There are chords that are labelled explicitly with the colours Messiaen hears (somewhat naively, to be communicated to and by the players); blocks of music based on 'interversions' with Greek rhythms, and birds from around the world. Partly following Tournemire (although in a radically different language), Messiaen explicitly connects his timbral, durationally coloured music to the colours of the apocalypse, and thence to his experience of *éblouissement*.[74] Messiaen states:

> When you look at a stained-glass window, you don't see all the colours straight away. You have a sensation of colour and you are

> dazzled – you have to close your eyes. [In the Sainte-Chapelle in Paris,] There are little figures depicting the lives of the Saints, the life of the Virgin Mary, the life of Christ, the lives of the Old Testament prophets; and they especially show the life of Christ to its full advantage There are all the scenes from the apocalypse, the end of the world that is, which is in effect a kind of pictorial catechism.[75]

Yet *Couleurs* requires more astute listening: Messiaen's writing is extremely precise, too classicist for this metaphor to be semantically exclusive. Rather, like rose-windows, Messiaen's music creates stories: he employs different levels of competing and completing paradigmatic narratives that are essential to the transparency and impact of this taut work. The modernist fracturing of form and content is reinterpreted: the fractured form organizes different layers of the content, with different degrees of narrative development. Most obviously, the melody of the 'Alleluia du Saint-Sacrement' at rehearsal fig. 32, approximately the golden ratio in *Couleurs*, is begun yet only completed at the end of the work following an 'Epôde'-like, bird-cadential section at rehearsal fig. 81. *Couleurs* has diachronic, evolutionary and developmental qualities, but it also has a circularity. It is a harvest home of Messiaen's techniques, a high-water mark of Messiaen's infusion of religious metaphor and meaning, and of avant-garde music and classicism, producing a satisfying musical narrative balancing a range of heterogeneous musical materials. There is even a strong sense of deformed or diffuse tonality in certain parts of the work. For instance, the A major of the 'Alleluia du Saint-Sacrement' is at the heart of the 'dazzlement' at rehearsal fig. 69 in the score. In a note Messiaen describes the effect:

> One must first of all hear the 'Alleluia for the dedication of a church.' All the instruments that play this (on the same level of level of intensity) must shoot forth [*jaillir*] their harmonics *spontaneously* from this [Messiaen is referring here to the clarinets 2 and 3 that double the trumpet and add harmonics, also marked *f*]. One must also hear the Alleluia for the eighth Sunday after Pentecost on the piano (and cencerros) . . . The ensemble must give the impression of the abundant colours [*des couleurs foisonnantes*] of a sunlit stained-glass window.[76]

Messiaen's notion of *des couleurs foisonnantes* refers to the irradiation of the 'deformed' A-major plainchant melody (in the 'small Trumpet'), diffused and saturated with other melodies and timbres. This demonstrates what the spectral composer and theorist Hugues Dufourt (b. 1943) has called 'inharmonic energy', associated with higher partials and the 'different forms of distribution of energy in the determination of timbre when it is superimposed', but what Messiaen is creating here could be recognized as a harmonic and inharmonic ecology, balancing materials and timbres.[77] Understood in this way, Messiaen's work is given a slightly different nuance from the kind of 'desubjectification' or 'blinding' quality associated with *éblouissement* proffered in the first preface of *Couleurs*.[78] It can instead be thought of as entraining the listener, or attuning them to Messiaen's aural images of worldly emancipation.

This part of *Couleurs* (at rehearsal fig. 69) is indicative of Messiaen's ideal of form as an evolution of colour, which acts as a revalorization of mysticism here.[79] The experience of colour in this work is phenomenological, psychoacoustic, psycho-visual and synaesthetic (*l'audition-intérieur*).[80] It is a visually diegetic paradigm of 'transitions, saturation [and] of crossing of thresholds' that reveals the *jouissance* of this 'dynamic morphology'.[81] Messiaen places the effect of the form of the work into the listener to give a semblance of what he hears in 'default' of the divine, engendering in them a new religious reality and spiritual experience that he would develop in his later music.

6
On Influence

Messiaen lived and worked in an ecology of musicians – mentors, colleagues, performers and students. The precipitous gradient of his evolution before and especially after the Second World War was partly due to 'le cas'. It evolved through his personal refiguration of other composers' works, and it developed through his pedagogical engagement – as teacher and as colleague – with Pierre Boulez, Iannis Xenakis, Karlheinz Stockhausen and others.[1] Messiaen provided an artistic exemplar for his students and others as to how artistic authenticity was coextensive with the forging of a unique listening experience. For Messiaen, this was informed by his own religious-modernist vision.

From very early on, Messiaen's originality was fuelled by a voracious capacity to listen and to absorb, to transform and to refine what he heard. His artistic originality is not merely a matter of nature or nurture, nor is it only dependent on his artistic environment and his mentors; instead it is a measure of his talent and aptitude for autodidactic growth. Messiaen's teaching became a reflection of his personal preoccupations: other music was interesting to the extent that it was useful, and certain composers, such as Brahms, Mendelssohn, Bruckner, Mahler and Italian opera composers (Rossini, Verdi and Puccini, for example), were excluded from his canon of teaching repertoire.[2]

From Messiaen's teachers came various formative traditions, conventions, approaches, aesthetics and sensibilities, but these precepts were no '*restriction*'.[3] From Dupré came counterpoint, formal rigour and classicism, modes (Gregorian modes, Hindu modes and rhythms) and organ improvisation; from Tournemire, mysticism, modes (Gregorian and Hindu modes) and organ improvisation (Hindu modes); from Emmanuel, Greek rhythms and Greek and Hindu modes; and from Dukas, Messiaen inherited classicism, an interest in rhythm and making his modes work as part of a musical narrative, orchestration, an interest in birdsong and a sense of his métier. Messiaen was not of the generation taught by the organist and pedagogue Nadia Boulanger (1887–1979), who expressed her distaste for Messiaen as both composer and improviser.[4] Despite her desire that Messiaen should not play for the memorial service (held annually from 15 March 1920) for her sister, the composer Lili Boulanger (1893–1918), and her mother, Messiaen did play once for this service at La Trinité, in 1934. Messiaen later, perhaps out of respect for Nadia's antipathy towards him, respectfully asked his assistant Jean Bonfils (1921–2007) to play for her funeral on 26 October 1979 at La Trinité.[5]

The classicism that informed Messiaen's modernism is manifested in clear formal structures, transparency and purposefully employed musical language. This is not neo-classicism (imitating or deforming older styles and genres) but a modernist remaking of the past, reconfiguring the relationship between form and content. Had Messiaen followed his forebears and teachers, he may perhaps have written operas, symphonies, sonatas (Widor, Vierne, Emmanuel, Dukas), organ symphonies (Widor, Vierne, Tournemire, Dupré, Langlais, Fleury) and triptyques, such as Dupré's 'symphonic poems' for organ: *Evocation*, op. 37 (1941), or *Psaume XVIII*, op. 47 (1949). However, works such as Dukas' *Ariane et Barbe-bleue* (1899–1907), Emmanuel's *Salamine*, op. 21 (1921–3, first performed 1929), Dupré's *Symphonie-Passion*, op. 23 (1924), and *Le Chemin de la Croix* (1931) and Tournemire's *L'Orgue Mystique* (1927–32) were the crucibles that informed Messiaen's development.

Messiaen did not publish any explicitly liturgical works, like Duruflé's *Requiem* (1947), based on the plainchant *Missa pro defunctis*, or Langlais' *Messe Solennelle* (1949), a work Messiaen analysed and admired,[6] or even works such as Dupré's devotional memorial oratorio *La France au Calvaire*, op. 49 (1953). He was not a choral conductor, as are many organists in anglophone countries, and indeed did not conduct his own works, but participated in the performances of his works as adviser, impresario, pianist and organist. Dupré had expressed a desire to mould an organist equal to himself and had focused on Messiaen. As Demessieux put it: 'He [then] found rich skill and promise [*riche nature*] in Messiaen and procured an engagement in Brussels for him; Messiaen refused, wishing to make his career as a composer and only wanting to be an organist to play his own works, in the way he wanted.'[7] Unlike many of his fellow organist composers who set the Mass ordinary – Alain (three times in 1938), Charpentier

(2006), Duruflé (1966), Falcinelli (1947), Jolivet (1940 and 1962), Langlais (eleven settings) and Litaize (1954, 1959) – Messiaen never published his setting for eight sopranos and four violins (ostensibly completed in manuscript).[8] Instead, he professed his faith through para-liturgical works that have an evangelical and Catholic function, proclaiming the Church's mission outside ecclesiastical confines.

Messiaen's path was fuelled by contact with other iconoclasts of his own generation. The connection with Jolivet, who was strongly influenced by Schoenberg and by the teaching of Varèse, helped to fuel his own spirit of research, and this was informed by an awareness of the intense, incantatory and ritualistic language of the six short piano pieces of Jolivet's *Mana* (1935, published 1946), his *Danse incantatoire* (1936) and his *Cinq danses rituelles* (1939).[9] For Messiaen, Jolivet's *Mana* revealed research into 'sound space': acoustic phenomena and the resonance, register and spacing of chords.[10] In his preface to the score, Messiaen notes the interest in 'sound space', '*inharmonic*' harmonies and 'overheard waves' consonant with acoustic research and 'magic spells'.[11] Messiaen notes 'the extreme mobility of the rhythm' and that Jolivet 'proceeds above all by variation and dislocation' and 'by opposition'. Jolivet treated the piano as a resource for the exploration of timbre and sonority, duration, density and intensity of sound. As in *Vingt Regards*, 'the low and high registers are opposed, blended, interpenetrated or separated in a constant change.'[12] The rhetoric and shaping of phrases in *Mana* often sets up a sense of disfigurement of tension and release, repetition and development; there are climaxes, codas and cadences, but there is also melody, and elegantly controlled violence. These features can be heard in Messiaen's piano music of the 1940s, and indeed in the early piano music of Boulez.[13] The shadow of the monodic passages in Jolivet's 'Pégase' (*Mana*, VI) can also be heard in 'Force et agilité des Corps Glorieux' (*Les Corps Glorieux*, V, 1939) and in the piccolo and bassoon duet at the start of 'Chant d'amour II' (*Turangalîla-Symphonie*, IV), as well as in *Visions de l'Amen*, *Trois petites Liturgies*, *Harawi* and the *Catalogue d'oiseaux*.[14] Messiaen took what he needed.

Like Jolivet, Messiaen was enchanted by Asian music; French colonialism here merged with modernist internationalism. After the short-lived experience of compositional fraternity through the concerts of La Spirale, La Jeune France and the Concerts de la Pléiade, Messiaen had garnered a reputation as both a conservative and a radical. Although only in his thirties, Messiaen offered an alternative *esprit ouvert* to tradition, history and aesthetics, foreign music and modernist classics which contrasted with two other major pedagogical choices in Paris: Nadia Boulanger for technique and discipline and René Leibowitz for dodecaphonic music.

Messiaen's teaching at the Conservatoire was divided into periods: an 'aesthetics and musical analysis class' (1947–54), a 'musical philosophy' class (1954–61) under Dupré's leadership, then 'musical analysis' (1961–6) and finally a 'composition' class (1967–78).[15] Messiaen came from a generation of composer analysts, and for composers such as Boulez and later Levinas, these functions were coextensive.[16] He also taught in the USA and Canada, and throughout Europe.[17] Messiaen's teaching was holistic, interdisciplinary and almost unfailingly positive; it 'made his students participate in their own level of creativity', while also sharing his 'problems and preoccupations'.[18] When he spoke in class or of his music, he talked clearly and with certainty, without any affect (or jeremiads), without hesitation, often with humour and a sense of camaraderie and mutual discovery, but sometimes with long pauses where he was clearly formulating and clarifying his next words.[19] Messiaen's interest was in the sound of music, as George Benjamin (b. 1960), a composer and student of both Messiaen and then Alexander Goehr, observed. Messiaen did not speak to Benjamin much of counterpoint, the organic structuring of composition or the connections between different types of materials, nor of the 'way' of writing, such as the making of sketches and the relationship between the (final) surface of the score and the background materials – these things were the provenance of Goehr's teaching.[20] Messiaen's faith was carried into his teaching. He was well aware that Christ came as servant and teacher, and, in a secular environment, Messiaen exported this mission of embracing others through patience, kindness, empathy and love.

His teaching belonged to an *explication de texte* tradition, a form of objective analysis of structure and style embracing an engagement with the aesthetics or poetic aspects of art. It was not a systematic or formal means of analysis (such as that of Heinrich Schenker, for example). But the giving of information was not what made the classes special for generations of students. First, Messiaen made seemingly obtuse but in fact intelligent and purposeful connections between very different types of music from different periods, such as between plainchant and Mozart, Berlioz, Chopin, Debussy and others.[21] Second, Messiaen's taste in music was extremely diverse; he embraced Western and non-Western music (the music of Bali, Java, Japan, Tibet and India, a country Messiaen wished to visit).[22] Third, he brought in guests each year, including composers such as John Cage in 1949, whom he described as having an 'attitude' of 'taking stock of the radical powerlessness of creation in the faces of the mysteries surrounding us', and, in 1972–3, Horațiu Rădulescu, whom he called 'one of the most original young musicians of our time'.[23] Messiaen invited instrumental specialists into his class to explain the mechanics and capabilities of particular instruments. Yet it was Messiaen's personal charisma that excited students through a style that was both formal and collegial, but also passionate and sincere. He made time to share his knowledge, was generous with students' work, not shying away from technical faults but revealing students to themselves. As Messiaen put it himself: 'I've changed my waistcoat thousands of times.'[24] The class achieved a kind of celebrity status; it was filmed and photographed for magazines, most notably by the French photographer Robert Doisneau.

Pierre Boulez had petitioned the head of the Conservatoire, Claude Delvincourt, officially to recognize Messiaen's analysis class and move it from the home of Guy Bernard-Delapierre to the Conservatoire (Boulez received his premier *prix* in 1944–5). From the start, Messiaen discerned in Boulez a personality in revolt against everything, but he was sage enough to realize that this was a necessary path to maturity for the young composer. For Boulez, Messiaen's attention to detail and analysis of Stravinsky's *Le Sacre du printemps* later fuelled his own analysis of that work, which, focused on rhythm, is subtly but significantly different from that of Messiaen. A comparison of Messiaen's and Boulez's analyses of rehearsal fig. 13 of Stravinsky's *Le Sacre* is instructive.[25] Messiaen analyses only the first iteration of this 'rhythmic theme',[26] while Boulez also examines other variants and features such as elision, augmentation, doubling and elements of symmetry. Boulez's focus is on rhythmic cells, on which he provides a deeper level of analysis than Messiaen, while Messiaen's investigation, later described by Boulez as 'biased', is focused on the accents and the actorial agency that created musical cells, which Messiaen called *personnages rythmiques*.[27]

The manuscript of Messiaen's analysis is lightly written in pencil (double-sided) on extremely thin, delicate paper, and it has the appearance of a 'final version' or summation of his teaching.[28] In fig. 13 of *Le Sacre*, Messiaen identified what he calls 'the first purely rhythmic theme in music', but also a quantitative order (long and short durations), a dynamic order (densities and intensities) and a phonetic order (timbre and attack), ideas derived from the philosopher Gaston Bachelard (1884–1962) and that feature in the sketches for the *Quatre Études*.[29] In Messiaen's and Boulez's music and thought there is concern for the materiality of sound: the way hierarchies of elements of music can be shaped using the properties of instruments, and the perception of their infusion in time and musical space.[30]

In Messiaen's hearing, the accents (from bar 3 of fig. 13 of *Le Sacre*) are fortified by the eight horns. The following unaccented values are heard as a 'unity of value', that is, the durational value of the rests (silence) is conjoined with the value of the accented note. He then divides these values into two sets: A, which increases in rhythmic value, and B, which decreases. This thinking prefigures what Messiaen calls the 'law of the rapport between attack and duration', used in 'Les Mains d'abîme' (*Livre d'orgue*, III). Boulez would later refer to such a clear event as a 'signal': a 'musical object' for 'orientation' that in 'Les Mains d'abîme' is differentiated from the ethereal melodic and ornamental music that follows it and that may have acted as a model for the relationship between the material at the opening of Boulez's *Rituel in Memoriam Bruno Maderna* (1974–5).[31] Messiaen's analysis of fig. 13 reveals his own compositional preoccupations, as do other examples, such as his analysis of the final section of *Le Sacre*, the 'Danse sacrale', where his analysis of *personnages rythmiques* and rhythmic values is translated into the thought that underpins the large-scale retrograde canon at fig. 25–32 of 'Joie du sang' (*Turangalîla-Symphonie*, V).[32]

Boulez's analysis of Stravinsky's fig. 13 of *Le Sacre* begins when the accents start, rather than at the beginning of the passage. His concern is with cells and their development. This thinking can also be seen in his understanding of the second movement of Webern's piano *Variations*, op. 27 (1935–6), as well as his own *Piano Sonata No. 2* (1946–50),[33] which was played by Loriod at Darmstadt on 19 July 1952 and then recorded by her in 1961. In Boulez's sonata, small musical cells are consciously destroyed and creatively reformed as a mode of narrative development.[34] Boulez's own career as a conductor, advocate for and public educator about new music was significantly different from that of his teacher. His music, like that of Messiaen, is characterized by autodidactic research, intellectual rigour and precision, and attention to the material qualities of sound.

These are prominent features in Boulez's *Le Marteau sans maître* – three intermingled cycles of three Surrealist songs by the poet René Char, making nine pieces, a formal thinking that is recognizable from Messiaen's *Turangalîla-Symphonie*, despite Boulez's antagonism towards that work. The cell technique is a surface feature here, along with the diverse ensemble that exploits the relationship between plucked, hit, metallic, wooden, bowed instruments and the alto voice, which, as Messiaen noted, bears the marks of his excitement 'about Balinese and African music'.[35] 'Commentaire II de "Bourreaux de solitude"', piece IV of *Le Marteau*, reveals research into the ways in which registral variance (often with pointillist textures) and instrumental attack and decay can create cohesion through a volatile musical surface that seemingly resists narrative development.[36] Behind the surface is a form of serial multiplication technique, a kind of algorithmic principle, but also research into the relationship between harmonic aggregates, and musical materiality that pointed back to Messiaen's analysis of *Le Sacre*.

Messiaen's analytical technique at fig. 13 of *Le Sacre* can be applied to the flute monody of 'L'Artisanat furieux' (III) from *Le Marteau*, a fitting counterpart to the opening of Debussy's *Prélude à l'après-midi d'un faune* that Messiaen also analysed rhythmically.[37] Messiaen notes how the pause at the end of bar 1 of 'L'Artisanat furieux' 'suspends the rhythmic effect', and how this is complicated by the grace notes in bar 2, a feature of Boulez's later music, notably *Mémoriale* (1985). But what is made clearer in Messiaen's rhythmic analysis (without the pitches) is the internal sense of development. Applying Messiaen's 'unitary' thinking from his analysis of fig. 13 to bars 2–5 of the Boulez piece, there is reduction from two minims to one-and-a-third of a minim, to three-quarters of a minim and thence back to a minim. Once again using the same thinking, there is an internal sense in which the short versus long durations in bar 1 are repeated and amplified in bar 2.[38] If Boulez's style of musical analysis from fig. 13 of *Le Sacre* is applied, the sense of rhythmic augmentation and diminution become clearer, such as the grace notes in bar 2 that are transformed in bar 5. The same kinds of analysis, examining deformation, symmetry and reversal, can be applied to the slow movement (II) of Boulez's second sonata.[39]

In his discussion of 'valeurs irrationelles' (triplets, quintuplets and so on), Messiaen first unpacks examples from Debussy, Ravel, Varèse, and Jolivet, showing the use of ties (from one duration to another) to demonstrate how rhythm can produce expressive accents and rhetoric, but, perhaps most fascinatingly, how rhythm participates in the developmental narrative of his chosen examples through repetition and variation. Jolivet is used as an exemplar here, leading (for Messiaen) to Boulez's and Stockhausen's music.[40] This interest in rhythmic theories is developed in both his students' writings through their structural generation of more complex music from simpler values and interrelationships, and the engagement between tempo, pitch, pulse and narrative perception.

Despite some negative and hurtful comments about certain pieces by Messiaen, Boulez retained a sincere respect and affection for his *maître*. His invective reactively critiques Messiaen's work and was part of the 'fertile ground' perceived by his other avant-garde colleagues. Boulez stated that 'Messiaen's method never manages to fit in with his discourse, because he does not compose – he juxtaposes – and he constantly relies on an exclusively harmonic style of writing; I would almost call it accompanied melody,' a description that could be thought of in relation to the discussion of the central section of movement II of the *Quatuor pour la fin du Temps* earlier, and 'Le Parc de Nara el les lanternes de pierre' (II) and 'Miyajima et le torii dans la mer' (V) from the *Sept haïkaï*.[41] Boulez's tenet, also reformulated five years later by Barraqué, does not adequately describe the sophistication and dynamics of Messiaen's textures.[42] Boulez also stated:

> The whole German-Austrian musical tradition is fundamentally alien to him [Messiaen] in its need to express *evolution* and *continuity* in the handling of musical ideas – what the Germans themselves call *durchkomponieren*. (Just as we can speak of eclecticism in his choice of composers, so his actual style of writing – juxtaposing and superimposing rather than developing and transforming – may be called eclectic.)[43]

Boulez is referring to Messiaen's adaptation (through Stravinsky) of *personnages rythmiques*, and his approach that contrasts with traditional ideals of development through processes of repetition and variation, phrase and formal development (compression and extension), and especially tension and release. While these things do not exist in Messiaen's music in the same way that they do in a Beethoven symphony, for example, through processes of tonal mediation and through what Boulez himself called 'recognised "markers" in recognised forms,'[44] concerns for development and for narrative are found almost everywhere in Messiaen's music; his altered conception of these precepts is integral to his modernism.

Superimposition was important to Messiaen, for example in *Turangalîla-Symphonie* or in the 'Strophes' of *Chronochromie*; 'accompanied melody,' and indeed the love of melody,[45] was likewise fundamental to Messiaen's thought, but Boulez's comments point to other partisan ideas.

First, there is a desire to distance himself from Messiaen (understandable for such an independent and equally autodidactic character), perhaps as a reaction to the strength of his teacher's personality. Stockhausen wrote of the 'explosive confrontation' of Messiaen's teaching and his ability to engage different musical parameters, and Michel Fano described him as 'above all a "triggerer"'.[46] Speaking of himself in 1945 at the time of the 'cas Messiaen', Boulez stated: 'I don't think it is possible to separate the technique an individual possesses, from the shocks one has received.'[47] In the final set of conversations with Michel Archimbaud, Boulez noted that teaching 'must have the function of a detonation, and for this to happen, there must be a detonator, but also an explosive charge'.[48] For Boulez, following Messiaen, the past should be taught 'with reference to the present'.[49] Yet analysis should not merely be an *explication de texte* but function as part of a developmental artistic process. Boulez explains this telos: analysis 'should display doubt and dissatisfaction' that is not merely affirmative or descriptive – a criterion that Boulez applied to others as much as to himself – but a 'surprising encounter', finally 'to make room for inner experience' and for composition.[50] Messiaen's teaching had this function for Boulez and Stockhausen, but the 'explosion' of his teaching initially sent Boulez away from ground zero in order to distance himself from Messiaen and his school of thought.

Second, Boulez defined Messiaen's music against hegemonic Germanic traditions. There is also perhaps a little criticism of Messiaen's limited engagement with music of the Second Viennese School (Schoenberg, Berg and Webern), which was so important to Boulez's own intellectual and musical development. Third, Boulez points to what he sees as a reluctance in Messiaen's work (despite its many innovations) to free itself from traditional means of structuring and thinking that could be described somewhat crudely as 'bottom-up' harmonic thinking. Musical pointillism, as found in *Le Marteau* or in Stockhausen's *Kreuzspiel*, is briefly explored in 'Mode de valeurs', but Boulez perceived a reluctance to go beyond this experiment. In a rudimentary way, although Boulez does not put it like this, Messiaen remained essentially wedded to the organ with the pedals for the bass and the manuals for the higher sounds.

Fourth, there is an implicit critique of Messiaen that he does not seek to reinvent himself; once he arrived at the language of birdsong, the forms change, but the materials do not evolve significantly. And finally, there is an implicit critique of something that Messiaen states of his own music:

> I'll take this opportunity to plead my own case: Japanese music is static, and I myself am a static composer because I believe in the invisible and in the beyond; I believe in eternity. Now, Orientals are on much closer terms with the beyond than we are, and that's why their music is static. The music written by me, a believer, is equally static.[51]

Yet the musical complexity and multivalency of Messiaen's music challenges the exclusive and ideological category of 'staticism' that has become a *mot juste* of the Messiaen literature.[52] 'Staticism' seems to deny the eclectic *esprit de jeux* between elements in Messiaen's music, instead promoting the immutable properties of the divine from Neoplatonic philosophy while providing a panacea to certain negative aspects of modernism.[53] Most importantly, it also seems to marginalize the particular narrative experience afforded to the listener by Messiaen's music – the 'curve in the ear's response' to musical signs and changing hierarchies between musical parameters.[54]

In *Boulez on Music Today* (1971), Boulez does not mention any names but attempts to provide a mirror to current tendencies. He sets out his stall on analysis, informed by his own analyses of Stravinsky and especially Webern. There is a shift from thinking about the Schoenbergian paradigms of 'the musical idea: the logic, technique and art of its presentation' to thinking about structure, and a type of '*active*' analysis that examines 'musical facts', 'internal laws of organisation' and interprets such deductions to grasp the 'internal rigour' of a work.[55] For Boulez, this critical and self-reflexive learning process is essential to a writing that is not only free of formulae but relies on the ear and intelligence to use pre-compositional information as part of a generative and evolutionary process. Messiaen noted that Boulez had adopted certain ideas from Greek and Hindu rhythms but that serialism was only a 'theoretical point of departure':[56] rhythmic and structural formulae were only a beginning, and he understood Boulez's form of creative transgression. Boulez shares with Messiaen an understanding of analysis as an active preparatory means for musical creation, but for Boulez, the 'responsibility' of ideas to each other, to a classicist balance of internal cohesion and creative transgression, is vital. In Boulez's music and writings there is a search for order and clarity, structure, hierarchy, proportion and balance, and sensuality that is abundantly French, but always drawn from a profound understanding of the historical evolution of musical language: lessons learned from Messiaen's class.[57]

Such concerns were interpreted in a different way by the Romanian-born Greek composer Iannis Xenakis (1922–2001), who, after being injured in the Second World War, graduated in civil engineering but fled from Greece to Paris in 1947. Xenakis had been a member of the resistance against the British and had suffered facial disfigurement as a result of an injury sustained while fighting.[58] In Paris he gained employment in Le Corbusier's atelier as an engineer, and then worked as an architect, designing the Philips pavilion at the 1958 Brussels World's Fair and composing music for it – *Concret PH*, which sought an 'extremely rich sound (many high overtones) that has a long duration, yet with much internal change and variety'.[59]

Messiaen visited the pavilion and gave a lecture there known as the *Conférence de Bruxelles* in September 1958.[60] He approved of Xenakis's architectural creation, according to a letter of 19 October 1958, in which Xenakis included an architectural study and the calculations for the Philips pavilion, 'hoping this will interest you', and a 'theoretical study on the introduction to calculus and probability in musical composition', asking Messiaen's advice before publication in 1961.[61]

Xenakis wanted to study composition. After being rejected by Boulanger and Honegger, he studied briefly with the composer and teacher Darius Milhaud (1892–1974), whose music Messiaen admired. He then turned to Messiaen for advice, who noted:

> I understood straight away that he was not someone like the others . . . He is of superior intelligence . . . I did something horrible which I should do with no other student, for I think one should study harmony and counterpoint. But this was a man so much out of the ordinary that I said . . . No, you are almost thirty, you have the good fortune of being Greek, of being an architect and having studied special mathematics. Take advantage of these things. Do them in your music.[62]

Messiaen helped Xenakis, as he did Gérard Grisey and Tristan Murail, to 'find his own music'. Grisey later studied briefly with Xenakis in 1972 (as well as Stockhausen and Ligeti) at the Darmstädter Ferienkurse (for which Messiaen wrote a reference), and despite Grisey's later reflection on Messiaen's teaching as austere and hermetic, he was awarded the prix de Rome (1972) by the two-man jury of Messiaen and Xenakis, the latter praising Grisey as 'most gifted' and possessing an 'outstanding imagination in new music'.[63] Messiaen told Xenakis that he was 'talented . . . even very talented', yet he composed in 'a naive fashion'. Upon seeing his shock, Messiaen added (in Xenakis's words): 'Please don't take it as an insult. I hope I am also naive and will remain so as long as I live.' Xenakis qualifies this: 'By naivety he meant lack of bias, openness,' quite a different complexion on this concept from Maxwell Davies's or Stravinsky's negative judgements (discussed earlier).[64] Alexander Goehr recalled another ramification of this openness. Messiaen was silent and sometimes reduced to tears by the disagreements in his class between 1955 and 1960. He told them: 'Gentlemen let us not argue like this. We are all in a profound night, and I don't know where I am going: I'm as lost as you.'[65] This 'night', perhaps a reflection of the need for theory to explain the complexity of modern music, was also a place of artistic possibility, which Xenakis sought to address in his own ways.

Xenakis became an *auditeur* in Messiaen's class from 1951 to 1954, later describing his teacher as 'practically unknown' at this time.[66] Messiaen exhorted him to listen to and get to know as much music as possible rather than pursue academic training and, uniquely, for Xenakis at this time, 'to make what you want to make', giving him courage to 'risk things'.[67] He enjoyed Messiaen's analyses and current compositional preoccupations (birdsong) and remarked on 'his pure combinatorial thought. He used a language I could immediately understand.'[68] On 15 November 1952, Xenakis noted Messiaen's approval of *Zyia* for soprano, flute and piano. Messiaen wrote: 'You have made fantastic progress . . . You now have a musical language, a style. It is very, very good,' and noted the 'exceptional . . . combination of timbres, melodies and rhythms' in the centre of the work.[69] Xenakis also detailed Messiaen's fascinating lessons in 'Hindu rhythms' and 'the way he combined and transformed them', alongside his 'interversions', but he also commented that Messiaen lacked the necessary mathematical means to continue developing these.[70] While Xenakis remarked that 'I drew the conclusion that his methods were actually very rudimentary and that it was possible to do much more complex things,' he also hailed Messiaen's 'genius' for his 'intuitive insight into maths'.[71]

Xenakis was fascinated by Messiaen's interest in scales and modes and saw parallels with his own work using sieve theory, a selection (through omission) and organization to create relationships between sets of material using different musical parameters, including algorithmic and stochastic principles. Xenakis therefore further extended the idea of scales and modes to the 'characteristics of sound, provided that the values of that characteristic can be ordered'. His description of sieve theory is clearly an extension of Messiaen's 'interversions', *permutations symétriques*, the 'law of the rapport of attack and duration' and indeed Messiaen's own extension of 'modes' beyond pitch to duration, dynamics, attack and register in 'Mode de valeurs', a piece that inspired the 'mechanism, automatism, and algorithmic' nature of Xenakis's work *Le Sacrifice* (1953) for large orchestra, the second part of *Anastenaria* (1952–4).[72]

Xenakis's *Le Sacrifice* (and his later stochastic thought in *Pithoprakta* (1955)) can be understood as a creative response and reaction to integral serialism.[73] In *Pithoprakta*, there is a different extension and revalorization of Messiaen's thinking through the calibration and interrelationships of musical parameters: 'time, pitch, intensity and/or, degree of disorder [for clouds of events]; also the smoothness of sound', and a concern with the organization of sonority (the composition of sound) as a structuring principle.[74] Messiaen taught Xenakis's music (*Metastasis*, *Pithoprakta*, *Eonta* and *Herma*),[75] and he gave a speech for Xenakis's reception into the Académie des Beaux-Arts on 2 May 1984. In it, he praised his work as a 'force of nature, a torrential power capable of annihilating the listener. That is his genius.'[76]

Messiaen and Iannis Xenakis, Salle Pleyel, Paris, 1980.

Messiaen also had an enormous admiration for the composer György Ligeti (1923–2006), whom he described as 'one of the great musicians of the twentieth century; using only his instinct, his brain and his sensibility, he created some of the most advanced works of this epoch'.[77] Messiaen commented on Ligeti's originality, his capacity to create previously unheard sounds and his sense of structure and rigour: 'His writing is a lesson. He has an extraordinary technique.'[78] Although Ligeti was not a student of Messiaen's, they broadly shared in a modernist search for an alternative synthesis between tonality and atonality through forms of modality; an interest in non-Western music, polyrhythm and metre and the ways in which density and intensity of sound can inform and shape a musical narrative, and a care for the effect of music on the listener.

Messiaen and Ligeti are both hybridic composers: 'bricoleurs' who achieved unique modernist syntheses; compare, for instance, the way two modes create a hybrid 'super-mode' at the opening of 'Action de grâces' (*Poèmes pour Mi*) – which Levinas described as an 'ensemble of enharmonic registers' that he calls a 'harmonic pedal',[79] – and in Ligeti's first piano étude, 'Désordre' (1985). In both pieces, rhythmic and structural procedures, involving forms of organized asymmetry, generate new harmonic and contrapuntal relationships that inform their respective languages. Both composers created systems that could be reformed organically and retasked in different contexts, which also allowed the balance and opposition of musical elements to coexist subdermally. However, Ligeti does not appear in Messiaen's analyses of other composers, which most often reveal his own preoccupations and certainly his own hearing.

Messiaen's rhythmic analyses of Stockhausen revealed his interest in freedom from metre and a concern with rhythm as an expressive device. In his discussion of Stockhausen's *Klavierstücke* I–IV (1952), Messiaen is concerned with the way 'irrational values' are contained within other 'irrational values', and in the polyrhythmic possibilities of these rhythms in the wind quintet *Zeitmasze* (1955–6). Again, this is exactly what Messiaen had done in the 'Entrée' of the *Messe de la Pentecôte* (1950–51) by deforming Greek rhythms (although the way Messiaen did this is not clearly shown in the sketches for that work).[80] Messiaen read his own and other composers' rhythmic thought through a range of eclectic sources that reflected his own (French) musical education and taste: Vincent d'Indy (masculine and feminine cadential endings), plainchant theory (concentrating on expression and shape: 'anacrusis – accent – termination'), and Dupré's and Emmanuel's teaching. Mozart, plainchant and Indian

Stockhausen, Boulez and Messiaen at the Théâtre de la Ville, Paris, 26 January 1987.

rhythms for instance could therefore be unpacked and related to contemporary music in ways that showed fundamental musical confluences, concentrating on the revalorization of underlying features and principles of music, devolved from a discussion of historical period attributes or of ideals of musical-historical progression.[81]

Such an *esprit ouvert* and syncretism impressed Stockhausen: Messiaen effectively 'raised the dead' and became a 'glowing crucible' for the 'invention of the new'.[82] Stockhausen encountered Messiaen's music first at the Darmstädter Ferienkurse. He and Goeyvaerts had played Messiaen's recording of the *Quatre Études* after Goléa played an early pressing of it at a lecture on 26 June 1951. Stockhausen admired the 'punctual style' of the *Études*.[83] Messiaen himself was also present at Darmstadt as a teacher in 1951 and 1952.

Stockhausen moved to Paris on 8 January 1952 (in the middle of the academic year) and joined Messiaen's class as an *auditeur*, writing the first version of *Punkte* for orchestra by 24 October that same year.[84] Jonathan Harvey noted the presence of Indian music in 'Les Yeux dans les roues' (*Livre d'orgue*), which 'attaches pitches and durations' and permutates them in a similar way to Stockhausen's *Kreuzspiel*.[85] Stockhausen's hearing of Messiaen's *Quatre Études* in *Kreuzspiel* is evidenced (despite Stockhausen's criticisms of Messiaen's *Livre d'orgue*) in the connection between rhythm, register, duration, attack and timbre, and his use of what Messiaen would later call 'minting' found in various pieces of the

Livre d'orgue, including 'Les Yeux', in both *Pièces en trio* and in the final movement 'Soixante-quatre durées'. *Kreuzspiel* is also marked by the sense of process as form and by a sensitivity to the material qualities of sound (attack and decay). These features are all also presented in *Kontakte* (1958–60), which exists in two versions: for electronic sounds, and for electronics sounds, piano and percussion. Stockhausen's later description of what he called 'momente-form', in relation to this work, is redolent of the language used by Messiaen in the preface for his *Quatuor pour la fin du Temps*. Stockhausen describes it as a focus on the 'now . . . a vertical slice dominating over any horizontal conception of time and reaching into timelessness, which I call eternity: an eternity that does not begin at the end of time, but is attainable at every moment'.[86]

Stockhausen's rapport with Messiaen was also realized through a shared but different sense of spirituality that can be seen in in the introduction to *Kontra-Punkte* (1952) for small ensemble:

> a series of the most clandestine yet palpable transformations and renewals – no foreseeable end. One never hears the same things. Yet one has a sense of never departing from a unique and extremely unified construction. A hidden force which creates cohesion; related proportions: a structure. Not the same figures in a changing light. Rather this: different figures in the same, all-penetrating light.[87]

Messiaen's universal Catholic 'biblical' thought becomes a universal 'spiritual' ideology in Stockhausen, typified (later) by his engagement with the writings of Sri Auribundo (1872–1950) and the *The Urantia Book* (first published in 1955).[88] For Stockhausen, spirituality was 'very concrete', a way of expressing 'supernatural things' that 'words cannot say', though an 'analogous approach', as Messiaen put it, to Messiaen's 'reality of the invisible'.[89] Their concerns with time and space (and human perception of these phenomena) and the properties of sound and spatialization (harmonic and physical) mark Stockhausen and Messiaen as patriarchs of spectralism.[90] Also crucial for both composers was the interaction between timbre, pitch and duration, colour, numerical symbolism and permutation.[91] Likewise, reinterpretation of musical notation (Messiaen's 'Neumes rythmiques' was important for Stockhausen),[92] rhythmic layering, and creating taxonomic systems such as in Messiaen's 'Mode de valeurs', was refigured in the nine scales of notational variability in *Zyklus*

(1959) for one percussionist. Both composers maintained a vital interest in world musics and astronomy, and Stockhausen retained a love of Mozart garnered from Messiaen's teaching.

They shared an interest in theorizing about their own music in particular, with the place of the composer considered not as a 'liberator' (Messiaen) but, for Stockhausen, as shaman: a vessel that is a higher form of being.[93] They both owed much to the totalizing, absolute vision of the arts as a unitary binding force for humanity promoted by Wagner, which is played out in Stockhausen's 'monumental' works such as *Momente* (1962–9), *Hymnen* (1966–7), *Fresco* (1969), *Sternklang* (1971), *Inori* (1973–4), *Sirius* (1975–7), *Licht* (1977–2003) and *Klang* (2005–7). Messiaen remarked that Stockhausen is an example of a composer who is 'capable of constantly renewing and changing himself . . . he's a formidable character'.[94] The engagement of both composers with theory, system, intuition and belief, and their tu(r)ning of modernism towards the sacred, was crucial to their vision and originality.

7
On the Monumental, 1964–83

The increasing mondialization of Messiaen's music is intimately connected with his establishment as a venerable figure of twentieth-century music. Messiaen's international status can be assessed through his honours and prizes. This recognition begins in the 1940s with the Blumenthal Prize (1941), and it increases from the late 1950s with his award of the Chevalier de la Légion d'Honneur (1959) and the Grand Croix (1987), his appointment as a member of the Institut de France, and being awarded the Koussevitsky Prize (1967), the Calouste Gulbenkian Prize (1969), the Erasmus Award (1971) and the Ernest von Siemens Award (1975). There is a crescendo into the 1980s with honours bestowed from all over the world, including the Prix Paul VI, awarded to him at Notre-Dame de Paris by the Cardinal-Archbishop of Paris, Jean-Marie Lustiger (1926–2007), on 28 March 1989 (Messiaen donated the money to Médecins sans Frontières for their work in Afghanistan).[1] Another way of understanding Messiaen's presence is through his many trips to the United States and Canada, and his visits to Japan (1962), Iran (1969), New Caledonia (1975), Israel (1983) and Australia (1988), during which he collected birdsong.[2]

From the 1960s, Messiaen's work became increasingly known outside France through recordings and tours, and through composer studies and books of conversations. Messiaen's circle of influence widened beyond his home country and students, and he began to influence peers such as the Catholic composer James MacMillan (b. 1959).[3] His music and religious aesthetics gave a form of permission to new generations of composers to express faith through musical modernism.

Monumentalism is important to Messiaen's works in this period, and it takes in many meanings: in the natural world and the sublime (mountains and birds), interior and exterior spaces (the 'Summa' of St Thomas

Aquinas and outer space) and Messiaen's presence as progenitor and patriarch of the avant-garde.[4] Through monumentalism, there is also a return to mysticism, to the task of embodying the unknown and the invisible. *Et exspecto resurrectionem mortuorum* (1964) uses a title from the Latin Nicene-Constantinopolitan Credo:

> *Et exspecto resurrectionem mortuorum,*
> *et vitam venturi soeculi. Amen.*
>
> And I look for the resurrection of the dead:
> and the life of the world to come. Amen.

This is a statement of belief – of a 'fact' understood but yet to be manifested. *Et exspecto* could be understood as a protest against *Sacrosanctum Concilium* (SC), passed on 4 December 1963 as part of the Second Vatican Council (1961–5) under Pope John XXIII and then Pope Paul VI, but it could also be appreciated as a reconfiguration of some of its precepts. This is the document that instituted liturgical reform in the Catholic Church; Latin was to be maintained for Latin rites, but the use of the vernacular was to be 'extended' and controlled (article 36).[5]

Olivier Messiaen

GRAND ~~OFFICIER~~ CROIX DE LA LÉGION D'HONNEUR
COMMANDEUR DES ARTS ET LETTRES
GRAND CROIX DE L'ORDRE NATIONAL DU MÉRITE
COMMANDEUR DU MÉRITE FÉDÉRAL ALLEMAND
COMMANDEUR DE L'ORDRE DE LA COURONNE ROYALE DE BELGIQUE
COMMANDEUR DE L'ORDRE DU CHÊNE DU LUXEMBOURG

COMPOSITEUR DE MUSIQUE

PROFESSEUR DE COMPOSITION
AU CONSERVATOIRE NATIONAL SUPERIEUR DE MUSIQUE DE PARIS
ORGANISTE DU GRAND ORGUE DE LA SAINTE TRINITÉ A PARIS

ORNITHOLOGUE ET RYTHMICIEN

MEMBRE DE L'INSTITUT DE FRANCE
MEMBRE DES ACADÉMIES DES BEAUX ARTS DE BAVIÈRE, DE BERLIN, DE HAMBOURG
DE L'ACADÉMIE SAINTE CÉCILE DE ROME, DE L'ACADÉMIE AMÉRICAINE DES ARTS ET LETTRES,
DES ACADÉMIES ROYALES DE LONDRES, DE STOCKHOLM
MEMBRE D'HONNEUR DE L'ACADÉMIE SAN FERNANDO DE MADRID, DE L'ACADÉMIE DES ARTS ET SCIENCES DE BOSTON (USA)
DOCTEUR HONORIS CAUSA DE L'UNIVERSITÉ CATHOLIQUE AMÉRICAINE, DE LOUVAIN (BELGIQUE)
DOCTEUR ÈS-LETTRES HONORIS CAUSA DU CORNELL COLLÈGE (IOWA)
MÉDAILLE D'OR DES ARTS, SCIENCES ET LETTRES DE PARIS
PRIX ERASME (HOLLANDE) · SIBELIUS (FINLANDE) · VON SIEMENS (RFA) · L. SONNING (DANEMARK) · BACH (HAMBOURG) · LIEBERMANN (RFA) · WOLFF (ISRAËL) · ACADÉMIE BERLIN (RFA) · INAMORI DE KYOTO (JAPON) · VILLE DE PARIS (FRANCE)

TÉL. (1) 46 27 99 34 230 RUE MARCADET 75018 PARIS F

Messiaen's visiting card, given to Felix Aprahamian with correction by Messiaen.

Et exspecto was Messiaen's first major work with a Latin title. It was written for forty players, including wind, brass and metallic percussion. Messiaen stated that this 'instrumentation is destined for vast spaces: churches, cathedrals and even open-air spaces and mountain tops'. *Sacrosanctum Concilium* asks that composers 'filled with the Christian spirit . . . produce compositions which have the qualities proper to genuine sacred music . . . [and provide] for the active participation of the entire assembly of the faithful'.[6] *Et exspecto* was 'addressed to all who believe – and also to all others'.[7] It was therefore a form of proclamation in which 'active participation' is reconfigured as an internal response to the dazzlement of God's divine glory and the perception of humanity's heavenly telos.

Messiaen's vision for this work is universal. In the preface to the work, he described as inspiration the pyramids and stairs of ancient Mexico, ancient Egyptian statues, Gothic and Roman ecclesiastical architecture, texts of St Thomas Aquinas on the Resurrection, and the practice of working amid the high alps of France near his holiday home in Petichet. It was conceived to be played in front of the glacier of La Meije,[8] but it was first performed (at Messiaen's choice) at 11 a.m. on 7 May 1965 under Serge Baudo and in the presence of André Malraux, the minister of culture who commissioned the work, in a relatively small ecclesiastical space with a very high ceiling – the Sainte-Chapelle in Paris, 'the summit of religious art'.[9] Messiaen's friends and students were present, including Barraine, Charpentier, Daniel-Lesur, Langlais, Litaize and Xenakis.[10] Here, the dazzling colours of the medieval stained-glass windows acted, in Messiaen's opinion, as an ideal visual companion to the colours of his music. The second performance was in Chartres Cathedral (another UNESCO world heritage site noted for its stained-glass windows) on 20 June 1965 in the presence of General de Gaulle and Malraux. Boulez gave the third performance in the Odéon – Théâtre de France, described a little sanguinely by Messiaen as 'without presenting the same mystical splendours' but 'no less glorious'.[11]

The ideal of glory is important in Messiaen's thought and connected to monumentalism. Messiaen had read the Swiss theologian (and musician) Hans Urs von Balthasar's work on glory.[12] Glory in *Et exspecto* is present in the premonition, promise or 'guarantee', as Messiaen puts it, of our own future resurrection in the image of Christ.[13] This is not merely mystical idealism but belief in action: glory can be understood as the revelation of this future promise *now*. For Messiaen, this was belief affirmed through musical irradiation – colour allows the invisible and intangible (the domain of God, angels, heaven) to become sensible.[14] The environment for the first two performances was crucial. The architecture and stained glass in these buildings facilitated participation in the monumental and sublime, understood as appreciable and yet beyond our imagination, allowing access to a representation of Messiaen's internal vision and promoting eschatological desire. *Et exspecto* is in five short movements. Messiaen uses texts from various sources (Psalm 130 – *De profundis*, Romans, St John, St Paul's letter to the Corinthians and the Apocalypse), each tinged with the mystical *promesse de bonheur* of the resurrection. There are also familiar sounds of birds, the abyss and of plainchant – not forbidden, but in fact 'given pride of place' in *Sacrosanctum Concilium*.[15]

The first movement envoices the text 'Out of the depths have I cried unto thee O Lord, Lord hear my cry' (Psalm 130). The precipices of the abyss are dramatized through a multi-voiced monodic chorale as a representation of the awe, austerity and majesty that erupts from and extends the colour chords or 'complexes of sound' below.[16] Each chord is coloured in different ways, 'like a new race of chords' – a principle used throughout the work – that 'dazzles the eye' like stained glass, in which 'a thousand colours become one sole colour'.[17]

The second movement evokes 'Abîme des oiseaux' (*Quatuor pour la fin du Temps*) and *Couleurs de la Cité céleste* (without the plainchant), and contains a fascinating *Klangfarbenmelodie* effect in bar 3 that Messiaen calls 'mélodies par manques' (melody by loss).[18] This concern with different 'orders' of sound and the relationship between dynamics, timbre and duration had caught his ear in Act I, scene III of Debussy's *Pelléas et Mélisande* and was important in his teaching of this work.[19] Boulez later demonstrated how a duration 'can be manifested by a group of pitches, and a pitch can be realised with a group of durations, so [that] use will be made of a multiplicity of timbres, with a general dynamic envelope'.[20] A comparison of bar 3 of *Et exspecto* (II) and Ex. 19b from *Boulez on Music Today* shows complementary research into the materiality or use of the properties of sound in music.

The third movement of *Et exspecto* is memorable for the extraordinary solos for bells, gongs and tam-tam crescendos that follow the titular epigraph (John 5:25), announcing the hour when the dead will hear Christ's voice. Messiaen had studied Aquinas's writings on the resurrection before composing this piece. In this movement, he uses the Uirapuru (musician wren), an Amazonian bird traditionally understood to be heard immediately before the moment of death. Here it symbolizes Christ waking the dead (the Resurrection). Woodwind chords with repeated notes, crescendos and diminuendos inside them (brass and metallic percussion) again explore changing sonic densities and intensities. Messiaen described himself as a pioneer in the use of combinations of metallic percussion that 'in their extraordinary resonance were a sort of representation of mystery and of the dream that one is looking for in music'.[21] The third and fourth pieces explore 'four musics, four shimmerings of colours and four sound complexes'.[22] They engage the ways in which the liminal saturation of loudness and sonic density, connected with birdsong and plainchant, is effected in acoustic space.

In the final chorale-like movement, time is marked relentlessly by six gongs, as though waiting for the voice of an immense crowd (Revelation 19:6) through an 'enormous fortissimo, unanimous and simple'.[23] This idea is adapted in the sound world of Boulez's *Rituel in Memoriam Bruno Maderna* (1974–5) where the percussion functions as a rhythmic anchor to the increasing density and elaboration of the material.[24] Austerity is didactically impressed upon the listener (in both these works), a monumentality that is solemn, rich and overwhelming rather than merely 'simple'. Following Messiaen's ideal of stained-glass windows, the white unitary light of God shines through the window (his harmonies) to dazzle the listener with colour. This complex and traumatic experience leaves the listener to complete the action of revelation as their 'active participation' (SC), effectively following the light back through the window to God.

Sacrosanctum Concilium was concerned with the 'eternal' and universal Church. In the Second Vatican Council, the composer Maurice Duruflé participated in a commission of expert musicians (appointed 26 May 1964) that advised the Commission Épiscopale de la Liturgie. This subgroup of 22 members, 12 being clerics, also included the composers Jean Langlais and Gaston Litaize, as well as Duruflé's second wife, Marie-Madeleine Duruflé-Chevalier. In a series of articles, beginning in an issue of the journal *L'Orgue* (July–September 1965), Duruflé observed that the precepts of *Sacrosanctum Concilium* were being ignored: the position of the organ and the role of organists was being undermined. He lamented the lip service given to Gregorian chant (in French) and its loss in favour of 'new songs in French, of such vulgarity and musical platitudes that act in the name of the "renovation of liturgical music"'.[25] This practice effectively reversed what Pope Pius X decried as 'profane and theatrical art' in his

Tra le Sollecitudini (1903), and the explicit connection between participation 'in divine worship' and the singing of Gregorian chant endorsed in *Divini cultus* (1928).[26] Gregorian chant and the pre-eminence of the organ were also reinforced by later missives: Pius XII's *Mystici corporis Christi* (29 June 1943), *Mediator Dei* (20 November 1947) and *Musica sacra disiplina* (25 December 1955), in *Sacrosanctum Consilium* and in *Musicam Sacram* (5 March 1967). However, following the French Church's 'interpretation' of *Sacrosanctum Concilium*, Duruflé lamented that Gregorian chant was effectively 'condemned to death'.[27] Messiaen also recognized the impoverishment of music and the role of the organist.[28] In Duruflé's writings, for a musician with a 'Gregorian soul', it is evident that this practice created a sense of bewilderment and betrayal.[29]

Langlais had written music in the vernacular, but infused with the Gregorian spirit, from 1954; however, in letters and articles before the Second Vatican Council he decried the new music written for the Church and affirmed the true religious spirit of Gregorian music and the place of beauty and artistry in religious music. This led in 1967 to a complete rift between Langlais and the French Church authorities.[30] Rolande Falcinelli resigned from the Basilique du Sacré-Cœur in 1973, citing her differences with the clergy and her inability to play modern music in the liturgy like 'the great Messiaen', implying that Messiaen had a licence not afforded to others.[31] A form of liturgical antagonism also set in, whereby trite songs in French from the east end of the church were answered by sophisticated organ plainchant improvisations from the west end.[32] Therefore, the kind of liturgical role of the organ in the liturgy envisaged in Tournemire's music, and inherited by Messiaen's generation, was fractured.

Messiaen's works in Latin can be thought of as an open critique of this ecology. Messiaen was not involved with the liturgical debates in France but commented that 'the statue comes down from its pedestal!': for him, Gregorian chant sung in French removed its 'majesty and dreamlike quality'.[33] He noted that Latin created a certain distance between the listener and the meaning behind the words that is beneficial to spirituality.[34] Boulez sanguinely noted the way Latin provides 'religious identity', and a 'feeling [of being] Roman Catholic' that was 'all the more arcane for being irrational'.[35] But Gregorian chant is about more than beauty, patrimony and tradition. It is a form of prayer, exaltation and exhortation that points to a way of thinking and living. For Messiaen, it was 'the "only" liturgical music which possessed at the same time, purity, joy and the ability to transport the soul towards the Truth'.[36]

In his oratorio *La Transfiguration de Notre-Seigneur Jésus-Christ* (1965–9), Messiaen sought to 'renew the tradition' and to 'prove that Latin texts are very beautiful and that their unintelligibility adds to their mystery. The statue remains on its pedestal.'[37] Gregorian chant was a form of sacramental, eternal and universal material that remained truthful beyond contemporaneous liturgical fashion. *La Transfiguration* was a long-cherished idea. In the early 1930s, he had noted to himself: 'faire aussi oratorio sur *La Transfiguration*'.[38] It uses chant-like material in Latin, almost always in unison or harmonized as chorales; the text therefore has the sort of admirable clarity demanded by the Council of Trent in 1562–3.

La Transfiguration was commissioned by the Calouste Gulbenkian Foundation in Lisbon, and it was first performed on 7 June 1969 in their festival.[39] The work is in fourteen movements divided into two 'Septenaires'. Each 'Septenaire' ends with a chorale, and the second one is considerably longer. The transfiguration is part of the narrative of Christ's life – birth, baptism, transfiguration, crucifixion, resurrection, ascension – and it is considered to be one of the miracles of Jesus and a revelation of Christ's real eternal and godly nature. Messiaen stated:

> Christ was radiant at the moment of the transfiguration. He was radiant at the moment of the resurrection, and we too shall be radiant when we rise again . . . It was while I was in the mountains that I had the idea for this work. Looking at the glaciers of La Meije, I was suddenly aware of the difference between the dazzling whiteness of the snow, and the even more dazzling splendour of the sun. That is how I understood the difference between our tiny man-made lights and the great light of the Resurrection and the Transfiguration.[40]

The monumental is celebrated in this work. Messiaen's mother wrote of 'My alps, those of my childhood, those which I love', and *La Transfiguration* can be partly understood as a tribute to his mother's love, which nurtured Messiaen's poetic sensibility and his appreciation of glory.[41] It is one of his longest pieces to date and it required the largest forces of any work thus far. The score was the first of Messiaen's works to be published *en grand format* (31.3 × 41.4 cm (12 × 16 in.)). It is sometimes described as an oratorio, but unlike many of the well-known works in this genre – Händel's *Messiah* or Mendelssohn's *Elijah* – it does not tell a story but rather surrounds the event with a commentary drawn from scripture and the theology of Aquinas.

Messiaen is a musician of ellipsis. He points to the event (such as the Transfiguration or the Resurrection) and evokes it through a form of theatrical representation. Arguably, in maintaining a certain distance, the holiness and uniqueness of the event is preserved.[42] The monumental and iconic function of the event therefore acts to entrain desire through participation, but also reveals our own human inadequacy, as intimated in the ideal of the sublime, where we can perceive an event (a sunset, for instance) but yet the event itself overwhelms our imagination.[43] Messiaen's music therefore brings both perception and imagination into sharper focus through his personal yet universal vision of such events. His music creates an experiential refiguring of the real world (as well as mysticism and theology) rather than providing an escape from it, while pointing towards the 'luminous, unchanging Reality' of God.[44]

La Transfiguration is a harvest home for Messiaen's rhythmic and harmonic techniques. In his chorales (especially movements VII and XIV), flashes of tonal chords erupt like the sun through clouds to illuminate the texture and impart monumentality. Chorales also function as liminal quilting points, fulcrums or plateaus of material that structure each movement, just as they did in Tournemire's *L'Orgue Mystique* and his *Sept Chorals-Poèmes d'Orgue pour les sept paroles du Xrist*; they titrate religious glory and presence to the listener.

Messiaen uses North and Central American and Australian birds (pieces III, IX and V) and presents a striking image of the peregrine falcon (XII) – the fastest animal on earth in its dive – as well as trills and glissandi to impart the effects of light (III) and lightning (VIII), and a halo of sound (brass without percussion, III) to colour the name of Christ, a technique redolent of that which is used in Bach's *St Matthew Passion*. Also present are brass 'sound-pedals', like those in *Couleurs* that express 'the abyss' (XII), wordless vocalization (IX), the effects of sonic saturation and counterpoint (VI) and an abundant use of harmonics above classified chords (in XIV, for example) through his orchestral technique, something that had been noted of Messiaen's orchestration by Virgil Thomson in 1945.[45]

Messiaen's spatialization of harmony relates to his own kinaesthetic hearing of the organ; he can use notes in the right hand to irradiate pitches in the left so that his music becomes coextensive with organ pipe voicing. This approach to harmony was already present in Messiaen's 'chord of resonance', in which the right hand contains higher harmonics above the fundamental that effected his later concept of *éblouissement*, or sound-colour dazzlement.[46] The percussion contributes potently to this harmonic dazzlement in *La Transfiguration*, not as noise or to provide textural 'glitter' (as in Boulez's *Pli selon pli*, and other contemporaneous scores) but as an enhancement and dramatization of the theological and mystical sense of presence and imagery. There is much harmonic and textural premonition of scores to come, especially the *Méditations sur le Mystère de la Sainte Trinité* for organ (1969), *Des canyons aux étoiles...* (1972–4) and *Saint François d'Assise* (1975–83).

Méditations had its genesis in improvisation. The organ at La Trinité was rebuilt from 1962 to 1966, with the addition of seven stops, a crescendo pedal and general pistons that obviated the need for registration assistants.[47] The year 1967 marked the centenary of the church. On 23 November, Messiaen gave a concert of improvisations entitled 'Le Mystère de Dieu', responding to homilies on the Trinity from Maxime Charles (1908–93, the rector of the Basilique du Sacré-Cœur from 1959–85).[48] These improvisations formed a basis for the written *Méditations*, premiered privately by Messiaen at La Trinité on 8 November 1971, and then publically by the composer at the National Shrine of the Immaculate Conception in Washington, DC, on 20 March 1972. Messiaen subsequently recorded it at La Trinité from 29 May to 3 June 1972.[49]

Messiaen's preface describes 'le langage communicable', which he thought of as functioning like leitmotifs, and through which he 'tried to construct a language . . . to express the inexpressible' because 'the invisible reality is more real than the visible reality.'[50] Perhaps the idea derives from Arthur Rimbaud's sonnet 'Voyelles' (1871), or from his friend the artist Sonia Delaunay's 'simultaneous alphabet, based on the investigation into the correspondence between vowels and colours conducted in the 1920s'.[51] But through his *langage*, he reinscribed the issue of the absence of specific meaning inherent in absolute (wordless) music, invoking, following Aquinas, the ability of angels to communicate without words and inciting each other (and humanity) to listen 'by some sensible sign'.[52] Following his previous scores, where colours, concepts and birds are labelled, Messiaen creates a musical 'alphabet . . . grouping the letters according to the type of phonic production. Furthermore, I have given each letter a *sound*, a *pitch*, and a *duration*', thereby attaching semantic meaning to the materiality of sound. The use of the vernacular (rather than Latin) perhaps implies a personal locution, useful for the player but not particularly so for the audience; criticism of the transmission of meaning in Messiaen's *langage* was

Messiaen at the organ of the Église de la Sainte-Trinité, Paris, 1963.

made after the European premiere of *Méditations* in Düsseldorf by Almut Rössler in 1972.[53]

Messiaen also provides extensive texts for each piece (often citing Aquinas) that explain the narrative of the work for the listener. The pacing, colour and use of devices, internal rhythmic processes (in pieces I, III and VII especially) and birdsong create a satisfying meditative concert experience. Whether the music is theological or becomes theological through performance is debatable. *Sacrosanctum Concilium* recommends: 'The texts intended to be sung must always be in conformity with Catholic doctrine; indeed, they should be drawn chiefly from holy scripture and from liturgical sources.' Messiaen fulfils this mandate in *Méditations*, in a para-liturgical work that employs organ music to represent and elaborate upon scriptural texts. This emphasis on communication perhaps could be understood as related to various imperatives in writing about avant-garde music by Stockhausen and Luciano Berio (1925–2003), and also perhaps in the turn to vocal music in the work of Mauricio Kagel (1931–2008), Berio, Ligeti and Stockhausen.

Méditations was Messiaen's longest organ cycle thus far, and, apart from the short conservatoire piece *Verset pour le fête de la Dédicace* (1960), his first major work for the instrument for eighteen years. The *Verset* (December 1960) was premiered in the *concours* at the Conservatoire de Paris by Messiaen's student Raffi Ourgandjian and others. It is a work that uses the Gregorian chant for the Feast of the Dedication of a church

(25 October), which effectively stands in for the text, acting symbolically as a 'communicable language' without words. The work is in rondo form with two varied repetitions of the opening section, punctuated by two strophes from the song thrush (used in *Catalogue d'oiseaux* and *Livre d'orgue*), marked 'rhythmic, with a strange joy'.

Méditations are a point of consolidation. Like *Catalogue*, *Couleurs*, *La Transfiguration* and the *Verset*, the listener is asked (in pieces II, IV, VI, XIII and IX) to hear the relationship between discrete musical sections across spaces of musical time. Unlike previous organ cycles, the pieces are not given titles but are instead built around ideas. Like *Les Corps Glorieux*, *Méditations* has a clear highpoint in the middle of the work (VI); the final piece (although containing toccata figurations) revises ideas and provides a form of summation. Messiaen's adaptation of the 'hallucination chords' from Act I, scene II (b. 1–4) of Berg's *Wozzeck*,[54] where Wozzeck has visions of the end of the world, appear at the opening of the 'Offertoire' (*Messe*), in *La Transfiguration* (movements II and VII), *Méditations* (movement VII) and *Des canyons aux étoiles...* (movement III), and they represent the darkness of the Crucifixion at the opening of 'La Résurrection du Christ' in movement X of *Livre du Saint Sacrement* (1984). Registrations and textures in *Méditations* also reoccur in the *Livre*.

The same chords also appear, associated with night, on page three and eight of another extended birdsong work, *La Fauvette des jardins* (1970). Like 'La Rousserolle effarvatte' (*Catalogue*, VII), which charted 27 hours centred on this bird and its ecology, this work marks seventeen hours of nature, depicting the familiar area around Messiaen's summer home in Petichet. The mountain Grande Serre and Lake Laffrey accompany the protagonists, eighteen of them including the Loriot (a nod again to Messiaen's wife Yvonne Loriod, the dedicatee of the work), the moon, the undulations of water, the colours of the sun in the lake, the threat of a summer thunderstorm and the silhouettes of trees in moonlight. Messiaen's bird writing creates different forms of proximity to the listener, with careful character and textural differentiations. He contrasts and juxtaposes bird material with his modes and other types of chords (the nightingale and the 'chord of the total chromatic' on page 9 of the score for example) and mirror- and row-like constructions. Irruptions of tonality and the return of material create narrative connections for the listener across the approximately thirty-minute duration of the work.

The parade of avian icons in *Fauvette* intensifies during the day. Nature is observed, implacable, disinterested, monumental and existing in parallel with humanity. The garden warbler is Messiaen's lead protagonist in this musical dumbshow. Messiaen's colour chords permeate and underline the virtuosic volley of its song. Colour is imparted through a fracturing effect created by the bird's *vitesse*. As Messiaen states: 'each note is provided with a chord, not a traditional chord but a complex of sounds destined to give the timbre of that note.'[55] Messiaen's portrayal of the bird is intrinsically concerned with the listener's psychological perception, something that was important to the spectralist composers present in Messiaen's class from 1969 to 1970.

Hugues Dufourt has noted that 'the harmonic structure of sound' – that is, in Messiaen's case, birdsong heard as an inherently unstable material – 'can be prolonged by its timbre.'[56] Tristan Murail's comment on Messiaen's role in his own thinking supports this interpretation: 'You didn't need to think about music in terms of accompanied melody or counterpoint . . . [but rather] the importance given to timbre, as a way of structuring the form.'[57] This is indeed a potent way of hearing Messiaen's music, as evolving colours shaping forms from within. The speed of Messiaen's birdsong creates its own separate ornithological paradigm, giving the listener a semblance of the bird's world. The succession of timbres, registers, durations, accents and colours imply but significantly

Messiaen, class of 1969–70 (Conservatoire de Paris), including Michaël Levinas (standing far left), Michel Béroff (standing third from left), Gérard Grisey (standing fourth from right) and Tristan Murail (far right).

Messiaen and Loriod at Bryce Canyon, Utah, 1972.

diverge from tonal grounding – instead 'underheard' (Dupré) and 'overheard' sounds (Jolivet) help facilitate the liminal quality of this music.[58]

This liminal perspective is developed in *Des canyons aux étoiles...*, which 'is at once geological, ornithological, astronomical, and theological.'[59] Here, there is a reflection between inner and exterior experience, between metaphor and what it attempts to evoke. The colours, especially the different reds in the rocks in the canyons of Utah and the colours of mountains, trees, vegetation and birds (figured iconically),[60] are humanly sensible images for Messiaen in which eternity and the glory of God are manifested. But for Messiaen, this eternity is also present within ourselves, awaiting realization, partially through image and symbol, religion and theology, but then fully through death and resurrection.

Des canyons aux étoiles... was commissioned by the singer and philanthropist Alice Tully (1902–1993) and inspired by a voyage to the great canyons of Utah: 'Mount Messiaen' was officially named on 5 August 1978 and marked with a plaque at the site. Messiaen had a stone from the mountain in his private collection of objects.[61] The work is in twelve movements and was premiered on 20 November 1974. The third performance, in London on 12 November 1975 at the Royal Festival Hall, was conducted by Boulez, who never recorded the work.[62] The work is written for a small orchestra and includes an aeoliphone (wind machine) and geophone (a new instrument commissioned by Messiaen that gives the sound of creaking dry earth),[63] and parts for solo piano and horn.

Des canyons aux étoiles... begins appropriately in the desert, an ascetic, lonely place beneath the stars where kenosis (spiritual self-emptying) and the 'interior conversation of the spirit' can be activated. Extreme timbres (piccolo, violin harmonics, the aeoliphone for the desert wind), birds and the unnamed sonic image of 'the abyss' (Revelation 9:1–3) all define Messiaen's sonic and sensual landscape. This sound world is familiar from earlier works, but in *Des canyons* there is above all a sense in which the discrete segments, which Boulez might have critiqued as 'obstinately segmented forms', individuate and characterize each movement while still being confined to their 'inviolable space', as Boulez states.[64] For the most part, these segments enable a sense of balance and continuity between different types of materials. Messiaen uses subtle changes in figuration – for example, the new piano cadential material in movement VII – and changes in the harmonic teleology, timbre (reorchestration), register, density (addition or subtraction of material) and the dilation of radiance through tonal chords to signal narrative change. Such recognizable 'markers' abound in his music and help demarcate Messiaen's forms.[65] These are the ways in which Messiaen embeds what Boulez would call the 'responsibility' of the composer and the 'deductive methods to amplify, transform and proliferate' the material to create narrative experience.[66] There is in *Des canyons* a sense of evoking majesty through restraint, perhaps mediated through the bass-light quality of Messiaen's orchestration. There is also an attention to delicacy and to clarity in the combination of instrumental groups, and a respect for the way the properties of the instruments can contribute to the narrative.

Des canyons aux étoiles... contains exquisite spectral orchestration (movements II and X), chorales in III and XII (and in other movements), a wider use of glissandi than in *La Transfiguration*, 'communicable language' (in movement III), and the Trisagion in V (a text for Good Friday), extended instrumental techniques (V, VI (the solo horn movement) and X), the presence of the idea of the 'abyss' (from *Couleurs*) and 'sound-pedals' (although sometimes not named, they occur in movements I, III, V and VII), often combining lower brass (bass trombone), tam-tams and gongs. There are two birdsong piano works: movement IV and IX; movement IV uses the cossyphe de Heuglin (white-browed robin), an East African bird used later by Florentz in his *Asun: conte symphonique sur l'Assomption de Marie*, op. 7 (1986–8), a bird also used by Messiaen in *Un sourire* (1989).[67] Messiaen's textures are irradiated by tonal colours, indicative of sunlight on the red rocks of Utah, of spiritual bliss and radiance, especially E major in the long coda of movement VII, C Major in X and XI, and A major in VIII, which prefigures the angel's music in tableau 3 of *Saint François* and, at the conclusion of the work (in XII), points back to the resonant conclusion of *Visions de l'Amen*.

Messiaen's use of Ernest Hello's and Romano Guardini's theology makes fascinating connections with scripture and nature. For example, Messiaen uses Hello in movement V: the replacement of the existential *la peur* (fear) by the personal *la crainte* (also 'fear') is interpreted by Messiaen as 'reverence of the sacred, and of divine presence': a 'conduit to adoration'.[68] Messiaen evokes this reverence through musical colours that present his unique vision of rocks, trees, snow and wind. For 'Appel Interstellaire' (*Canyons*, VI), he uses the sounds of the horn's 'call' to connect the human abyss of misery, as Hello conceives it (the work was originally a memorial piece to a student, Jean-Pierre Guézec),[69] to the abyss of God; abasement is conjoined with adoration. In movement VIII, Messiaen connects interior radiance (the heart of Jesus and the love underpinning creation) and the radiance of the star Aldebaran as an image of the resurrection through the sort of blissful music (harmonics and percussion) heard in 'Jardin du sommeil d'amour' (*Turangalîla-Symphonie*, VI).

The development of interior grace and human predestination to follow Christ through death and resurrection is the subject of Messiaen's largest work, his four-hour opera *Saint François d'Assise* (1975–83). Published *en grand format*, the scores weigh over 20 kilograms (44 lb). Messiaen loved opera and taught operatic works of Monteverdi, Mozart, Wagner, Mussorgsky, Debussy and Berg especially, but was uneasy about the Swiss composer and director of the Paris Opera Rolf Liebermann's request for an opera. Messiaen had been to Assisi as early as autumn 1959, and again in April 1980, bringing back a small tree branch from the Carceri that he kept in a custom-made box, noting that the branch was the 'exact colour of the Franciscan's dress'.[70]

The idea of the opera was mooted as early as 1971, but Messiaen only signed the contract on 25 April 1976.[71] Although he considered St Paul's conversion on the road to Emmaus, Messiaen chose the subject of St Francis for his opera because 'of all the saints, he most resembles Christ by his poverty, his chastity, his humility and, bodily, by the stigmata that he received on his feet, his hands and side.'[72] Francis's love of birds meant that, for Messiaen, he was a 'colleague and friend'.[73] The opera can be understood as partly autobiographical, partly didactic, but mostly as a worldly attempt not merely to theologize or allegorize but to demonstrate the growth of grace within a human soul.

Messiaen wrote the libretto using historical sources – the *Fioretti* and St Francis's writings. He gave careful instructions for staging, lighting and costumes that were inspired by paintings and frescoes of Cimabue (*c.* 1240–1302) and Giotto (*c.* 1267–1337). He left out the character of St Clare (a follower of St Francis) and created the Angel as the only female character. Messiaen's opera is in three acts and eight 'tableaus' (distributed as three, three and two, respectively), a term he uses in preference to the tradition 'scenes' and which is redolent of the frescos of Giotto and Fra Angelico (*c.* 1395–1455), and is also found in medieval mystery plays including didactic 'miracle' or 'Saint's plays' which re-enact saintly miracles rather than biblical events. The opera uses an extremely large orchestra (especially the percussion) and requires a choir of 120 singers. The orchestration was an immense work for Messiaen, who suffered from various illnesses, including back trouble (partly caused by standing to do this work).

Messiaen retired from the Conservatoire at the end of September 1978.[74] Langlais described Messiaen as being almost uncontactable in 1982 and working 'at least twelve hours a day' on the opera. The Messiaens had bought La Sauline, a house in the Sologne, on 6 June 1981 as a refuge for work, and they moved in on 26 October.[75] During the orchestration, Messiaen confided to Langlais: 'I am not sure if it [this opera] is a good one.' Langlais asked him, 'What do you wish for the performance of this work?' Messiaen responded somewhat facetiously: 'I wish [for] seven men and one angel.'[76] The work was premiered at the Paris Opéra (Palais Garnier) on 28 November 1983 with Seiji Ozawa (1935–2024) conducting and José van Dam in the title role.

Saint François d'Assise is rarely staged, perhaps due to the huge expense of mounting a production including the extensive rehearsals required. It uses leitmotifs for characters and ideas. Francis's leitmotif is employed to reveal the state of his soul or its progress towards grace, made possible

Messiaen giving Jean Langlais the Officier de la Légion d'Honneur, 20 October 1968.

through suffering,[77] reflection, prayer, chant, the effect of God's will or desire, kenosis and sacrifice, illumination, sonic saturation and other factors. For Messiaen, the subjective intuition of God's presence and love was manifested through his synaesthesia, described in 1978 in words that prefigure the end of his opera:

> When I hear music, when I read music, I see colours, which are marvellous and impossible to describe because they are moving like the sounds themselves, and as the durations are in movement, these are the things that move and which interpenetrate. One is not able to write them down, but one is dazzled [*ébloui*]. And it is this dazzling that brings us closer to a leap beyond time, to a leaving of oneself that will be eternity.[78]

The opera has an interior narrative centred on the main character, St Francis, and perhaps, therefore, lacks some of the theatricality of nineteenth-century opera. The first act introduces Francis and his fellow monks. Francis's fear of the Leper naturally precipitates a confrontation with this character through the agency of the Angel in tableau three, in which the Leper is healed and Francis grows in holiness. The fourth tableau speaks directly of predestination. Francis comes to experience God's presence as he swoons in tableau five. The audience listens in to Francis's blissful unconscious state through the diegetic music of the (musician) angel tuning up (not the character of the Angel, but another angel that appears to St Francis), using music that was refigured by Messiaen from the end of movement II ('L'Ange au sourire') of Daniel-Lesur's chamber work *Suite médiévale* (1945). Messiaen did not want to represent Christ on stage, so the audience diegetically hears the invisible chorus (in C major at rehearsal fig. 87 – the key of light and resurrection that ends the opera) as a representation of Christ's voice accompanying the otherworldly sound of the angel (played by the ondes Martenot).[79] The wordless angel's musical pace differs from the human characters around it, an aspect inspired by Japanese Nō theatre.[80]

In the sixth tableau, St Francis preaches to the birds, and here Messiaen uses a form of controlled aleatoricism in the 'Grand concert d'oiseaux' (rehearsal fig. 118–24). A major (associated with the angel from tableau three) shines through the miasma of Messiaen's colourful writing at fig. 120. This key is also directly elaborated through colourful spectral chords to embody the words *par surcroît* (in excess) at five bars before rehearsal fig. 137, and then followed by chords based on E♭ major (associated with the angel's 'Thème de la vérité'), and C major (Resurrection). In a synaesthetic sense, therefore, motives and keys are connected (for the listener) with the developments of characters and religious ideas.

In the final two tableaus, Francis receives the marks of Christ's crucifixion on his body (and in making Christ's presence visible, the choir becomes visible also), and then he dies in the final tableau. St Francis is seen resurrected with the Leper, and the choir (Christ) sings of 'la joie', realizing Francis's final words, adapted from Aquinas: 'Saviour, Saviour, music and poetry have brought me towards you, by image, by symbol, and by default of truth . . . Deliver me, intoxicate me, dazzle me with your excess of Truth.'

Through this work, Messiaen offers the hope that humanity can be raised above itself. The opera refigures nineteenth-century romantic aesthetic precepts: desire and longing become eschatological and heroism becomes a form of religious triumphalism. In places such as the healing of the leper (tableau three), the angel's music (tableau five), the stigmata (tableau seven), and at the conclusion of the work, Messiaen's opera invokes the sublime. This concept is understood through this opera not only as that which can be perceived but yet overwhelms our imagination, but as a revelation of 'the impossible made possible' through Christian redemption. The work therefore attempts to transcend the theology that inspired it, and to lead thought out of its own ideological and aesthetic aporias through 'the shock of the positive' in the Resurrection:[81]

> it acts as a pressing fundamental; the most considerable to take place since creation. At the opposite of certain representations, I do not see the resurrection as an effort made by Christ: it was sudden, like the explosion of an atomic bomb.
>
> The shroud of Turin is a witness. I believe in it, not because this appears to me to be like a miracle, but [because it is] a natural phenomenon. At Hiroshima, the bodies of the victims were found photographed on the walls. In the same way, the resurrection was an atomic shock. Christ was raised in one stroke and his effigy was imprinted on the shroud.
>
> I have tried in my music to render the resurrection – this very concrete and extraordinary thing – in multiple ways, without ever having achieved it. I am not able to render this moment as it was. The resurrection of Christ gives to us all the right to be resurrected also, and the presentiment of this moment particularly disturbs me.[82]

Messiaen's opera presents a fantasy of ontological transformation that embodies an example of human and divine love: 'carnal' and 'spiritualized'.[83] The erotic love-death of Wagner embodying renunciation and sacrifice is refigured through Christ's love in the character of St Francis.[84] His self-overcoming and *éblouissement* is a didactic call to humanity, achieved through ecstatic, spiritual and violent means, to become more like Christ. Belief configured through trauma reflexively asks the listener to examine their own spiritual compass. Wagner's realization of the sacred in art and within humanity itself through a music that was of *das Volk*, for *das Volk* and to be transformative of *das Volk* (Wagner does not put it this succinctly) was an ethos reframed by Messiaen in a manner boldly congruent with *Sacrosanctum Concilium*. Messiaen's *Saint François d'Assise* is a work of a composer 'filled with the Christian spirit' that provides 'for the active participation of the entire assembly of the faithful'.[85] It can be regarded as a para-liturgical work (outside but doing the work of the Church) that provides a 'foretaste of that heavenly liturgy which is celebrated in the holy city of Jerusalem', not merely for 'the glory of God and the sanctification of the faithful' but as a potent form of *Verklärung*, as enlightenment, awakening and enchantment.[86]

8
On Final Works and Legacy

The thinking that surrounds the concept of 'late style' – notably from the philosopher Theodor W. Adorno and the literary critic Edward W. Said – provides critical avenues into understanding Messiaen's last works.[1] The focus in Adorno's work is on the way that late style provides a critique of earlier style, and of the ways in which the craft, style and aesthetics of art diagnose a form of social truth – that the Enlightenment promise of freedom, rationality and progress had failed.[2]

Messiaen's music engages with the emancipatory *promesse de bonheur* of the Enlightenment, reinterpreting Adorno's negative dialectics of modernity with a 'shock of the positive' that also forms a potent form of social-historical critique.[3] It provides a riposte to modern secular Enlightenment values and discourse and empirical and scientific inquiry through Messiaen's revalorization of mysticism and musico-theological discourse. Freedom has constraints, and Messiaen's religion demands discipline, observance, obedience and piety; the 'binding' (*ligere*) in *religio* is operative. In Messiaen's religious-modernist music and aesthetics, the Enlightenment 'social contract' is supplanted by a more primal covenant – a participation in Christ's legacy through divine filiation (the doctrine that through the sonship and redemption of Christ, Christians are adopted into a filial relationship with God), and even a desire to imitate or figure, in and through art, the form of Christ's divinity and his attributes.[4]

In Messiaen's music, the private nature and particularity of his vision is made public; his music comes from Catholicism, but it is not orthodox. It does not deny human failure – Messiaen's music celebrates human frailty and mortality while looking beyond this to what we will become after death – but instead provides a form of blessing in sound, resonating an ideal of God's unconditional love and the Christian redemptive message. This is not merely a particular panacea but a pathway to goodness, certainty, truth and wisdom embodied in a strange beauty that exists beyond appearance.

In many ways, it is not 'of our time' to speak of the eternal, the universal, through personal belief and the intimacy of art. Yet Messiaen's music re-enchants a 'post-ideological' age in which Christian salvation is bracketed off from secular reality.[5] It is a critical tool that acts to remind humanity of its predestined state, suggesting that we should be joyful and glorious and so live out the action of God's grace. But this is also why Messiaen's music is useful for the 'non-believer': it gives a semblance of retasking or relativizing this order.[6] This music can be enjoyed through the appeal to the religious absolute, and its colour and sense of transcendence can be appreciated without necessitating belief, or as even as a surrogate form of religious engagement. Part of Messiaen's legacy was to create a space for a new form of 'contemporary spiritual music' that fulfils this non-religious mandate.[7]

Igor Stravinsky sardonically remarked that he esteemed Messiaen's music highly, but he noted that 'one of those great hymns of his might be the wisest choice of all our music for the deck-band concert on the *Titanic* for our sinking civilization.'[8] The composer George Crumb (1929–2022), who met Messiaen in the 1960s, noted the 'spiritual exaltation' of his music 'against the academic greyness and the sterile pretensions of much music composed since the middle of the twentieth century'.[9] This is partly why there is 'intransigence' in Messiaen's late music. The pursuit of his mission to 'revive the faith in the luminous and positive elements of the Christian faith', as he put it in 1992, remained a potent sacred flame.[10] This project was attempted through a personal, subjective and yet universal music using modernist twentieth-century resources in its complexity, speaking through his dissonant musical language of a Catholic redemptive wholeness. The sometimes fragmentary realization of musical taxonomies of *TMLM* already revealed this complexity. The music of the 1940s acted as a 'deforming prism' or intensification of complexity understood as a form of enrichment.[11] Messiaen's works after the 'experimental' period (1949–51) can therefore be thought of as a dialectic between the centripetal security of systems, techniques, patterns and perhaps also mannerisms (see below), and the reality of his music that centrifugally pulls away from such concerns through the more volatile nature of the musical material itself.

In Messiaen's late music that followed the opera, it could be argued that the fresh 'new blood' of the *Turangalîla-Symphonie*,[12] or the granite-like iconoclasm of *Chronochromie*, had largely disappeared. The aspects of 'drive' discussed earlier are reduced. Certainly, there is *agapē* (and desire), but with a diminished sense of the verve and passion inherent in Eros and Thanatos (love and death), or the 'obsessional' qualities of Messiaen's music observed by Harrison Birtwistle.[13]

One of the fundamental issues in Messiaen's late music is that the ideas – inseparable from their realization, as Boulez states – are sometimes not very strong.[14] The spectrum between music that is merely well made and that which is inspired is operative. This is not a question of development or 'progress' in the language. Messiaen's essential modernist classicism remains. Movements and sections of cycles are still contrasted, even fragmented as mosaics in sometimes consciously antagonistic ways, yet the content of the 'tiles' is often less potent or astringent than in some parts of *Catalogue d'oiseaux*, *Couleurs de la Cité céleste* and *Méditations sur le Mystère de la Sainte Trinité*, for example, and there is not always the dynamic blend of relative stabilities and instabilities that was a feature of Messiaen's earlier work.[15] Yet in Messiaen's late music there is a renewed command of his musical language, a greater objectivity, rethinking and repetition of personal musical tropes, transparency of thought amid its complexity, and an audacity that affirms, critiques and enriches his previous thought. The ideal of 'simplicity', promoted by the composer, is present in the sense of the assuredness of his own language, but not always necessarily in the music itself.[16]

Messiaen's 'lateness' is also a reminder of the many spiritual preoccupations that appear in the twentieth century partly in response to capitalism and materialism, and its sense of being out of time with French music and other contemporary art music.[17] French music had 'moved on' through Boulez and the Institut de Recherche et Coordination Acoustique/Musique (IRCAM); the spectralists, including the Finnish composer Kaija Saariaho (1952–2023), resident in Paris from 1982; in the music of Pierre Henry (1927–2017) and the work of François Bayle (b. 1932), both Messiaen students who engaged with *musique concrète*, and in the Groupe de Recherches Musicales (GRM) from 1966. Composers such as Pascal Dusapin (b. 1955), a pupil of Xenakis, Philippe Manoury (b. 1952), and Jean-Claude Risset (1938–2016), who was a student of Jolivet, have pursued paths independent of Messiaen's legacy.

For Messiaen, the end was approaching. In the year before his death, he stated: 'I please myself always by meditating on the glorious mysteries. I am of an age when it is necessary to think of the beyond [*à l'au-delà*] with the hope that it will be glorious.'[18] Messiaen had been physically exhausted and ill during the orchestration of *Saint François d'Assise*, and he considered this work both a *summa* and his final work. He stated that he felt he had 'nothing more to say. I was like a man who was finished.'[19] Despite this despondency, others still had enormous faith in him. Falcinelli wrote: 'For me, Messiaen is the ideal musician of the Apocalypse . . . I wait to see what comes from his pen after his Saint Francis, the supreme point of his immense creation: what will he write?'[20] It was therefore a form of refreshment to return to the organ as a confirmation of renewal.

The *Livre du Saint Sacrement* (1984) was commissioned by the American Guild of Organists, and it was first performed by Almut Rössler on 1 July 1986 in Detroit and then in Paris at the Maison de la Radio on 5 May 1987 in the Salle Olivier Messiaen. Messiaen visited Israel and the West Bank twice, in May 1983 and then from 31 March to 14 April 1984 in which he (again) visited Gethsemane, and (in 1984) the desert of Judea where Christ had repented and Ein Gedi (near the dead sea). He tried to bring the birds of Christ's life to a truthful realization in this work.[21] Even before publication, the *Livre* had been taken up by leading organists throughout the world. It was the only major organ work that Messiaen did not play in public or record.

Messiaen's *Livre* continues the theme of monumentality present in his works of the 1950s onwards; it is his longest organ piece – its eighteen movements last around one hundred minutes. It was begun as early as 1979 as an idea for 'organ études of complementary colours – on acciaccaturas, clusters'.[22] Conceived from improvisations, it was written to be heard in its entirety in an evening.[23] Messiaen had reread Marmion's *Le Christ dans ses mystères* on the liturgical year, with its understanding of 'each anniversary of the mysteries carrying specific graces' that we receive again each time in the Communion (Eucharist) because these mysteries are 'contained within the host'.[24] The first eleven pieces take the listener through forms of adoration at the altar rail. They revisit the catechistic subject-matter of Messiaen's output, moving from the mystery of Christ's birth to his death, resurrection and the resurrected Christ's appearance to Mary Magdalene.[25] The final seven pieces of the *Livre* figure Christ's abiding post-resurrected absence and yet his presence in the community of believers and the Church through the sacraments, mystical symbols of grace that were instituted by Christ.[26]

The *Livre* forms a set of musical stained-glass windows (like Messiaen's *Vingt Regards*) through which the listener can experience a sonic immersion in, even possession by, the Logos, while allowing it to remain numinous and mystical.[27] The real presence of Christ, like the burning bush, is made more potent because we cannot touch it,[28] but the immersive sound of the organ attempts to embody Messiaen's compositional mission 'revive the faith in the luminous and positive elements of the Christian faith', making the grace of Christ an embodied experience for the listener.

In this cycle, there is a reinvigoration of Messiaen's modes and other chords, of plainchant, interversions and theological imagery realized through gesture and timbre. For instance, the toccata patterns and then central cascades of sound in 'Les deux murailles d'eau' (XIII) symbolically connect the walls of water on either side of the Israelites (Exodus 14:22) and the two halves of the broken bread in the Mass, and dissonant three-note chords on a swell mixture stop creates an image of religious asceticism and Christ's sojourning into the implacable Sinai desert in 'La manne et le Pain de Vie' (VI). There is an extension of the organ's resources: new registrations, new textures, such as using the pedal coupler to extend the number of notes played by the hands in 'La Source de Vie' (II). There is less reliance on juxtaposition of material and more on harmonic and textural exploration. The *Livre* returns to the music of the 1930s, in the sense of vertical, harmonic organization rather than linear contrapuntal elaboration (parts of 'L'apparition du Christ ressuscité à Marie-Madeleine' (XI) and 'La Transsubstantiation' (XII) are exceptions). In 'La joie de la grâce' (XV) there is virtuosic writing for three different birds, all tinged with Messiaen's proto-spectral harmonies and with a clear sense of each bird's narrative development created through the repetition, expansion and contraction of material. Different registrations and textures delineate the birds for the listener, while the white-throated robin is the only bird to range over all three organ manuals.

In the *Livre*, there is a powerful complement between the spiritual and natural darkness and the rending of Christ's body in 'Les ténèbres' (IX), and the audaciously titled 'La Résurrection du Christ' (X), which moves through colour chords from darkness (Messiaen's adaptation of Berg's 'hallucination chords' from *Wozzeck*) to the light of F# major, the key of *Le Banquet céleste* and 'Le Jardin du sommeil d'amour' (*Turangalîla-Symphonie*, VI). The ending of 'La Résurrection du Christ' attempts to capture the radiance of Christ, shown for example in Matthias Grünenwald's Resurrection panel of the Isenheim Altarpiece (1515), which was one of Messiaen's favourite images.[29] This conclusion is adapted from the pianissimo end of Dupré's *Le Chemin de la Croix*, VI (1931); music signifying Christ's humility (his meeting with Veronica on the way to Calvary) therefore becomes rethought as a triumph over death. The key of F# can retrospectively be heard as anchoring, drawing and shaping the work from the opening; the narrative arc of the piece acts as a progressive answer to the rhetorical question of the scriptural epigraph accompanying the work: 'Why seek ye the living amongst the dead?' (Luke 24:5). Messiaen's continual use of the organ fortissimo signals the monumentality of his rhetorical answer articulated through a sense of liminality and obsession. Crucially, it signals that despite the phantasmatic support of noumenal meaning, and the organ's immense volume and shifting sonic densities of sound, this piece figures human inability to comprehend the extraordinariness of the Resurrection – even the magnificence of the ending of this piece remains a necessarily insufficient symbol.

This piece is followed by the only narrative single piece in Messiaen's organ output, following the examples of 'La Rousserolle effarvatte' (*Catalogue,* VII) and *La Fauvette des jardins*. But 'L'apparition du Christ ressuscité à Marie-Madeleine' is concerned not merely with the observation of nature through time but with the time of biblical narrative and the real-time human perception of divinity. It begins with the sound of psychological confusion, shaking off the spiritual somnolence of night (the Crucifixion) on the dawn of the third day (the day of Christ's resurrection). Messiaen uses ascending 'confused chromatic counterpoints', as he calls them – similar to those used at the start of his 1977 improvisations on his mother's poetry that there represented the primordial amniotic sphere of his own life.[30] Quiet, ethereal words of Christ to Mary Magdalene follow, not expressed with 'communicable language' but merely through harmony, harmonic spacing and timbre. There follows the gradual recognition of and the joy of Christ's presence (still with the five wounds) represented for the listener as witness and participant. Christ's charge to Mary Magdalene: 'Go and find my brothers and repeat my words: I go to my Father and your Father, to my God and your God,' is followed by Messiaen's 'communicable language' to spell out themes of 'your Father' and 'your God', and immediately then 'Apocalypse' in octaves. The work ends like the opening, now with 'chromatic counterpoints', and finally chords like those used for Christ's recognition of Mary Magdalene, here symbolizing Christ's disappearance from his earthly life.

Both the *Livre du Saint Sacrement* and the opera have a sense of a journey that concludes with the believer's realization of Christ; they employ mysticism and theology to ask questions of the believer, to affirm, renew and expose the listener anew to Christian ideology and teleology. Many 'Messiaens' can be heard in the *Livre*: the suavity of *Le Banquet céleste*; the monumentality of *Apparition de l'Église éternelle*; the chorales, ecstasy and vehemence of *L'Ascension* and *La Transfiguration*; the classicism and theology of *La Nativité du Seigneur*; the visionary and dramatic imagery of *Les Corps Glorieux*; some of the eclecticism of the *Messe de la Pentecôte* and the *Livre d'orgue*, and the *langage communicable* of *Méditations*.

Likewise, in Messiaen's 29 liturgical improvisations, recorded live on Sundays or other liturgical occasions between 1984 and 1987, past, present and possible future 'Messiaens' appear.[31] In these performances Messiaen is heard searching for new ideas and sonorities, but more typically repeating and elaborating upon certain learned patterns, conventions and rhetorical gestures and improvising within the Catholic tradition prescribed by his forebears, especially Tournemire and Dupré. These improvisations are a reminder that Messiaen's language was continually evolving through his contact with the organ at La Trinité. In the last three years of his life, Messiaen played two masses per Sunday and did not play for vespers; it was his custom to pray before the service.[32] He also began planning an (unrealized) renovation of the organ at La Trinité, adding many new stops, including new higher harmonics (mutation stops), inspired by new developments in organ building and the organ music of Florentz, and 32' stops in the swell box and on the pedal.[33] This renovation did not come to pass.

In 1971 Henri Dutilleux gently chided Messiaen that he had '"annexed" birds'. Messiaen 'responded pleasantly: "But there still remain many others!"' Dutilleux commented on the difficulty of writing birdsong after Messiaen, something that would be taken up in different ways by Einojuhani Rautavaara (1928–2016) in *Cantus Arcticus* (1972) and in a number of Florentz's works, such as *Asun*, and *Debout sur le Soleil: chant de résurrection*, op. 8 (1990) for organ, which ends quietly on various mutation stops not found on most organs.[34] Messiaen described *Debout* as an 'extraordinary work' whose ending is a 'reflexion on the abyssal character of the divine mystery'.[35] Birdsong also features in David Lumsdaine's (1931–2024) *Four Soundscapes* (1990), Jonathan Harvey's *Bird Concerto with Piano Song* (2003) and in several works by Tristan Murail, including *Le Rossignol en amour* (2019) for piano.

The *Petites esquisses d'oiseaux* for piano returned to some staples of Messiaen's musical aviary. They were written in summer 1985 and premiered by Loriod on 25 January 1987. These six short pieces (each around two minutes in duration) use now-familiar means (chords and textures), but without the detailed topographical information of *Catalogue* or *Fauvette*. These are intensified distillations that form windows embodying Messiaen's delight in his medial ornithological world.

The *Chant dans le style Mozart* (1986) is a mostly tonal Conservatoire test-piece for clarinet and piano – part pastiche, part tribute; Mozart's 22 piano concertos had been played by Loriod in November–December 1964 with Boulez, Bruno Maderna and Louis Martin as conductors, and the late operas had been firmly established in Messiaen's teaching repertoire.[36]

Messiaen's last three small orchestral pieces can be understood as being modelled on one of his favourite images: the stained-glass window. If for Messiaen sound-colour dazzlement provided an 'excess of truth',[37] there is also a more nuanced sense in which the mind, ear and eye are called on to participate in making this truth, following *Sacrosanctum Concilium*, and to move between the whole image and the way in which the panes, colours or musical segments imply a sense of modernist fragmentation. There are, therefore, strong centrifugal and centripetal forces at play in these works, and the question, in a more dialectical paradigm, of whether these fragments move towards a form of synthesis is left in the listener's ear.

It is tempting to see these final small orchestral works in the light of the first three orchestral works (*Les Offrandes oublieés*, *Le Tombeau resplendissant* and the *Hymne au Saint Sacrement*). In this sense, they are not merely summations, or revisitations of Messiaen's modernist ideal of nineteenth-century tone poems, but instead can be understood as embryonic works that may have, perhaps in the light of the improvisations above, been developed in ways unknown.

Un Vitrail et des oiseaux (1987) is the first of these three late works. It is for 25 musicians – woodwind, one trumpet, piano solo, five percussionists and no strings. It was commissioned by Boulez for the Ensemble Intercontemporain and premiered on 26 November 1988. In the preface to the score, Messiaen notes: 'But the birds are more important than the tempi, and the colours more important than the birds. More important than all the rest is the aspect of the invisible.'[38]

Stained-glass windows and birds are two of Messiaen's chosen portals to perceive the 'invisible'. For the theologian Thomas Merton (1915–1968), 'Christ alone is the way and he is invisible,'[39] but for the artist Paul Klee (1879–1940), 'Art does not reproduce the invisible; rather, it makes [it]

Messiaen reading Thomas Merton on the summit of Grand Galibier, France, 14 September 1977.

visible.'[40] There is therefore a return in *Un Vitrail et des oiseaux* to Messiaen's Sisyphean project of 'making the invisible visible'.[41] In the modernist, fractured qualities of this and the other works, there is transparency and a form of lyricism produced through a balance of stable and unstable material presented in a narrative of discrete sections. The sense of the invisible made visible is made symbolically appreciable through such formal means and, as in *Couleurs de la Cité céleste*, through the experience of colours, the infusion of diachronic and synchronic time, and the superimposition of different narrative levels of information in the work.

Un Vitrail et des oiseaux is constructed in three sections, or what Messiaen calls 'periods', and a coda. His material undergoes transformation through accretion of material, refiguration, diminution or augmentation, superimposition and different orders of juxtaposition. Each period is signalled by bird material for tuned percussion (xylophone, xylorimba and marimba), sounds that had been heard at the start of *Saint François d'Assise*, and contains sections for untuned percussion, chorales and the homophonic harmonization of birdsong. The cadenzas for each period – using the 'hors tempo' technique, where birds fly free of any metrical constraints[42] – are scored for the piano with respectively two, four and six instruments. They include some of Messiaen's favourite birds, such as the garden warbler, the blackbird, the robin, the blackcap and the subalpine warbler. These remain connected to the cadenzas, as other birds do to other discrete sections. Different bird species are therefore used as a form of internal structural demarcation.

La Ville d'En-Haut (1987) is a short piece for piano solo and an orchestra of 39 players, including fourteen brass, woodwind and percussion, again with no strings. It was premiered by Boulez with the BBC Symphony Orchestra at the Salle Pleyel, Paris, on 17 November 1989. It uses many of the same textures as its predecessors but is perhaps more radiant (owing to its use of triadic material in the chords) and more intense, awesome and monumental in its vision of the 'changing colours' of the celestial city as it 'descends from heaven'.[43] There is once again a focus on composite timbres and balanced homophonic writing, and a sensitivity to the orchestral voicing of the chorales. There is a clear sense of melody and harmonic direction, of primary colours and contrasting timbral colours (as at fig. 69 in *Couleurs*). There is also a sensitivity to the way in which timbral counterpoint within these chorales provides an intensification of the primary material, and how register (led by the trumpets especially) directs the narrative.

Mannerism – the tendency to repeat stylistic formulae – could be a fair criticism aimed at Messiaen's late works, and indeed many of the works that use birdsong. Yet such a broad-brush criticism belies the difference between Messiaen's textures, timbral and temporal scaffolding, birds and chorales. Messiaen's response to birdsong is not that of the automaton; there is always a sense of excitement in the refashioning of this material, and indeed in the refiguring of other composers' music. There is a sense of the past, including his own history, speaking through him here, but this material also acts as a prosthesis: birdsong changed Messiaen as he changed it, and as listeners we are invited into this process.

Un sourire (1989) for woodwind, trumpet, strings (no double basses) and percussion, premiered on 5 December 1991 by the conductor Marek Janowski and the Orchestre Philharmonique de Radio France. It is not only a tribute to Mozart for the bicentenary of his death but benevolently joins itself to the ecology of Mozart's legacy. Messiaen describes it in terms of the composer's transcendence of his impoverished circumstances: 'despite the struggles, the suffering, the hunger, the cold, the incomprehension, and the proximity of death, Mozart always smiled.'[44] This is a somewhat tendentious and romantic caricature of Mozart's last year, but it was nevertheless Messiaen's inspiration.[45] As Messiaen stated in the score, the work 'continually alternates a very simple melody in the violins [also featuring woodwind solos], and an exotic birdsong [strangely for Messiaen, unnamed in the score] with repetitions by the xylos [xylophone and xylorimba], woodwind, and horns'. The work concludes first with a radiant chorale moving towards A major (*fff*), and then a long denouement that concludes definitively in that key, perhaps a homage to Mozart's clarinet Quintet KV 581 (1789) and his clarinet Concerto KV 622 (1791).

The short *Pièce pour piano et quatuor à cordes* (1991) was written at the request of Messiaen's student Thomas-Daniel Schlee (b. 1957) and for the ninetieth birthday of his father, the publisher Alfred Schlee (1901–1999), who was editor of Universal Edition, which was founded in 1901. It was first performed on 18 November 1991 with works also written for the occasion by Berio, Boulez, György Kurtág (b. 1926), an *auditeur* in Messiaen's class of 1957–8,[46] and Alfred Schnittke (1934–1998). It has an ingenious ternary structure in which the first section, comprising five musical panes of stained glass (rehearsal fig. 1–5), is reversed to conclude the work (from rehearsal fig. 10–14) with various aspects of extension, registral change and reordering of the instruments (such as the interversions at rehearsal fig. 4 and 11) and rewriting. The central garden warbler section uses some antiphonal writing between the piano and the strings. This *Pièce pour piano et quatuor à cordes* and the three small orchestral works are all in the orbit of Messiaen's final major completed work, *Éclairs sur l'au-delà...*, a work for a large orchestra written in eleven movements for the conductor Zubin Mehta (b. 1936) and the New York Philharmonic.[47]

Messiaen's final years are astonishing not simply for the amount of music composed, against a background of illness, but for the way he and his wife crossed the globe. There was a series of concerts from 16 to 22 March 1987 at the Royal Academy of Music in London – organized by the composer Melanie Daiken (1945–2016), who had been an *auditeur* in Messiaen's class in 1967–8 – which included performances of works by Stravinsky, Debussy, Ravel, Poulenc, George Benjamin, Boulez and others. The week included an exhibition, an organ competition (adjudicated by Messiaen), lectures, a lecture-demonstration of the ondes Martenot by Tristan Murail and masterclasses given by Messiaen, at which Loriod advised: 'You must play all the notes all the time; play with your fist, your arm, whatever is necessary!'; and Messiaen told one pianist sagely: 'you can't play wrong notes in my music, because of the modes.'[48] At a party at Felix Aprahamian's house at the end of the festival, Messiaen sang Figaro, accompanied by Loriod.[49]

In 1988, as part of a bicentennial delegation for the founding (colonization) of modern Australia, Messiaen and Loriod, along with a number of other musicians, were invited to Australia, staying in Melbourne (where he went, along with Yvonne and Jeanne Loriod, to St Patrick's Cathedral for the 9.30 a.m. Sunday Mass and then to St Francis' Church on Lonsdale Street for the 11.00 a.m. Mass on Pentecost Sunday), Sydney and Brisbane for concerts.[50] Messiaen's interest was in the birdsong to be found in Sherbrooke Forest, in the Dandenong ranges to the east of Melbourne, Tidbinbilla in the Blue Mountain ranges to the west of Sydney (an encounter with three Superb lyrebirds from 11 June 1988 is recorded in his *Cahiers* and forms the basis of the third movement of *Éclairs sur l'au-delà…* (Visions of the Beyond)) and Tamborine Mountain, just south of Brisbane.[51] Messiaen's sketch of a lyrebird created 'in Sherbrooke Forest' (twice underlined) on 30 May 1988 (see opposite) includes sketches for three other birds not used in the score of *Éclairs*, nor in his other late music.

These areas are not part of the Australian 'outback', but from a European perspective it is easy to imagine them seeming exotic and symbolic of 'the beyond', with their enormous trees and exotic flora and fauna. It is therefore unsurprising that birdsong, and Australian birdsong especially, features so heavily in Messiaen's *Éclairs sur l'au-delà…* Birds act as mediators – as *fil conducteurs*, in a Surrealist sense – between the phenomenal and noumenal divine worlds: they make audible the invisible.

In Melbourne, the Messiaens stayed in the Robin Hood motel for five nights with Harold and Isobel Bradley, lyrebird observers from the

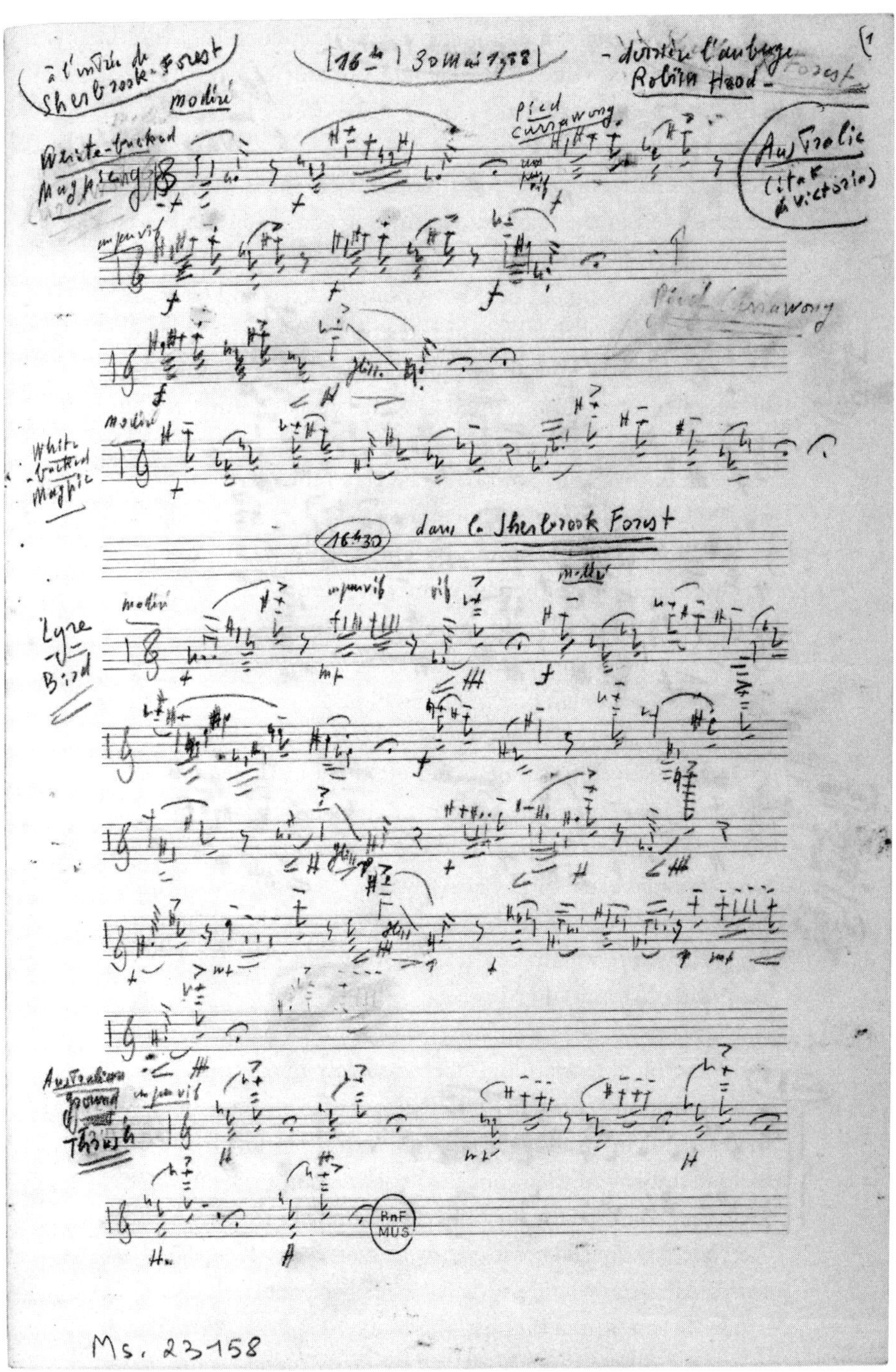

Messiaen's birdsong sketch, 30 May 1988, MS 23158, p. 1.

Sherbrooke survey group, and the journalist and translator Anna Murdoch, who provided this wonderful intimate portrait of the couple. She describes the composer in his

> astrakhan hat, serge trousers and traditional shirts worn by the peasant men in the Camargue, his long coat and gum boots. Although he is quintessentially European he looked strangely appropriate among the massive mountain ashes and ferns and mists and lights of that ancient forest. Both solid and ethereal.
>
> . . . Messiaen, who walks in small steps, curved forward over his feet like a penguin, seemed to gather momentum going up hills.
>
> . . . At dinner, she [Loriod] made very funny lyrebird imitations. Her imitation of a kangaroo, though energetic, was less successful . . . She ate enormously and was always first to finish . . . One night, she finished his dinner standing beside him at the table with her fork. 'I need energy,' she said.
>
> . . . His manners are more formal. He gives no kisses, only gentle handshakes, although one night, he did do a gay imitation of a centipede putting on trousers. He was completely childlike.
>
> Messiaen and his wife never talked about their marriage; Messiaen is a very private man. It was how he was with his wife that was revealing; if she fussed too much, he could give her a long, irritated glare, but he also gave her the most tender smile, and was protective of her hands; he often took things from her when they were walking in case she strained them. They called each other Yvonne and Messiaen.
>
> Messiaen asked to hear the Australian national anthem one night at dinner, so Harold, Isobel and I gave him a lame version of 'Advance Australia Fair' with many of the words missing. We then sang them 'Waltzing Mathilda' with a lot more heart. The melody impressed them but my explanation of the words left them very confused. By the third day, Yvonne Loriod was kissing everyone, standing on her toes to exuberant '*Bonjour!*'s and '*Bonne nuit!*'s. Messiaen would watch his wife's behaviour helplessly.
>
> He was interested in most of our conversations, particularly if we were talking about birds, but his face would become completely impassive if he wasn't interested or didn't approve and he would say nothing. He looked completely indifferent when

> Harold wanted to talk about the possibility of extra-terrestrial life. [Astronomy was a subject close to Messiaen's heart and that featured in many of his works. Astronomy provided images of God's glorious creation. Messiaen stated in this article that 'Astronomers and Catholics are in agreement that there is no life apart from [that on] earth. . . . Why did Jesus come here? . . . Because there was nothing to save anywhere else.' For Messiaen, as a Catholic, humanity was made in the image of God.][52]
>
> . . . Harold was very frustrated that he could not find him a lyrebird for his next composition. There are only about 70 lyrebirds left in the 800 hectares [1,975 ac] of Sherbrooke forest. The forest rang with calls 30 years ago, Isobel said.
>
> We were there at the right time for mating. The male stands on a dirt mound in a ray of light as if on a stage and makes incredibly accurate and piercing imitations of the birds around him, pulling his long, silver feathers over his head and shaking them. Day after day we heard nothing from the 28 males of the forest.
>
> On the way out of the forest one day, he told me the parable of the six wise virgins and the six foolish virgins from St Luke. The wise virgins have oil for their lamps but the foolish virgins have none and when they ask for some, they are denied it. 'Oil is the symbol of grace,' Messiaen explained. 'Those who have prepared themselves for death are ready when it comes.' . . .
>
> What music would he take to an empty place? 'The song of birds.' . . .
>
> [The next morning] in the forest, for the first and last time, we heard a male lyrebird singing passionately deep in the forest.
>
> Messiaen's concentration was absolute. Yvonne Loriod gave her husband his glasses, he took from his bag a book of five-line paper and wrote straight down in music the sounds of the amorous lyrebird. If someone spoke to him when he was listening, he didn't hear.
>
> On our last morning, there was not a sound in that cathedral of trees except the wind hundreds of metres above us.[53]

Messiaen had known Australian birdsong from recordings sent to him by the Australian composer Nigel Butterley (1935–2022) and material sent by ornithologists; he had used Australian birds in his music before (in *Des canyons aux étoiles...*).[54] Australia was therefore a desirous location

Olivier Messiaen and Yvonne Loriod in Sherbrooke Forest, Australia, published in *The Age* (11 June 1988).

for the composer. The lyrebird copies human-made sounds, and other birds, including the 'laughing' kookaburra – a characteristically ugly song that is transfigured by Messiaen in piece VIII of *Éclairs*. For Messiaen, the lyrebird represented an image of the Church as the bride of Christ. In his birdsong *Cahiers* he writes of the magnificent eucalyptus trees, the mountain ash and the terrain of the lyrebird where it 'dances and sings!!!'[55] His setting in piece VIII evokes the colour of the bird, but it is also quite orchestrally dense, and perhaps solo instruments might better have represented the specialness of this unusual animal (it is unclear if the bird Messiaen notated was imitating something).[56]

Many of the different 'Messiaens' are present in *Éclairs*. This is not uncommon with composers in so called 'late music' – the same could be said for Beethoven's last five string quartets, Mahler's last three symphonic works or Stravinsky's *Requiem Canticles* (1966). The chorale of the first piece, 'Apparition du Christ glorieux', returns us to the world of 'Majesté du Christ' (*L'Ascension*) and the chorales of *La Transfiguration* in their sense of awe and wonder. The second movement revisits many previous ideas (from *La Nativité* and *Poèmes pour Mi*, *Et exspecto* and *Des canyons* to *Saint François d'Assise*), but presents them with renewed transparency, new forms of orchestral delicacy and texture (such as the passage for three horns, cellos, cymbals and gongs in *Éclairs*, II). *Couleurs de la Cité céleste* and the 'Strophes' of *Chronochromie* can be heard in the background of movement IV, and the 'Prière du Christ montant vers son Père' (*L'Ascension*) and 'Jardin du sommeil' (*Turangalîla-Symphonie*, VI) behind movement V.

There is within the idea of late style the critical expectation of final thoughts and final music that will somehow impart great secrets and new visions. It should not be expected that artists suddenly grasp something altogether new or develop 'gifts of prophesy'. There is also, through Adorno, the notion of an alienation from and critique of earlier styles. But as in Beethoven's *Missa Solemnis*, op. 123 (1819–23), Adorno's chosen litmus test for late style, with its dialectic of an 'archaizing tone' and 'humanistic aspects', there is a sense not of atavism, 'exclusion' or 'permanent renunciation' but of subtly reconfiguring conventions, styles and techniques in Messiaen's late music.[57]

These features are complemented by the lyrical warmth of Messiaen's late music (a concept that might have reinforced Adorno's observations of Beethoven), which speaks through artistic assuredness. What Adorno hears as subverting the affirmative in Beethoven *as* post-Enlightenment 'truth'[58] can be heard in Messiaen's final works as affirming and desiring his own spiritual telos. Both Beethoven's *Missa Solemnis* and Messiaen's late works provide ways of engaging with what cannot be easily 'reconciled'.[59] In *Éclairs* there is sincerity and refinement, tribute rather than parody, *suavité* (in movements V and XI) and shock (such as the unison full orchestral 'gloria' at the end of VIII). There are favourite birds – a solo blackbird in *Éclairs*, VII and the garden warbler playing *hors tempo* in movement VIII – and new theological sources such as Dom Jean de Monléon's *Le Sens Mystique de l'Apocalypse* as inspiration for the saturated 'Épôde'-like image of the elect (birds) in the tree of life, 'spooning' the fruits from the 'humanity of the word', as well as familiar images of the seven angels and seven trumpets of the Apocalypse from *Couleurs* (in *Éclairs*, VI). There is testimony and triumph, sensuousness and ecstatic joy, but there is also a sense of attempting to reconcile diverse materials. For the listener, there is drama, pacing, contrast, imagery and new manifestations of celestial and musical radiance throughout the cycle.

Messiaen's visions are uncompromising, intransigent both with reference to himself (his own history) and his sense that the world needed to rehear the message of salvation. *Éclairs* acts as a reaffirmation as well as a proclamation. Messiaen's 'beyond' is far from the staticism imparted to his music by many commentators; rather, as the images in the book of Revelation (the last book of the New Testament) testify, it is full of life, full of movement and joy. Part retrospective, part sunset, *Éclairs* is also both public testament and a personal work, looking backwards on a life of eschatological hope and the near possibility of its fulfilment.

The lyricism of *Éclairs* is continued in the *Concert à quatre* (1991–2), a homage to Mozart, Rameau and Scarlatti. Messiaen had originally considered an oboe concerto for the composer and oboist Heinz Holliger, and then a work on the subject of grace for oboe, cello, piano, harp and orchestra. Messiaen began it in summer 1991, and it was to be a concerto in five movements (a genre that Messiaen had avoided) for five musicians (Loriod, the cellist Mstislav Rostropovich, Holliger, the flautist Catherine Cantin and the conductor Myung-whun Chung), but it remained incomplete at Messiaen's death (the fifth movement was to be a fugue). The second half of the first and all of the fourth movements were orchestrated by Loriod with the composer George Benjamin and Holliger, with birdsong additions in the last movement (IV) drawn from sketches from the opera. The *Concerto* was premiered on 26 September 1994.

The first movement, 'Entrée', is in a large binary form, with five parts in each half, and is notable for its radiance (C major), lyricism and some wonderful subtle orchestral effects using the solo strings (the three solo cellos accompanying the solo oboe is delightful). The second movement, 'Vocalise', is an orchestration of Messiaen's *Vocalise-étude* (1935) in A major (modes 2 and 3), which he wrote for A. L. Hettich's collection of 120 such works by various composers, including Aaron Copland, Darius Milhaud, Carl Nielsen, Poulenc and Ravel.

The 'Vocalise' perhaps pays tribute to Debussy's *Prélude à l'après-midi d'un faune* in the use of its incantatory lines.[60] Most notable at the opening is Messiaen's incantatory use of a Hindu mode, no. 15: *Māyāmālavagaula* (flute), then at the beginning of verse two, no. 46: *Ṣaḍvidhamārgiṇi* (flute and oboe), and then again *Māyāmālavagaula* (flute, oboe and cello) at rehearsal fig. 8, just before the final cadence. This is possibly Messiaen's only known use of Hindu modes, placing him alongside Emmanuel, Dupré, Tournemire and Jolivet, who had all used them in their music. Messiaen uses the orchestra under the piano part as a kind of piano pedal, continually shifting the density of the sound to irradiate the texture and highlight certain parts of lines, but adding birdsong (the rock thrush) played by the celesta in verse two.

The 'Cadenza' (III) contains extensive solos for all the major instruments (as the title implies), especially for the piano (Messiaen's favourite garden warbler) and the cello (the Australian lyrebird). The movement finishes with a short string cadenza of a triangle accompanying the sixteen first violins (divided into six), playing interversions derived from the opening oboe solo (a version of which is repeated just after). There is then a spellbinding ending with contrary motion flourishes from the celesta, a long silence and then a solitary note from the tam-tam in the depths, like a half-heard 'inferior resonance'.

In the 'Rondeau' (IV), Messiaen uses the classical sectional form to spotlight the different instruments. It includes a section from fig. 20 that is redolent of the first movement of the *Quatuor pour la fin du Temps*. Two *hors-tempo* cadenzas are bifurcated at rehearsal fig. 30 by the rhythmic and timbral interplay of the piano with tubular bells. The superimposition of material, orchestration and the tonal orientation of the ending brings to the ear the layered sounds of 'Joie du sang des étoiles' (*Turangalîla-Symphonie*, V) especially, which also adapted rondo form.

Messiaen's final works reveal the ways in which he kept ploughing his own modernist fields. They show reversion and revision, an assertion (as in his early music) of melody and colour as phantasmatic means of sustaining and regulating religious belief, and they demonstrate anew how his ecology of techniques concerning rhythm, time, timbre and birds could be integrated into his musical narratives. But repeating this economy

Last known photo of Messiaen, at home (rue Marcadet), 25 March 1992.

and reinscribing excess brings questions of sustainability, and the way this music normalizes, yet shows different facets of, religious-modernist *jouissance*. Certainly, for Messiaen there was a necessity and an obsession to make faith performative. The aspiration to what is beyond finitude is not only a form of worldly renunciation (which brings its own pleasure) but a means through which Messiaen enables a participation in our world – an exhortation to examine our own motivations, beliefs and libidinal investments.

Other movements and artistic fashions, including the flowers that grew on the rubbish dump of postmodernism, had passed by Messiaen. Some of his music has arguably already been consigned to the museum case; it has become art that is periodically pulled out, inspected and then returned to store. This has been largely the fate of much avant-garde music, but certain pieces of Messiaen in his lifetime became standard repertoire – the *Vingt Regards*, the *Turangalîla-Symphonie* and the organ music (up to and including parts of the *Messe de la Pentecôte*) are works that have assured his legacy.

Messiaen died on 27 April 1992 after a short period of hospitalization at the Hôpital Beaujon de Clichy-la-Garenne. His legacy and heritage have continued to be served by recordings, including various compilations of his works. Messiaen's work has been performed worldwide and his status outside France, including through a considerable strain of Anglo-American scholarship, has advanced more considerably than in his home country.[61]

Over his lifetime, many of Messiaen's students, including Alain Louvier (1962), Gilbert Amy (1965) and Betsy Jolas (1968), dedicated works to him, and composers sent him dedicated copies, including Varèse's *Arcana* (1925–7, revised 1931–2), Jolivet's string quartet (1934), Giacinto Scelsi's (1905–1988) *Anahit* (1965), Xenakis's *ST/10–1, 080262* (1956–62), Boulez's *Le Soleil des eaux* (1947, revised 1950, 1958, 1965), Kurtág's *Quartetto per archi* (1959) and Barraqué's *Séquence: pour voix, batterie et divers instruments* (1950–55).[62] After his death, various composers created memorial works, including Takemitsu's *Rain Tree Sketch II* (1992) and Murail's *Cloches d'adieu, et un sourire* (1992). Naji Hakim's *Le Tombeau d'Olivier Messiaen* (1993) for organ (dedicated to Loriod), and Harvey's *Tombeau de Messiaen* (1994) for piano and electronics both pay homage to the composer. Jacques Charpentier's *Ubi Caritas* (2008) for women's voices and organ (perhaps a homage to the *Trois petites Liturgies*) was composed for the centenary of Messiaen's birth and was first performed on 12 June 2008 in La Trinité

Olivier and Alain Messiaen at Petichet, 1964.

(and recorded on 26 June 2008).[63] The colour of Messiaen's music can be heard in the legacy of French spectralism[64] and in the legacy of the organ as a medium for religious expression and apocalypticism in the music of Florentz, Thierry Escaich and Valéry Aubertin (b. 1970).

A piano competition, the Olivier Messiaen International Competition, was established in 1967 as part of the Royan Festival and was held in Paris in 2000, 2003 and 2007. There was a year-long festival of Messiaen music at the Southbank in London in 2008. The Messiaen competition was relaunched in Lyon in 2019 and dedicated to organ performance, and then revived, after cancellations due to COVID-19, in 2022.[65] The annual Festival Messiaen au Pays de la Meije was founded in 1998; its concerts and events have involved Messiaen's former students (including Boulez, Murail and Levinas) and scholars of Messiaen's music. The Fondation Olivier Messiaen was created after his death in 1994 by his wife, and in 1997 a rue Olivier Messiaen was created in the 13th arrondissement of

View from the balcony of Messiaen's house, Petitchet, 2023.

Paris, and another in Toul in 2022.[66] Messiaen's and Loriod's papers and documents were donated to the Bibliothèque Nationale de France in February 2015 to create the Fonds Messiaen. On 1 July 2016, Messiaen's restored house and gardens at Petichet were opened and have served as a locus for concerts, teaching, an artist's retreat and memorial events.[67]

The making of Messiaen into a kind of saintly figure had started many years before his death. On 14 August 1978 (Vigil of the Assumption), the year of a major festival of Messiaen's music in which his music was played across France,[68] Messiaen's brother Alain wrote:

> Olivier, my brother, is, above all, a metaphysical musician, and the metaphysical – in the sense of a Thomist intellectual – is a domain where impunity cannot penetrate . . . My brother Olivier is a SUBLIME being – one of the greatest beings, not only latterly [*temps dernier*] . . . I want to say, after his death, Olivier, my friend, my brother, will belong to the 10th circle of the angels that form the 'chosen' – and the heavenly city shall ring with the strains of his 'resurrection' from the dead![69]

This image fits well with the iconoclasm of Messiaen, but his public and private lives were complex as a son, father, husband and carer. There was the man that Goléa described as an 'extraordinarily delicate man, of a timidity that is moving, and an exquisite politeness', but who wrote music of 'torrid eroticism'.[70] There was the *maître* whom the composer Gérard Grisey lauded as 'God the Father'[71] – the spiritual godfather of many other composers in the latter twentieth century. For his students there was the *professeur* who imparted 'luminous explanations' of music, who had 'the most fabulous ears of the twentieth century', who taught with 'humility' and 'spontaneity' and who also demanded great faithfulness and rigour from performers of his music.[72]

There was also the 'secret' Messiaen. Messiaen remained silent about aspects of his music, other composers and family members. His appearance as 'poverello' artist and church organist belied his wealth, yet he was largely uninterested in – and also charitable with – money.[73] Messiaen's early life as a performer gave way to his life as a church organist and as an improviser. Improvisation was a resource brought into a productive engagement with musical research that embodied a spirit of 'audacious iconoclasm' beyond academicism.[74] Yet musical analysis, self-assessment and theorizing were foundational for the composer, as they were in very different ways for Boulez, Stockhausen, Cage and Elliott Carter, but not for composers such as Maxwell Davies and Birtwistle. Carter, Maxwell Davies and Birtwistle, who venerated Messiaen and shared with him a concern for memory, block forms, ritual and intricate layering techniques, including complex counterpoint,[75] were non-religious high modernists. Yet they also shared with Messiaen a vocation for aesthetic iconoclasm (not pluralism) and a search for new forms of lyricism.[76] The Surrealist poet Paul Éluard called lyricism a 'développement d'une protestation' (development of a protestation), and this can be understood in Messiaen's music as a form of volatile, allusive and intransigent modernist beauty that functions as a renewal of musical language for these composers – what Levinas called, referring to the integration of a 'multiplicity of currents' in Messiaen, 'the contemporaneity of the eternal'.[77]

For Messiaen, lyricism is also part of his claim for truth, underpinned by the divine. His particular insufflation of musical history can be understood in terms of cultural memory and as a form of generosity. At the heart of Messiaen's music is the capacity for him to embrace God, to see and understand his own agency in this embrace, and to create a music that communicates not only the resurrected life (to come) but to impart that God is here for humanity *now*. In Messiaen's image of the stained-glass window as a metaphor for the timbral-colouristic effect of his music on the listener, we may 'see' it, but sound is refracted into our bodies and resonates within us, allowing us, following Messiaen's thought, to realize ourselves as subjects configured by his music and therefore placed into an understanding of Messiaen's relationship with God.

Messiaen had an immense capacity to listen internally to this resonance, and to make different forms of sense from it.[78] There is with Messiaen a capacity to be spoken to and to speak.[79] But there is also in Messiaen's work a deep sense of responsibility for his actions, and a sense of a discourse addressed to an unspecified but universal locus. His language perhaps does not always readily welcome the stranger, but its strangeness acts as an invitation, a fascinator to those who encounter it.[80] The invitation can be thought of as a call to our own capacities to be and to act, which may spontaneously open up unexpected and serendipitous pathways. His music touches, regardless of belief or prejudice, upon human inadequacy as much as our capacity. It therefore asks us to interrogate the nature and limits of our own perception, subjectivity and our relationship to God.

When a person enters into one of the great Gothic cathedrals in France – Notre-Dame de Paris, the cathedrals of Amiens, Bourges, Chartres and Reims, or Messiaen's beloved Sainte-Chapelle in Paris, it is not necessary to hold the same beliefs as the artisans who made these edifices, nor to see their faces; it is enough to sense the spirit and intention, the spiritual ambience of these places that testifies to human capacity and gestures to what is beyond it. Such buildings allow us to feel that the absence of God is perhaps as profound as our images of divine presence. Messiaen's music speaks beyond doctrinal beliefs, but it also reinscribes and critiques institutional faith in ways that both embody and exceed it. His music exposes and makes an attempt to understand and affirm deeper ontological, ethical and humanist truths that exist and are yet to come, and whose promise informs religion.[81]

Human desire and our perception of God's desires then enter into this paradigm – desire that stems from the unconscious before being symbolized in language and translated through the eschatological fantasy of Messiaen's music. Understanding our desire and the reading of this desire is essential to our capacity to interact with the divine. Messiaen's music expresses not only a humanist desire to be with God but a desire to name God through sound that must remain unfulfilled. This is why the non-symbolic nature of sound is so appropriate to the task: it is a quality that helps facilitate a universal access to this art.[82] It is through the poetics of sound (structured by Messiaen's discourse) that we are enabled to approach asymptotically this sacred function of naming the unnameable. Poetics become an affordance of the sacred, but in reverse, the sacred is verified, articulated and made present through Messiaen's religiously structured poetics.

Messiaen's ideal of *éblouissement* is surely also about a remaking of the subject through reformation and self-discovery, and a relocation of the subject with reference to what the French protestant philosopher Paul Ricoeur has called 'the voice behind the voice . . . the absolute subject of discourse'.[83] When Messiaen invokes the image on the coin (Matthew 22:15–22 and Mark 12:13–17) in Act II, tableau 4 of *Saint François d'Assise* through the character of Brother Bernard's response to the voyaging angel, his question might, with hindsight, appear to be a self-reflexive one. Bernard sings: 'I have often thought, after my death, that our Saviour Jesus Christ will look at me as he regards the tributary money and say: "Of whom is this image and this inscription?"' He sings this to music reminiscent of Francis's theme, revealing both Bernard's holiness and that Francis has God's sacramental imprimatur. Messiaen consecrated his work to the glory of God, whose inscription he sought to imprint upon himself. To listen to Messiaen is to hear how he heard the 'voice behind the voice' and the ways in which he sought to live both in and through this image. It is to bring others into relationships with this voice of God through his art.

Select Discography

Many of the recordings mentioned here, and indeed many others, are available on the Internet from various sources, and these can in general be easily found. It is certainly worthwhile listening to Messiaen's own recordings and indeed others made on the organ at the Église de la Sainte-Trinité. *Messiaen par lui-même* was recorded in 1956 by Ducretet-Thomson (Mono, 1957) and rereleased by EMI Classics in 1992. It contains four discs of recordings by the composer of the published organ works from 1928 to 1951. For a clearer account of the organ at La Trinité, listen to Messiaen's stereo recording of *Méditations sur le Mystère de la Sainte Trinité* (1973). Messiaen's recordings, although fascinating in many ways, have issues of editing and tempi, but they also have great solemnity, suavity, lyricism and languor.[1]

There are recordings of Messiaen playing the piano: his *Quatre Études de rythme* (made on 30 May 1951),[2] accompanying Lisa Arséguet in *Poèmes pour Mi* (1964) and Marcelle Bunlet in *Harawi* (along with Debussy's *Cinq poèmes de Charles Baudelaire*), recorded on 13 September 1954 at the Festival de Vichy, but released in 2002. He also recorded the *Quatuor pour la fin du Temps* with Jean Pasquier, Étienne Pasquier and André Vacellier (1956) and played second piano in *Visions de l'Amen* to Yvonne Loriod (piano 1) in 1949 (Dial Records, 1950), with a spoken introduction by Messiaen, and again in 1962 for Véga. Yvonne Loriod has recorded the complete piano music of Messiaen, including the *Préludes* (1958 and 1968), the *Vingt Regards* (1956, 1973 and 1985 (live)) and the *Catalogue d'oiseaux* (1959 and 1970). She was Messiaen's ideal pianist on the many seminal recordings of his orchestral music. Her recordings are notable for their brilliance, authenticity, precision and subtlety. All of her Véga recordings (1956–63) were rereleased in 2019.[3]

Here are some other recommendations:

For the organ music there is the question of what type of instrument best suits this music. Purists would argue that these scores were written with La Trinité in mind, but the greatness of this music can be reflected through a wide variety of instruments, and this is arguably demonstrated through interpretation on different instruments. The heart of Messiaen's instrument at La Trinité was built by Cavaillé-Coll in 1868, but in accordance with the changes in neo-classical organ building in France from 1926, he changed it a number of times, essentially providing new forms of brightness to the instrument and a wider tonal palette. This was a trajectory for organs in many major Parisian churches, notably the Cathedral of Notre-Dame de Paris, and the churches of Sainte-Clotilde and Saint-Étienne-du-Mont, but not Saint-Sulpice, which, along with other great Cavaillé-Coll organs at Orléans Cathedral, the Abbey of Saint-Ouen in Rouen and the Basilica of Saint-Sernin in Toulouse, have remained unchanged apart from restorations.

For those interested in hearing the music on French instruments, there are interesting historical recordings of Messiaen's music by Jean-Jacques Grunenwald (*Le Banquet céleste* and 'Dieu parmi nous') on the Gonzales organ at Soissons Cathedral (1959); Marcel Dupré at Saint-Sulpice from 1960 playing *Le Banquet céleste* and 'Les Bergers' from *La Nativité du Seigneur*; Gaston Litaize in 1963 (*Le Banquet céleste*, *Apparition de l'Église éternelle*, *L'Ascension* and *La Nativité*) on the Fermis/Gonzales/Müller organ of Saint-François-Xavier (Paris); and Pierre Cochereau, who recorded *Le Banquet céleste*, *Apparition* (this is particularly majestic in its pacing and dynamic scope) and extracts from *La Nativité* at Notre-Dame in February 1972.

Simon Preston was the first English organist to record Messiaen: *L'Ascension* in 1962 (at King's College, Cambridge), and *Les Corps Glorieux* and *Le Banquet céleste* in 1969 at St Alban's Abbey. Allan Wicks was the first to record *La Nativité* at St Paul's Cathedral in 1964; Preston's interpretation of this cycle from Westminster Abbey dates from 1965. The New-Zealand born organist Gillian Weir recorded *Le Banquet céleste*, *Les Corps Glorieux*, *Apparition*, the *Verset* and *L'Ascension* (II and III) at the Royal Festival Hall in 1966 (Decca Eloquence), and she later recorded the complete works at Århus Cathedral, released in 1994. There is also the recordings, much praised by Messiaen, of the organ works (up to the *Verset pour la fête de la Dédicace*) by the blind organist Louis Thiry, recorded on the neo-classical Metzler organ in the Cathedral of St Pierre in Geneva (released in 1972). Jennifer Bate's complete set of Messiaen's works was recorded on the Gonzalez organ of Beauvais Cathedral in 1981–3, except for her first recording of the *Livre du Saint Sacrement* (released 1987), from La Trinité. Susan Landale has recorded some of the works at Saint-Vincent de Paul in Paris, and the *Livre du Saint Sacrement* at the Abbey of Saint-Ouen in Rouen (1996). Tom Winpenny has recorded most of the works on a variety of organs (2014–19). Almut Rössler recorded all of the organ works from 1969–95. Olivier Latry's recording at Notre-Dame (released in 2002) is extremely fine, as is Hans-Ola Ericsson's from Luleå Cathedral in Lapland, northern Sweden (released as a set in 2009), which includes 26 recordings of birdsong used in Messiaen's organ works.[4]

Weir, Thiry, Bate, Landale, Rössler, Latry and Ericsson all had a close association with Messiaen. In the early 1960s, Jeanne Demessieux had been encouraged by Messiaen to record his complete extant works (in stereo) and he had offered her the organ at La Trinité, but she was also considering Coventry Cathedral and Liverpool Metropolitan Cathedral.[5] Demessieux recorded 'Transports de joie' (*L'Ascension*) at Liverpool (1967), and from the same year there is a live BBC recording of her playing 'Les Anges' (*La Nativité*) from the Colston Hall in Bristol.

I would also recommend Kevin Bowyer's recording of *La Nativité* from Salisbury Cathedral in 1993. It is interesting to hear this music on somewhat smoother-sounding English instruments, so it is worth comparing Bowyer with Wicks, David Titterington at Gloucester Cathedral (1987) and also Richard Tanner at Blackburn Cathedral (2018). Allan Wicks's performance of *L'Ascension* (II and III) from Canterbury Cathedral (1976) has terrific intensity. Other notable recordings include recordings of *Livre du Saint Sacrement* by Anne Page (Norwich Cathedral, 2002), Marie-Bernadette Dufourcet Hakim (La Trinité, 2008) and Paul Jacobs (St Mary the Virgin, New York, 2010). An important factor in all of these recordings is the placement of microphones and their distance from the organ, and it is worth listening to other recordings of these instruments to get an aural bearing on the degree of presence of the instrument and the inclusion of the building in the sonic picture.

For the piano works, aside from Yvonne Loriod, I would recommend the *intègrales* by Peter Hill (1985–92), who also recorded *La Fauvette passerinette* in 2014, as well as Håken Austbø (1994–2002) and Roger Muraro (2016). All of these pianists consulted Messiaen and/or Loriod, but they bring still different colours, senses of narrative, timing and touch to this music. For parts of the *Vingt regards* and 'Le Merle bleu' from the *Catalogue d'oiseaux* it is well worth listening to the Decca Studio recordings by Messiaen's friend, who became a Catholic priest, Jean-Rodolphe Kars. A later live recording by Kars, discovered in the archives of Netherlands Radio in 2018, exists from 1976, although this release was unauthorized by the pianist.[6] For the *Vingt regards* and the *Catalogue*, Pierre-Laurent Aimard's recordings are essential (2000 and 2018 respectively), as is Peter Serkin's recording of *Vingt Regards* (1975) and Michel Béroff's recording of that cycle from 1987 (Béroff had been an *auditeur* in Messiaen's class from 1969 to 1971).[7] John Ogden's (1969), Joanna MacGregor's (1996) and Steven Osborne's (2002) *Vingt regards*, and Robert Sherlaw Johnson's (1973) and Roderick Chadwick's (2020–) recordings of the *Catalogue d'oiseaux*, the latter with complementary piano music, are also important. For *Visions de l'Amen*, Katia and Marielle Labèque (1970), John Ogden and Brenda Lucas (1971), Martha Agerich and Alexander Rabinovitch (1990) are classic recordings. The live concert recording of this work from 1978 by Jean-Rodolfe Kars and Michel Béroff for Messiaen's seventieth birthday is a fascinating recording, available online at www.inamediapro.com.[8]

For the songs, aside from the records made by Messiaen and by Loriod with various singers, Jane Manning's set (with David Miller and David Mason) from 1985–6 is a classic, and more recently Ingrid Kappelle and Håken Austbø's 2007 version is also excellent. Noelle Barker's and Robert Sherlaw Johnson's recording of *Harawi* (1969) is also important. Sylvia McNair's recording of Messiaen's *Trois mélodies* with Roger Vignoles (1997) is fascinating and gives a refreshing image of what Messiaen's songs sound like without a heavy vibrato, a possibility that is worth developing by other artists. Signe Bakke and Liv Elise Nordskog (2013) have recorded the *Trois mélodies*, the *Poèmes pour Mi* and the eight songs of Claire Delbos' *L'Âme en bourgeon*. The Sixteen's recording of the *Cinq rechants* from 1996, along with a capella works by Daniel-Lesur and Jolivet, is essential for any collector, but other interpretations by French, German and Danish choirs make for excellent comparisons.

Four recordings of the *Turangalîla-Symphonie* are discussed in Chapter Four. The first is the live recording made of the European premiere of the work on 25 July 1950, conducted by Roger Désormière with the Orchestre National de la RTF, and Yvonne Loriod and Ginette Martenot (INA Musique), and the second is a live radio broadcast of the work on 20 January 1959 (INA Musique) with Maurice Rosenthal conducting the Orchestre National de la RTF, and Yvonne and her younger sister, Jeanne Loriod (ondes Martenot). The third is the 1961 studio recording conducted by Maurice Le Roux with the Orchestre National de la RTF, with Yvonne and Jeanne Loriod. Both Loriods were involved with many more recordings.[9] The final revised version of the *Symphonie* is conducted by Myung-whun Chung with the Orchestre de l'Opéra Bastille, with Yvonne and Jeanne Loriod (1990). Other fine recordings include those by André Previn (1978), Esa-Pekka Salonen (1987), Riccardo Chailly (1993), Simon Rattle (2003) with Tristan Murail playing the ondes Martenot and Kent Nagano (2004).

Leonard Bernstein's recording of the *Trois petites Liturgies* (1964) and Marcel Couraud's recording in 1954 make an interesting contrast with the first recording (Loriod/Ginette Martenot/Roger Désormière, 1945). The first performance of *Oiseaux exotiques* from the Domaine Musical with Loriod and Rudolf Albert conducting in 1956 was released in 1957. Loriod recorded *Réveil des oiseaux* in 1953 in Germany with Hans Rosbaud conducting, and *Oiseaux exotiques* and *Réveil des oiseaux* were recorded by Loriod with the Czech Philharmonic and Václav Neumann in 1968.[10] For *La Transfiguration de Notre-Seigneur Jésus-Christ*, Antal Dorati (1973), Reinbert de Leeuw (1999) and Myung-whun Chung (2002) are essential. Chung's recordings of *Des canyons aux étoiles...* and *Éclairs sur l'au-delà...* are likewise important, as is Rattle's recording of *Éclairs* (2004). Boulez's recordings of *Chronochromie*, *Couleurs de la Cité céleste*, *Et exspecto resurrectionem mortuorum* and other works on Sony, and his later DG recordings are essential for all those interested in Messiaen's music. Especially enjoyable is his eightieth-birthday concert with Loriod and the Ensemble Intercontemporain, released in 1994, which includes the world premiere of *Un Vitrail et des oiseaux*. The disc entitled *Messiaen inédits* contains first recordings of a variety of works (solo, chamber, orchestral/ choral), released in 2008.

For the opera *Saint François d'Assise* there is the excellent DG complete recording with Kent Nagano (1999), with José van Dam in the title role and Dawn Upshaw as the Angel. This can be compared with the Seiji Ozawa complete recording (made from live performances at the Théâtre National de l'Opéra de Paris in December 1983), and the Lothar Zagrosek recording of tableaus 3, 6, 7 and 8 from the Salzburg festival in August 1985, with Dietrich Fischer-Dieskau in the title role. There is also a superb DVD of the centenary Holland Festival production conducted by Ingo Metzmacher with stage direction by Pierre Audi from 2008 (Opus Arte, 2009).

Various large sets of Messiaen's works are available, including a Warner Classics *Messiaen Edition* (2005) of eighteen discs; Warner Classics' hundredth-birthday box of fourteen CDs, *Olivier Messiaen, 1908–1992* (2008); DG's *Complete Edition* of 32 CDs (2008); and Warner Classics' *Olivier Messiaen Edition* of 25 CDs (2017).

References

All translations, unless otherwise indicated, are by the author.

Abbreviations

SC *Sacrosanctum Concilium* (4 December 1963)
TMLM Olivier Messiaen, *The Technique of My Musical Language*, 2 vols, trans. John Satterfield (Paris, 1956); single-volume edition published 2001
TRCO Olivier Messiaen, *Traité de rythme, de couleur, et d'ornithologie*, 7 tomes (Paris, 1994–2002)

Introduction: 'All the birds of the stars'

1 Olivier Messiaen, interview with Patrick Szersnovicz (29 May 1987), in *Le Monde de la Musique* (July/August 1987), p. 33.
2 Messiaen (11 June 1972), in Almut Rössler, *Contributions to the Spiritual World of Olivier Messiaen*, trans. Barbara Dagg and Nancy Poland (Duisburg, 1986), p. 51.
3 Olivier Messiaen, 'Comment ils travaillent', *Musica*, XL (March 1958), p. 7 (Messiaen's italics). See also Messiaen in *Olivier Messiaen et les oiseaux*, dir. Denise Tual and Michel Fano (Sofracima, 1973), available online at www.on-tenk.com, accessed 16 November 2023.
4 Order of service for Messiaen's funeral at the Église de la Sainte-Trinité, 14 May 1992.
5 See Roger Scruton, *The Face of God: The Gifford Lectures* (London, 2012), pp. 1–21.
6 Claude Samuel, *Olivier Messiaen: Music and Color: Conversations with Claude Samuel*, trans. E. Thomas Glasow (Portland, OR, 1986), pp. 20–21.
7 Messiaen in conversation with Claude Samuel (1988), *Messiaen Edition* (Warner Classics WA-11431930, 2005) [CD]. Maritain stated that there is 'no style reserved for religious art', or any 'religious technique' specific to art, most especially nineteenth-century neo-medievalism. Jacques Maritain, 'Chapter V: Art and Beauty', in *Art and Scholasticism*, trans. Joseph W. Evans (1935), available online at https://maritain.nd.edu, accessed 16 November 2023;

and Maurice Denis, *Nouvelles théories sur l'art moderne sur l'art sacré, 1914–1921* (Paris, 1922), p. 228. Denis' work was an important iconographical source for Messiaen's opera *Saint François d'Assise* (1975–83). See Robert Fallon, 'Two Paths to Paradise: Reform in Messiaen's *Saint François d'Assise*', in *Messiaen Studies*, ed. Robert Sholl (Cambridge, 2007), p. 226.

8 Roger Scruton, *The Soul of the World* (Princeton, NJ, 2014), p. 11.

9 Messiaen in conversation with Samuel (1988).

10 See 1 Corinthians 15:55.

11 Roger Scruton, *An Intelligent Person's Guide to Philosophy* (London, 1996), pp. 90–91.

12 Olivier Messiaen, *Conférence de Notre-Dame* (Paris, 1978), pp. 7–13; Scruton, *The Soul of the World*, p. 24.

13 *The Confessions of St Augustine*, trans. E. B. Pusey (London, 1970), p. 40.

14 From the card sent to friends and relatives by Yvonne Loriod after the death of the composer, 27 April 1992.

15 Messiaen (23 April 1979), in Rössler, *Contributions*, pp. 91 and 92.

16 *Olivier Messiaen: The Music of Faith*, dir. Alan Benson (London Weekend Television, 5 April 1985).

17 Alister McGrath, *Making Sense of the Cross* (Leicester, 1992), p. 33.

18 Stephen Kern, 'Introduction: From Christian Unity to Modernist Unification', in *Modernism after the Death of God: Christianity, Fragmentation, and Unification* (London, 2017), p. 3.

19 Ibid., pp. 3–9.

20 On mourning, see Stephen Schloesser, *Jazz Age Catholicism: Mystic Modernism in Postwar Paris, 1919–1933* (Toronto, 2005).

21 Daniel K. L. Chua, 'Beethoven's Other Humanism', *Journal of the American Musicological Society*, LXII/3 (Fall 2009), p. 572.

22 Alain Badiou and Élisabeth Roudinesco, *Jacques Lacan, Past and Present: A Dialogue*, trans. Jason E. Smith (New York, 2014), p. 18. On Badiou and the event, see Andy McLaverty-Robinson, 'Alain Badiou: The Event. An A to Z of Theory', 15 December 2014, https://ceasefiremagazine.co.uk, accessed 16 June 2021.

23 Olivier Messiaen, 'Cahier beige' (1941–4), Bibliothèque Nationale de France, Paris (hereafter BnF) RES VMA MS-1490, p. 46. The composer Michaël Levinas, a student of Messiaen in his class of 1971–2, has stated that 'Messiaen pushed us to find the unheard.' Michaël Levinas, 'Messiaen nous poussait à trouver l'inouï, ce qui n'a jamaie été entendu . . .', episode 3/5, *Les Grandes Entretiens*, www.radiofrance.fr, 12 April 2017.

24 Catherine Massip, ed., *Portrait(s) d'Olivier Messiaen* (Paris, 1996); and Anik Lesure and Claude Samuel, eds, *Olivier Messiaen: le livre du centenaire* (Lyon, 2008). See Robert Sholl, 'Introduction: The Image of Messiaen', in *Messiaen in Context*, ed. Robert Sholl (Cambridge, 2023), pp. 3–9.

25 Notably Peter Hill and Nigel Simeone, *Messiaen* (New Haven, CT, and London, 2005). For other biographies, see Christopher Dingle, *The Life of Messiaen* (Cambridge, 2007); and Gaëtan Puaud, *Olivier Messiaen* (Paris, 2021).

1 On Beginnings

1 Brigitte Massin, *Olivier Messiaen: une poétique du merveilleux* (Aix-en-Provence, 1989), p. 19.
2 Pierre was educated by the Marists at Linselles, the Redemptorists at Les Urrier in Switzerland and the Jesuits in Amiens and at Le Sacré-Cœur in Tourcoing. I am indebted in this chapter to Pierre-Jean Hormière's chronology (using work by Béatrice Marchal and other sources), 'La Cage et l'oiseaux: Cécile Sauvage (1883–1927) and Olivier Messiaen (1908–1992)', in Cécile Sauvage, *Le Vallon* (Paris, 2020), pp. 1–12, also available online at https://lescoursdemathsdepjh.monsite-orange, accessed 12 February 2023. This edition contains a short discussion of Sauvage's poetry by Jean de Gourmont, 'Cécile Sauvage: Portrait et autographe', pp. 13–15.
3 Messiaen in 'Trois jours avec Olivier Messiaen: Une archive de 1962' (programme 1/3), conversation with Micheline Banzet, recorded in March 1962, at www.radiofrance.fr, accessed 16 November 2023.
4 Pierre Messiaen, *Images* (Paris, 1944), p. 136.
5 Claude Samuel, *Olivier Messiaen, Music and Color: Conversations with Claude Samuel*, trans. E. Thomas Glasow (Portland, OR, 1986), pp. 13–14, 200; José Bruyr, 'Olivier Messiaen', in *L'Écran des musiciens* (Paris, 1933), p. 125.
6 Olivier Messiaen, 'Préface', in Cécile Sauvage, *L'Âme en bourgeon* (Paris, 1987), p. 8; edition with corrections in Messiaen's hand, BnF VM FDS 30 Mes 4 (73). Messiaen marks this 'préface relue', p. 15.
7 Messiaen, 'Préface', pp. 9–10.
8 Verse 8 of 'Tu tettes le lait pur…', Cécile Sauvage, *Oeuvres complètes* (Paris, 2002), pp. 45–76 (see p. 56 for the verse quoted in the text), originally published in Paris (1929). See also Messiaen, 'Préface', pp. 10–11.
9 Liner notes to 'L'Âme en bourgeon', recorded in La Trinité (French Erato, Stereo LP STU 71104, released 1978). See Phillip Weller, trans., 'L'Âme en bourgeon', with an afterword, in *Olivier Messiaen: Music, Art and Literature*, ed. Christopher Dingle and Nigel Simeone (Aldershot, 2007), pp. 191–278. See also Adrian Foster, 'From Recorded Sound to Musical Notation: Reconstructing Olivier Messiaen's Improvisations on *L'Âme en bourgeon*', DMus, McGill University, Montreal, 2017.
10 Messiaen reads this poem on *Olivier Messiaen: les couleurs du temps: trente ans d'entretiens avec Claude Samuel*, disc 1, track 1 (16 December 1976) (Harmonia Mundi 211848, released 2000) [2-vol CD].
11 Cécile Sauvage, Grenoble 1917, 'Pensées et fragments de lettres', in *Cécile Sauvage, 20 juillet 1883–26 août 1927: études et souvenirs suivis de pages inédits de Cécile Sauvage* (Saint-Étienne, 1928), p. 73. See also Georges Bernanos, 'Cécile Sauvage ou le miracle de la vie intérieure', in *Cécile Sauvage: études et souvenirs*, pp. 45–7.
12 *Olivier Messiaen: The Music of Faith*, dir. Alan Benson (London Weekend Television, 5 April 1985).
13 P. Messiaen, *Images*, p. 135.
14 *Olivier Messiaen: The Music of Faith*.
15 Messiaen, 'Préface', p. 15.

16 Béatrice Marchal, *Les Chants du silence: Olivier Messiaen, fils de Cécile Sauvage ou la musique face à l'impossible parole* (Paris, 2008), p. 1, and p. 110, citing Sauvage, *Prière*, book 4, strophe 1.
17 Ibid., p. 14.
18 Jean Tenant recounts this story in *Cécile Sauvage: études et souvenirs*, p. 10.
19 Hormière, 'La Cage et l'oiseaux', p. 2.
20 Marchal, *Les Chants du silence*, p. 25; P. Messiaen, *Images*, pp. 117, 124, 126.
21 Marchal, *Les Chants du silence*, p. 50; Hormière, 'La Cage et l'oiseaux', p. 2.
22 P. Messiaen, *Images*, p. 83.
23 Ibid., p. 107.
24 Ibid., pp. 128, 146–7.
25 Pierre Messiaen published his complete translation of Shakespeare from 1939 to 1943 with Desclée de Brouwer.
26 Marchal, *Les Chants du silence*, pp. 30–31; P. Messiaen, *Images*, pp. 130–34.
27 Marchal, *Les Chants du silence*, pp. 32–3.
28 Ibid., pp. 35–6, 38, citing *Oeuvres de Cécile Sauvage* (Paris, 1929), pp. 332–3.
29 Sauvage, 'Pensées et fragments de lettres', in *Cécile Sauvage: études et souvenirs*, pp. 163–4.
30 Marchal, *Les Chants du silence*, p. 41. Sauvage wrote about another baptism at Ambert in 1910: 'It is for him the beginning of the world, of a world, because each [person] brings a world with them through birth and this world disappears at each death.' 'Pensées et fragments de lettres', in *Cécile Sauvage: études et souvenirs*, p. 167.
31 Cécile Sauvage, letter to Pierre Messiaen from Avignon, 25 March 1909, in Cécile Sauvage, *Lettres à Pierre Messiaen* (Saint-Étienne, 1930), p. 9; letter to Pierre from Grenoble, 14 May 1912, p. 20; and letter from Avignon, 12 August 1909, p. 11.
32 Cécile Sauvage, letter to Pierre Messiaen, Avignon, 2 February 1909, ibid., p. 7.
33 Cécile Sauvage, letter to Pierre Messiaen, Avignon, 4 February 1909, ibid., p. 8.
34 This term is used in Cécile Sauvage, letter to Pierre Messiaen, Grenoble, 23 April 1912, ibid., p. 17.
35 Cécile Sauvage, letter to Pierre Messiaen, Grenoble, 12 October 1912, ibid., p. 24.
36 Sauvage, Grenoble 1917, 'Pensées et fragments de lettres', in *Cécile Sauvage: études et souvenirs*, p. 174.
37 For more on Alain Messiaen's poetry, see Herbert Schneider, 'Alain Messiaen – Dichtungen über Musik', in *Olivier Messiaen: Texte, Analysen, Zeugnisse* (Book 2: Das Werk im historischen und analytischen Kontext), ed. Wolfgang Rathert, Herbert Schneider and Karl Anton Rickenbacher (Zürich and New York, 2013), pp. 319–70.
38 See *TRCO*, tome V (Paris, 1999), vol. 1, p. 254. See the verse from 'L'Âme en bourgeon', p. 11 (1987 edn), in Marchal, *Les Chants du silence*, p. 59; and another verse cited by Pierre Messiaen in *Images*, p. 141.
39 Béatrice Marchal, ed., *Cécile Sauvage: écrits d'amour* (Paris, 2009), pp. 26–32, 140–41, on the dates of these poems, and Pierre Messiaen's changes to these poems to conceal his wife's feelings.
40 P. Messiaen, *Images*, p. 152.

41 Hormière, 'La Cage et l'oiseaux', p. 4.
42 Ibid., p. 6.
43 See Marchal, *Cécile Sauvage: écrits d'amour*, pp. 26–32, 140–41.
44 P. Messiaen, *Images*, pp. 159–89.
45 Marchal, *Cécile Sauvage: écrits d'amour*, p. 21. This comprises *L'Étreinte mystique* (1915), a work that links a burgeoning Christian faith with love for Jean (see p. 43, and poem XIV on p. 71), fragments of *Prière* (1914–15), *L'Aile et la rose* (undated, but from the same epoque) and *Primavère*.
46 Marchal, *Les Chants du silence*, pp. 60–70, 90–94, 105–13.
47 Messiaen in Olivier Mille, *Olivier Messiaen: la liturgie de cristal* (Artline films–Arte France–INA Entreprise, 2002); Messiaen in 'Trois jours avec Olivier Messiaen: Une archive de 1962' (programme 2/3).
48 Messiaen in *Olivier Messiaen: la liturgie de cristal*. Sauvage notes in a literary fragment from Digne, 1907: 'I adore fairy tales.' 'Pensées et fragments de lettres', in *Cécile Sauvage: études et souvenirs*, p. 162.
49 See Sauvage, Grenoble 1917, 'Pensées et fragments de lettres', in *Cécile Sauvage: études et souvenirs*, p. 173.
50 *Olivier Messiaen: The Music of Faith*.
51 Marchal, *Les Chants du silence*, pp. 71–5.
52 P. Messiaen, *Images*, p. 153.
53 Samuel, *Music and Color*, p. 110.
54 See Lucie Kayas, 'Chronique d'une carrière d'enseignant exceptionelle', in *Messiaen 2008: Messiaen au Conservatoire: contributions du Conservatoire national supérieur de musique et de danse de Paris aux célébrations de la naissance d'Olivier Messiaen*, ed. Anne Bongrain (Paris, 2008), pp. 10–23.
55 Massin, *Olivier Messiaen: une poétique du merveilleux*, p. 38; *TRCO*, tome VI (Paris, 2001), pp. 51–93.
56 Records at the institute show that Pierre taught there from 1948 to 1956. Email communication to the author from the Archives de l'Institut Catholique de Paris (8 July 2022). Other scholarship gives the more likely commencement date of 1929, see Hormière, 'La Cage et l'oiseaux', p. 9.
57 Marchal, *Les Chants du silence*, pp. 88–9; P. Messiaen, *Images*, p. 235.
58 Messiaen in conversation with Samuel (1988).
59 Marchal, *Les Chants du silence*, pp. 14–15, 95.
60 Letter dated 28 August 1927 from Pierre Messiaen to Messiaen's stepmother, in Hormière, 'La Cage et l'oiseaux', p. 9.
61 Marchal, *Les Chants du silence*, p. 97; P. Messiaen, *Images*, pp. 153–4; Marchal, *Cécile Sauvage: écrits d'amour*, p. 47.
62 P. Messiaen, *Images*, pp. 238–40; Peter Hill and Nigel Simeone, *Messiaen* (New Haven, CT, and London, 2005), p. 223.
63 P. Messiaen, *Images*, pp. 238–40.
64 Ibid., pp. 243–52.
65 Marchal opines that Messiaen copied the works from *Prière* each year as both a homage and a form of forgiveness, and that *La Dame de Shalott*, a theatrical and inventive piano work written in 1917, was recorded by Loriod in 1973 as a homage to his mother (Marchal, *Cécile Sauvage: écrits d'amour*, pp. 110, 112).
66 Hormière, 'La Cage et l'oiseaux', p. 11.
67 Samuel, *Music and Color*, p. 16.

68 Sauvage, Paris 1925, 'Pensées et fragments de lettres', in *Cécile Sauvage: études et souvenirs*, p. 179.
69 P. Messiaen, *Images*, p. 157. Pierre refers to the poet John Keats (1795–1821), who also died of tuberculosis, but it is clear that this comment has a wider purview.
70 Sauvage, Paris 1927, 'Pensées et fragments de lettres', in *Cécile Sauvage: études et souvenirs*, p. 180.
71 Hill and Simeone, *Messiaen*, p. 16.
72 Henri Dutilleux, 'Jean Gallon' [1960], in *L'Esprit de variation, écrits et catalogue établis par Pierre Gervasoni* (Paris, 2019), p. 82.
73 Hill and Simeone, *Messiaen*, p. 18.
74 See Anne Bongrain, 'Les Professeur: les sources théoriques', in *Messiaen au Conservatoire*, ed. Bongrain, pp. 127–31; Christopher Brent Murray, 'Messiaen and the Paris Conservatoire', in *Messiaen in Context*, ed. Robert Sholl (Cambridge, 2023), pp. 27–36.
75 Samuel, *Music and Color*, pp. 111–12; Antoine Goléa, *Rencontres avec Olivier Messiaen* (Paris, 1960), p. 28.
76 Rolande Falcinelli, *Souvenirs et regards: entretiens avec Stéphane Detournay* (Tournai, 1985), p. 263.
77 Messiaen, liner notes to Yvonne Loriod's recording of Isaac Albéniz's *Iberia* (Véga, C 30 A 127 (disc 1)/128 (disc 2), 1958); Alexander Goehr, 'The Messiaen Class', in *Finding the Key: Selected Writings of Alexander Goehr*, ed. Derrick Puffett (London, 1998), p. 40, n. 7; Samuel, *Music and Color*, p. 114.
78 Jean Barraqué, 'Olivier Messiaen' [1953], in *Écrits*, ed. Laurent Feneyrou (Paris, 2011), pp. 60, 89, 102.
79 Preface to *Fugues à 4 parties des élèves ayant remporté le Premier prix au Concours de Fugue (Année 1926)* (Paris, 1926).
80 *Fugues à 4 parties des élèves*, pp. 6–10; other fugues in this volume are by Pierre Revel and Jean Rivier.
81 Marcel Dupré, 'Du temps où la gloire', in 'Olivier Messiaen a 50 ans', *Le Guide du concert et du disque*, Paris, XXXIX/229 (3 April 1959), p. 1090.
82 See the diary of Jeanne Demessieux for 6 June 1941 in *The Diaries and Selected Letters of Jeanne Demessieux*, ed. Lynn Cavanagh, trans. Stacey Brown and Lynn Cavanagh (n.d.), p. 125, available at https://opentextbooks.uregina.ca, accessed 16 November 2023.
83 *The Diaries and Selected Letters of Jeanne Demessieux*, entry for 16 April 1943, p. 198.
84 Dupré, 'Du temps où la gloire', p. 1090; Messiaen in 'Trois jours avec Olivier Messiaen: Une archive de 1962' (programme 1/3).
85 Dupré, 'Du temps où la gloire', p. 1090.
86 See Messiaen improvising in *Olivier Messiaen et les oiseaux*, dir. Denise Tual and Michel Fano (Sofracima, 1973), at www.on-tenk.com, accessed 16 November 2023; and 'Marcel Dupré Plays at Saint-Sulpice and at Meudon (3)', www.youtube.com, accessed 20 June 2023.
87 Testimony of Rachel Brunschwig, *auditeur* in the class, in Marie-Louise Langlais, *Jean Langlais Remembered* (2016), p. 38, available online at www.agohq.org, accessed 16 November 2023.

88 Dupré's advice to Falcinelli in 'Arcanes et pensées' (1950), available online at www.falcinelli.info, accessed 20 June 2023.
89 Dupré, 'Arcanes et pensées'. See also Dupré, 'Allocations aux élèves du Conservatoire', BNF RES VMB MS 85, in Lucie Kayas, 'Chronique', in *Messiaen au Conservatoire*, ed. Bongrain, p. 19, where Dupré advised: 'Search for the true harmony. Subtlety will come. Don't despise the analytical harmony. Be passionate about discovering the harmonic personalities of the great musicians.'
90 Henri Dutilleux, 'Divers aspects d'un langage contemporain' [1960], in *L'Esprit de variation*, p. 92.
91 Hill and Simeone, *Messiaen*, p. 179; Massin, *Olivier Messiaen: une poétique du merveilleux*, p. 74.
92 Roger Muraro, *Fauvettes de l'Hérault: textes* (Paris, 2020), pp. 16, 18.
93 M.-L. Langlais, *Jean Langlais Remembered*, p. 56.
94 Jean Langlais, ibid., pp. 51 and 37.
95 'Jean Langlais (Speaking in English) Remembers Vierne, Widor, Dupré, Messiaen, and Tournemire' (1982), www.youtube.com, accessed 9 December 2021.
96 Maurice Emmanuel, 'Art gréco-romain', in *Encyclopédie de la musique et dictionaire du Conservatoire, première partie: histoire de la musique*, vol. I: *Antiquité, Moyen-Âge* (Paris, 1913), pp. 377–534.
97 Olivier Messiaen, letter to Maurice Emmanuel, 29 December 1929, in *L'Enseignement de Maurice Emmanuel*, ed. Christophe Corbier and Sylvie Douche (Paris, 2020), p. 218.
98 Olivier Messiaen, 'Maurice Emmanuel: ses "trente chansons bourguignonnes"', *La Revue musicale*, special edition on Maurice Emmanuel (1947), p. 108.
99 Olivier Messiaen, letter to Maurice Emmanuel, undated (end of 1931), in *L'Enseignement de Maurice Emmanuel*, p. 219. For a full list, including second prizes, see Murray, 'Messiaen and the Paris Conservatoire', p. 29.
100 Christophe Corbier, ed., *Maurice Emmanuel: lettres choisies* (Paris, 2017), p. 504.
101 Alain Messiaen, 'Notre-Dame la musique' [6 April 1969], *Les Amis de St François* (January–February 1971), p. 26.
102 Olivier Messiaen, '*Ariane et Barbe-bleue* de Paul Dukas', *La Revue musicale*, 166 (May–June 1936), pp. 79–86.
103 Andrew Hussey, *Paris: The Secret History* (London, 2006), p. 267.
104 See Roger Nichols, *The Harlequin Years: Music in Paris, 1917–1929* (Berkeley, CA, 2003).
105 *TRCO*, tome II (1995), p. 154.
106 Hussey, *Paris: The Secret History*, p. 311.
107 *TRCO*, tome I (1994), pp. 9–12, 31–6.
108 George Antheil, *Bad Boy of Music* (New York, 1945).
109 Elsa Barraine, 'Olivier Messiaen, notre camarade chez Dukas', *Le Conservatoire*, 32 (April 1954), in *Bulletin de l'Association de Maurice et Madeleine Duruflé*, 7–8 (2008), pp. 31–4.
110 On the relation between transcendence of the norm and 'self-sublated perversion', see Slavoj Žižek, *Surplus-Enjoyment: A Guide for the Non-Perplexed* (London, 2022), p. 161.

111 See, for instance, Patrick Weil, *De la laïcité en France* (Paris, 2022); and Philippe Portier and Jean-Paul Willaime, eds, *Religion and Secularism in France Today* (Abingdon and New York, 2022).

112 Pope Pius X, *Tra le sollecitudini*, sections 3 and 25, available online at www.liturgyoffice.org.uk, accessed 20 June 2023.

113 See Katherine Bergeron, *Decadent Enchantments: The Revival of Gregorian Chant at Solesmes* (Berkeley, CA, 1998).

114 José Bruyr, 'Un entretien avec . . . Charles Tournemire', *Le Guide du concert* (11–18 April 1930), pp. 791–3, in *Bulletin de l'Association Maurice et Marie-Madeleine Duruflé*, 9 (2009), p. 170.

115 Jean-Marc Leblanc, ed., *Mémoires de Charles Tournemire, édition critique*, *L'Orgue*, 321–4 (2018), I–IV, p. 24.

116 Marie-Madeleine Duruflé-Chevalier, 'Entretien avec Marie-Madeleine Duruflé' (with Frédéric Denis on 7 April 1999), *Bulletin de l'Association Maurice et Marie-Madeleine Duruflé*, 17 (2019–20), p. 27.

117 Frédéric Blanc, ed., *Maurice Duruflé: souvenirs et autre écrits* (Paris, 2005), p. 28.

118 Ibid., p. 110.

119 See Cécile Auzolle, 'Daniel-Lesur et Charles Tournemire: une filiation', in *Musique, art et religion dans l'entre-deux-guerres*, ed. Sylvie Caron and Michel Duchesneau (Lyon, 2009), pp. 155–79. Florent Schmitt (1870–1958) set Sauvage's 'Si la lune rose . . .', from *L'Âme en bourgeon*, as the third of his *Six choeurs pour voix des femmes et orchestra*, op. 81 (1931).

120 Messiaen in Olivier Glandaz, *Messiaen à l'orgue* (Péronnas, 2014), p. 83.

121 Félix Raugel, review of *L'Orgue Mystique*, *La Revue musicale*, 10 (November 1929), p. 96.

122 Charles Tournemire, letter of 23 July 1931 from the Île de Ouessant, in Thomas Daniel Schlee and Dietrich Kämper, *Olivier Messiaen: La Cité Céleste, Das Himmlische Jerusalem* (Cologne, 1998), p. 141 (underlining in source). Messiaen's referees for this post were Dupré, Emmanuel, André Marchal, Widor and Tournemire. Hill and Simeone, *Messiaen*, pp. 34–6.

123 Dupré stated to Demessieux: 'I mistrust those who induce themselves to believe in mysticism, like Messiaen', and he agreed with Demessieux's 'definition' of this concept as 'partaking in blessedness'. Demessieux, diary entry for 2 September 1946, *The Diaries and Selected Letters of Jeanne Demessieux*, p. 345.

124 Letter to Stéphane Detournay, 29 January 1997, in Detournay, *Rolande Falcinelli: une esthétique de la synthése, les enjeux d'une pensée humaniste à l'ère postmoderne* (Lille, 2001), p. 279.

125 *Catechism of the Catholic Church* (London, 1995), pp. 114–30, 147–276.

126 To a lesser extent, Dupré's output for the organ also covers the topography of the church's year.

127 Olivier Messiaen, 'Musique religieuse' (5 February 1937), p. 1, in *Olivier Messiaen: Journalism, 1935–1939*, ed. Stephen Broad (Farnham, 2012), p. 63.

128 See Pope Pius XII, *Mystici corporis christi* (29 June 1943), available online at www.vatican.va, accessed 16 November 2023.

129 Olivier Messiaen, 'De la musique sacrée', *Carrefour* (June–July 1939), p. 75, in *Olivier Messiaen: Journalism*, ed. Broad, pp. 75–6.

130 See Lucie Kayas, *André Jolivet* (Paris, 2005), p. 205. See also Caroline Rae, 'Revitalising the Spiritual: Messiaen and La Jeune France', in *Messiaen in Context*, ed. Sholl, pp. 103–18.
131 Žižek, *Surplus-Enjoyment*, p. 161. See also Dylan Evans, *An Introductory Dictionary of Lacanian Psychoanalysis* (London, 1996), pp. 93–4; and Jacques Lacan, *Seminar VII: The Ethics of Psychoanalysis, 1959–60*, ed. Jacques-Alain Miller, trans. Dennis Porter (London and New York, 1992), pp. 235–68.
132 Messiaen in conversation with Samuel (1988).
133 Stephen Schloesser, *Jazz Age Catholicism: Mystic Modernism in Postwar Paris, 1919–1933* (Toronto, 2005); and Hussey, *Paris: The Secret History*, pp. 326–8.

2 On Becoming 'Messiaen', 1927–39

1 For 'the shock of lights and colours', see Brigitte Massin, *Olivier Messiaen: une poétique du merveilleux* (Aix-en-Provence, 1989), p. 153; for the 'unheard violence', see Peter Hill and Nigel Simeone, *Messiaen* (New Haven, CT, and London, 2005), p. 35; Messiaen, interview with Michel Archimbaud (1985), in Olivier Glandaz, *Messiaen à l'orgue* (Péronnas, 2014), p. 13; and Messiaen in conversation with Claude Samuel (1988), *Messiaen Edition* (Warner Classics WA-11431930, 2005) [CD].
2 Messiaen in conversation with Samuel (1988).
3 Carolyn Shuster-Fournier, *Un siècle de vie musicale à l'église de La Trinité: de Théodore Salomé à Olivier Messiaen* (Paris, 2014), p. 99.
4 Ibid., pp. 100–102 and 171–95.
5 Claude Samuel, *Olivier Messiaen, Music and Color: Conversations with Claude Samuel*, trans. E. Thomas Glasow (Portland, OR, 1986), p. 23; Messiaen, interview with Archimbaud (1985), in Glandaz, *Messiaen à l'orgue*, p. 13. Messiaen notes, sometime before 1972, that vespers was cancelled 'for various reasons', but comments on his love of improvising for this office because of the relationship between improvisation and the liturgy, especially the plainchant antiphon before the psalms and the relationship between registrations and the texts. Messiaen in *Olivier Messiaen et les oiseaux*, dir. Denise Tual and Michel Fano (Sofracima, 1973), at www.on-tenk.com, accessed 16 November 2023; and Messiaen (1969) in *Olivier Messiaen: la liturgie de cristal*, dir. Olivier Mille (Artline films–Arte France–INA Entreprise, 2002). See also *Olivier Messiaen: les couleurs du temps: trente ans d'entretiens avec Claude Samuel*, disc 1, track 3 (16 December 1976) (Harmonia Mundi 211848, released 2000) [2-vol CD].
6 Shuster-Fournier, *Un siècle de vie musicale*, pp. 109–11.
7 My thanks to the composer's great-grandson, Marc Bacon, for this information.
8 Samuel, *Music and Color*, p. 25; Messiaen, interview with Archimbaud (1985), in Glandaz, *Messiaen à l'orgue*, p. 13.
9 Glandaz, *Messiaen à l'orgue*, p. 35.
10 Jonathan Harvey, *In Quest of Spirit: Thoughts on Music* (Berkeley, CA, 1999), p. 2.
11 Messiaen cited in Anik Lesure and Claude Samuel, eds, *Olivier Messiaen: le livre du centenaire*, (Lyon, 2008), p. 59. Edvard Varèse, 'Amériques', in *Écrits*, ed. Louise Hirbour (Paris, 1983), p. 31.

12 Varèse, 'Les Nouveaux Instruments', in *Écrits*, p. 29; Glandaz, *Messiaen à l'orgue*, p. 32.

13 See www.organhistoricalsociety.org, accessed 15 May 2022.

14 Marie-Louise Langlais, *Jean Langlais Remembered* (2016), p. 53, available online at www.agohq.org , accessed 16 November 2023.

15 Other composers such as the German Max Reger (1873–1916) and the Czech composer Petr Eben (1929–2007) have also written important and extensive quantities of organ music.

16 Charles Tournemire, 'Des possibilités harmoniques et polytonales unies à la ligne grégorienne', *Revue Grégorienne*, XV/15 (September/October 1930), p. 174.

17 See Katherine Davies and Toby Garfitt, eds, *God's Mirror: Renewal and Engagement in French Catholic Intellectual Culture in the Mid-Twentieth Century* (New York, 2014), especially Chapter 6 by Stephen Schloesser, 'From *Mystique* to *Théologique*: Messiaen's "*ordre nouveau*," 1935–39', pp. 129–61; and Edward Baring, *Converts to the Real: Catholicism and the Making of Continental Philosophy* (Cambridge, MA, 2019).

18 *TRCO*, tome I (1994), pp. 7–9.

19 A brief comparison of performances shows that Messiaen's own recording of *Le Banquet céleste* is one of the slowest at 7.24, but Messiaen's fellow student Gaston Litaize took 5.14 to play the work. Other recordings of note are: Wolfgang Sieber (6.25); Pierre Cochereau (6.33 and 6.35 respectively); Jennifer Bate (6.55 and 7.14 respectively); Simon Preston (7.14); Olivier Latry (7.03); Gillian Weir (7.20); and Hans-Ola Ericsson (8.03).

20 Messiaen (16 December 1983), in Almut Rössler, *Contributions to the Spiritual World of Olivier Messiaen*, trans. Barbara Dagg and Nancy Poland (Duisburg, 1986), p. 140; Olivier Messiaen, letter to Maurice Emmanuel, undated (end of 1931?), *L'Enseignement de Maurice Emmanuel*, ed. Christophe Corbier and Sylvie Douche (Paris, 2020), pp. 219–20 and n. 46.

21 *Paroissien Romain* (Rome and Tournai, 1920), pp. 810–11; and Vincent d'Indy, *Cours de Composition musicale, rédigé avec la collaboration de Auguste Sérieyx d'après les notes prises aux Classes de Composition de la Schola Cantorum en 1899–1900* (Paris, 1909), vol. II, p. 449.

22 See for example the 'Offertoire' of no. 25 (*Pentecôte*) in *L'Orgue Mystique*, which uses 4' and 2' 2/3 stops in the pedals, or the 'Elévation' of no. 17 (*Pâques*), which uses a 4' stop in the pedal, as indeed does the 'Elévation' of no. 41.

23 *TMLM* (2001), p. 87.

24 *TRCO*, tome IV (1997), p. 33.

25 M.-L. Langlais, *Jean Langlais Remembered*, p. 53.

26 Hill and Simeone, *Messiaen*, pp. 26–7, 71; José Bruyr, 'Olivier Messiaen', in *L'Écran des musiciens* (Paris, 1933), p. 126.

27 Olivier Messiaen, 'Musique religieuse', p. 1, in *Olivier Messiaen: Journalism, 1935–1939*, ed. Stephen Broad (Farnham, 2012), p. 63.

28 Alain Messiaen, *Etats d'âme du paysage musical* (Rodez, 1969), p. 54.

29 Messiaen, liner notes to Yvonne Loriod's recording of the *Préludes* and *Quatre Études de rythme* (Erato STU 70433 , 1968).

30 Samuel, *Music and Color*, pp. 43, 45, 61–5. On Delaunay, see Almut Rössler in conversation with Messiaen (23 April 1979), in Rössler, *Contributions*, p. 79; see also *Olivier Messiaen: le livre du centenaire*, p. 159.
31 Rössler in conversation with Messiaen (23 April 1979), in Rössler, *Contributions*, p. 115; see also Olivier Messiaen, *Conférence de Notre-Dame* (Paris, 1978), p. 9.
32 Messiaen, *Conférence de Notre-Dame*, p. 11.
33 Ibid., pp. 9–13. Charles Tournemire, 'L'Orgue', *La Petite Maîtrise*, 203 (April 1930), pp. 16–18, cited in *Bulletin de l'Association Maurice et Marie-Madeleine Duruflé*, IX (2009), p. 180; Charles Tournemire, *César Franck* (Paris, 1931), p. 57; Charles Tournemire, *Précis d'exécution de registration et d'improvisation à l'orgue* (Paris, 1936), pp. 116–17.
34 *TMLM*, p. 83.
35 See Duncan Carmichael, 'Music in Colour: Messiaen and Synaesthesia', in *Messiaen in Context*, ed. Robert Sholl (Cambridge, 2023), pp. 240–47.
36 Messiaen describing Blanc-Gatti in *Olivier Messiaen: la liturgie de cristal*; Charles Blanc-Gatti, *Des sons et des couleurs* (Paris, 1934), p. 27 (original in italics for emphasis).
37 Messiaen in *Olivier Messiaen: la liturgie de cristal.*
38 Ibid. My thanks to Chrisopher Wintle for this idea from an unpublished paper.
39 Marcel Dupré, *Cours complet d'improvisation à l'orgue* (Paris, 1925), vol. II, pp. 25–7. Messiaen would have known this as a single-volume work.
40 Messiaen, 'Cahier vert' (1932–44), pp. 3 and 6, BnF RES VMA MS-1491.
41 Samuel, *Music and Color*, pp. 167–8; *TRCO*, tome I, pp. 66–8; tome VII (2002), pp. 1–22, 97–107.
42 Messiaen, liner notes to Yvonne Loriod's recording of Isaac Albéniz's *Iberia* (Véga, C 30 A 127 (disc 1)/128 (disc 2), 1958); see also *TRCO*, tome VI (2001).
43 Dupré, *Cours Complet d'improvisation à l'orgue*, vol. II, pp. 22–7; *TRCO*, tome VI, pp. 58, 63–5, 69–70, 89–93, 108, 110; Messiaen, *Ravel: Analyses of the Piano Works of Maurice Ravel*, ed. Yvonne Loriod-Messiaen, trans. Paul Griffiths (Paris, 2004).
44 Michaël Levinas, 'Prolégomènes', interview with Danielle Cohen-Levinas and Pierre Albert Castanet, in Levinas, *Le Compositeur trouvère: écrits et entretiens, 1982–2002* (Paris, 2002), p. 227.
45 Michaël Levinas, 'De la polyphony de la *Turangalîla-Symphonie* (1948) d'Olivier Messiaen à *Rebonds* de Michaël Levinas', in Levinas, *Le Compositeur trouvère*, pp. 112–13.
46 Michaël Levinas, 'La Loi et le hors-la-loi: l'ère du soupçon', in *La Loi musicale: ce que la lecture de l'histoire nous (dés)apprend*, ed. Danielle Cohen-Levinas (Paris, 1999), p. 14.
47 Ibid., p. 16.
48 Tournemire, 'L'Orgue', pp. 16–18, cited in *Bulletin de l'Association Maurice et Marie-Madeleine Duruflé*, 9 (2009), p. 180; Tournemire, *César Franck*, p. 57; Tournemire, *Précis d'exécution*, pp. 116–17.
49 Levinas, 'De la polyphony', p. 114.
50 Samuel, *Music and Color*, pp. 167, 64.
51 Julian Anderson, 'Messiaen and the Notion of Influence', *Tempo*, LXIII/247 (January 2009), pp. 2–6; Yves Balmer, Thomas Lacôte and Christopher

Brent Murray, 'Jolivet Revisited: Messiaen Borrowings from the Works of the 1930s', in *André Jolivet: Music, Art and Literature*, ed. Caroline Rae (Abingdon, 2019), p. 175; *TRCO*, tome VII, pp. 109–90.

52 Samuel, *Music and Color*, p. 193; *TMLM*, p. 71.

53 The others are *Le Banquet eucharistique* and *Jésus*. Neither work is extant.

54 Tournemire in *Le Courrier musical* (15 December 1931), reprinted in *L'Orgue: cahiers et mémoires*, 41 (1989), I, p. 83, n. 4.

55 Olivier Messiaen, letter to Maurice Emmanuel, undated (end of 1931?), in *L'Enseignement de Maurice Emmanuel*, p. 218.

56 See Nigel Simeone, 'Messiaen and the USA', in *Messiaen in Context*, ed. Sholl, pp. 46–53.

57 Hill and Simeone, *Messiaen*, p. 28; Nigel Simeone, *Olivier Messiaen: A Bibliographical Catalogue of Messiaen's Works, First Editions and First Performances* (Tutzing, 1998), p. 189. This work is not lost, as was thought, but can be consulted in BnF RES VMA MS-1489 (131 pages). For the preliminary round (1931 competition), Messiaen wrote a setting of *La Jeunesse des vieux* by Catulle Mendès. See Laura Hamer and Christopher Brent Murray, 'Olivier Messiaen and the Prix de Rome as Rite of Passage', in *Messiaen Perspectives 1: Sources and Influences*, ed. Christopher Dingle and Robert Fallon (Farnham, 2013), pp. 13–43.

58 Rolande Falcinelli, *Souvenirs et regards, entretiens avec Stéphane Detournay* (Tournai, 1985), p. 164.

59 Hamer and Brent Murray, 'Olivier Messiaen and the Prix de Rome as Rite of Passage', pp. 13–43.

60 Nicholas James Capozzoli, 'Messiaen's Forgotten Mie: Rediscovering the Organ Music of Claire Delbos', DMus, McGill University, Montreal, 2020, p. 7.

61 See Christopher Brent Murray, 'Messiaen and the Paris Conservatoire', in *Messiaen in Context*, ed. Sholl, p. 31.

62 Hill and Simeone, *Messiaen*, p. 43.

63 See Paul Festa's film about this piece, *Apparition of the Eternal Church* (2006), in which people who often know little or nothing about Messiaen's music listen and respond to this piece. Their responses evoke sadistic and masochistic imagery, often indicating that the overwhelming, sublime, gothic and 'astonishing' quality of the music threatens to desubjectify them, an ideal commensurate with Messiaen's later concept of '*éblouissement*'.

64 See BnF RES VMA MS-1937. This appears then to have been a 'working' score. BnF RES VMA MS-1936 is a neat score written on three pages.

65 Autograph (restored to the printed score in 1993): Sketches: BnF RES VMA MS-1938.

66 See 'Messiaen: Apparition de l'Église eternelle', www.youtube.com, accessed 16 November 2023. A brief comparison of performances shows that Messiaen's own recording of *Apparition* is one of the most magisterial at 10.13, but Messiaen's fellow student Gaston Litaize took 7.41 to play the work. Other recordings of note are: Louis Thiry (8.25); Thomas Trotter (9.48); Olivier Latry (9.45); Pierre Cochereau (8.37 and 10.04, both at Notre-Dame), (9.40 at Cologne Cathedral); Jennifer Bate (10.00); Gillian Weir (10.55); and Hans-Ola Ericsson (11.26).

67 The dedication reads: 'Au Maître Charles Tournemire homage de respect de sincère admiration Olivier Messiaen.' Author's private collection. See also Simeone, *Olivier Messiaen: A Bibliographical Catalogue*, pp. 26–7.
68 Messiaen, 'Billet parisiene: *L'Orgue Mystique* de Tournemire', *La Syrinx* (May 1938), pp. 26–7, cited in *Olivier Messiaen: Journalism*, ed. Broad, pp. 42 and 102. For the crossed-out dedication to Messiaen, see the front cover of Jean-Marc Leblanc, ed., *Mémoires de Charles Tournemire, édition critique*, *L'Orgue*, nos 321–4 (2018), I–IV.
69 Leblanc, *Mémoires de Charles Tournemire*, p. 298.
70 Olivier Messiaen, letter to Rolande Falcinelli, 4 March 1984, available online at at www.falcinelli.info, accessed 20 June 2023; Jon Gillock, *Performing Messiaen's Organ Music: 66 Masterclasses* (Bloomington and Indianapolis, IN, 2010), pp. 356–9.
71 Samuel, *Music and Color*, p. 176.
72 Hill and Simeone, *Messiaen*, p. 49.
73 M.-L. Langlais, *Jean Langlais Remembered*, p. 61.
74 Raugel, *Le Monde musical*, XLVI/2 (28 February 1935), p. 57.
75 Shuster-Fournier, *Un siècle de vie musicale*, p. 104.
76 Leblanc, *Mémoires de Charles Tournemire*, pp. 196–7, 203–4.
77 Suzanne Demarquez, *La Revue musicale*, 154 (March 1935), pp. 203–4.
78 Messiaen (7 December 1968) in Rössler, *Contributions*, p. 28.
79 Messiaen 'Cahier vert', pp. 29 and 25.
80 Ibid., p. 54.
81 Ibid., p. 55.
82 Boulez, 'Proposals' [1948], in *Stocktakings from an Apprenticeship*, trans. Stephen Walsh (Oxford, 1991), p. 49.
83 Olivier Messiaen, letter to M.-L. Langlais, 29 February 1936, in Marie-Louise Langlais, *L'Ombre et lumière* (Paris, 1995), p. 103; letter from Messiaen to Marcel Dupré from January or the beginning of February 1936, in *Olivier Messiaen: le livre du centenaire*, p. 18.
84 Excerpt published at www.archive.wikiwix.com, accessed 20 June 2023; source at BnF NAF 28312 (cote).
85 Massin, *Olivier Messiaen: une poétique du merveilleux*, p. 172.
86 Messiaen, preface to the score of *La Nativité* (Book I) (Paris, 1936).
87 Messiaen, 'Cahier vert', pp. 59–60.
88 Ibid., p. 61.
89 See Messiaen analysing this for his class of 1971–2 in *Olivier Messiaen et les oiseaux*.
90 Ibid.
91 This is a melodic idea that seems to have occurred initially to Messiaen (associated with the Father) in connection with a three-voice fugue (with a main subject, and specific ideas for concepts of the Father, Son and Holy Spirit). The last part of the theme of the Father corresponds very closely to the descending pedal theme in pieces IV and IX of *La Nativité*, and the theme for the Holy Spirit using the cornet stop used in piece IV of *La Nativité*, but also clearly the first piece of *Les Corps Glorieux*, which uses a cornet and makes a musical deformation of the 'Salve Regina'. See Messiaen, 'Cahier vert', p. 58.

92 BnF RES VMA MS-1493, p. 11.
93 Massin, *Olivier Messiaen: une poétique du merveilleux*, pp. 71–3.
94 Pope Pius XI, *Divini cultus* (20 December 1928), published for the 25th anniversary of Pius X, *Tra le sollecitudini*, available online at www.adoremus.org, accessed 7 August 2023.
95 Samuel, *Music and Color*, p. 67.
96 Messiaen in 'Trois jours avec Olivier Messiae: Une archive de 1962' (programme 1/3), conversation with Micheline Banzet recorded in 1962, at www.radiofrance.fr, accessed 16 November 2023.
97 On plainchant, see Jonas Lundblad, 'Universal Neumes: Chant Theory in Messiaen's Aesthetics', *Journal of the Royal Musical Association*, CXLVII/2 (2022), pp. 449–93.
98 *TMLM*, p. 8; *TRCO*, tome III (1996), p. 7.
99 Messiaen, 'Cahier vert', p. 49. This sketch in fact does not show the presence of plainchant and has different registrations from the final version of the piece, which contains a deformed version of the plainchant – Introit for Christmas Day 'Puer natus est nobis' – in the right hand.
100 *TMLM*, p. 42.
101 Tournemire, 'Des possibilités harmoniques et polytonales unies à la ligne grégorienne', p. 174.
102 Samuel, *Music and Color*, p. 69; *TMLM*, pp. 84–6; *TRCO*, tome I, p. 59, tome IV (1997), pp. 41–65, 131–70, and tome VI.
103 Hill and Simeone, *Messiaen*, p. 82.
104 Capozzoli, 'Messiaen's Forgotten Mie', pp. 54–6.
105 The four articles specifically reviewing works (musical and pedagogical) by Tournemire are found in *Olivier Messiaen: Journalism*, ed. Broad: 'Billet parisien: *L'Orgue Mystique* de Charles Tournemire', *La Syrinx* (May 1938), pp. 26–7 (Broad, pp. 41–2 and 101–3); 'Charles Tournemire: *Précis d'exécution, de registration et d'improvisation à l'orgue*', *Le Monde musical* (30 June 1936), p. 186 (Broad, pp. 53 and 115–16); '*Post Ludes Libres* (Charles Tournemire)', *Le Monde musical* (31 May 1937), p. 138 (Broad, pp. 54 and 117); and 'L'Orgue', *Le Monde musicale* (31 March 1938), p. 84 (Broad, pp. 56–7 and 118).
106 See Caroline Rae, 'Revitalising the Spiritual: Messiaen and La Jeune France', in *Messiaen in Context*, ed. Sholl, pp. 103–18.
107 Stephen Broad, 'Messiaen and Cocteau', in *Olivier Messiaen: Music, Art and Literature*, ed. Christopher Dingle and Nigel Simeone (Aldershot, 2007), pp. 1–12.
108 Lucie Kayas, *André Jolivet* (Paris, 2005), p. 205.
109 Ibid., pp. 220–23.
110 André Jolivet, *Écrits*, vol. I, ed. Christine Jolivet-Erlih (Sampzon, 2006), p. 289. The earliest-known correspondence between them is a telegram dated 13 May 1933, BnF NLA 46. My thanks to Caroline Rae and Christine Jolivet-Erlih for clarifications.
111 Yves Baudrier, letter to Daniel-Lesur, 6 January 1938, in Lucie Kayas, 'Le groupe Jeune France à travers sa correspondance', *Euterpe*, 35 (July 2020), p. 10.
112 Hilda Jolivet, *Avec . . . André Jolivet* (Paris, 1978), p. 83.
113 Shuster-Fournier, *Un siècle de vie musicale*, pp. 100–102, 177–4. Capozzoli, 'Messiaen's Forgotten Mie', pp. 10, 114–15.

114 M.-L. Langlais, *Jean Langlais Remembered*, p. 60 (letter dated 20 November 1932).
115 'Jean Langlais (Speaking in English) Remembers Vierne, Widor, Dupré, Messiaen, and Tournemire' (1982), www.youtube.com, accessed 9 December 2021.
116 André Breton, *Oeuvres complètes* (Paris, 1992), vol. II, p. 164.
117 Aurélie Decourt, *Une famille de musiciens au XXe siècle, la famille Alain* (Paris, 2011), p. 86; and François Sabatier, 'Histoire de l'orgue en France au XXe siècle, deuxième partie (1926–1970)', *L'Orgue*, 307–8 (2014), pp. 237–8.
118 See Christine Petch, 'Arnold Richardson, Director of Music May 1936–April 1942' (2004), available online at www.stalbansholborn.co.uk, accessed 21 June 2023.
119 See Lewis and Susan Foreman, eds, *Felix Aprahamian: Diaries and Selected Writings on Music* (London, 2015), pp. 341–2.
120 See ibid., pp. 300–301. Aprahamian gave the date as the 26 June, but in a letter to *Musical Opinion*, cited in Petch, 'Arnold Richardson, Director of Music May 1936–April 1942', he mentions that it was Saturday, 25 June 1938.
121 Hill and Simeone, *Messiaen*, pp. 79–82.
122 *TMLM*, pp. 57–62.
123 Hill and Simeone, *Messiaen*, p. 226.
124 Nigel Simeone, 'Messiaen's Family', in *Messiaen in Context*, ed. Sholl, p. 16.
125 Messiaen, 'Autour d'un Parution', *Le Monde musical* (3 April 1939), in *Olivier Messiaen: Journalism*, ed. Broad, p. 35.
126 *TMLM*, p. 57.
127 Hill and Simeone, *Messiaen*, p. 85.
128 Antoine Goléa, *Rencontres avec Olivier Messiaen* (Paris, 1960), pp. 34, 39. Messiaen also stated: 'In the Catholic religion, the marvellous that is given to us is true!' Massin, *Olivier Messiaen: une poétique du merveilleux*, p. 31; and 'In my religion we believe that the invisible is real.' *Olivier Messiaen: The Music of Faith*, dir. Alan Benson (London Weekend Television, 5 April 1985); *TRCO*, tome VII, p. 3.
129 Messiaen in 'Trois jours avec Olivier Messiae: Une archive de 1962' (programme 2/3).
130 Messiaen, 'Autour d'un oeuvre d'orgue', in *Olivier Messiaen: Journalism*, ed. Broad, pp. 74 and 135; and 'De la musique sacrée', *Carrefour* (June–July 1939), pp. 74–6.
131 Yves Balmer and Christopher Brent Murray, 'De l'harmonie à la composition: Messiaen, prophète de son propre style', in *De la libération au domaine musical: dix ans de musique en France, 1944–1954*, ed. Laurent Feneyrou and Alain Poirier (Paris, 2019), pp. 183–91.
132 *TMLM*, p. 52.
133 See Elizabeth McLain, 'Ressourcement Theology in the Interwar Works of Olivier Messiaen', in *Messiaen in Context*, ed. Sholl, pp. 95–102.
134 Falcinelli, 'La Spiritualité de la musique' (10 July 1977), in *Rolande Falcinelli: une esthétique de la synthése, les enjeux d'une pensée humaniste à l'ère postmoderne* (Lille, 2001), p. 618.
135 Marie-Madeleine Duruflé-Chevalier on Maurice Duruflé, 'Entretien avec Marie-Madeleine Duruflé' (with Frédéric Denis on 7 April 1999), reprinted in *Bulletin de l'Association Maurice et Marie-Madeleine Duruflé*,

17 (2019–20), p. 27. For the Gregorian books on his organ stand, see Messiaen improvising in *Olivier Messiaen: The Music of Faith*.
136 Charles Tournemire, preface to the scores of *L'Orgue Mystique* (Paris, 1928).
137 Ibid.
138 Rowan Williams speaking in 'Living with the Gods Omnibus: The Power of Images', at www.bbc.co.uk, accessed 25 January 2022.
139 Jacques Lacan, *Seminar XI: The Four Fundamental Concepts of Psychoanalysis*, ed. Jacques-Alain Miller, trans. Alan Sheridan (London, 2004), p. 113.
140 Williams speaking in 'Living with the Gods Omnibus'.

3 On Messiaen and the Second World War, 1939–45

1 See Thomas Lacôte, 'La forge de la Trinité: matériaux et timbres dans l'oeuvre d'orgue d'Olivier Messiaen', 6 December 2013, www.thomaslacote.wordpress.com.
2 Olivier Messiaen, interview with Antoine Goléa (1957), in *Le Charme des impossibilités*, dir. Nicholás Buenaventura Vidal (Les Films du Rat, Gloria Films, INA Entreprise, 2008).
3 Marie-Louise Langlais, *L'Ombre et lumière* (Paris, 1995), p. 114.
4 Messiaen in *L'Orgue*, 40–41 (December 1939), p. 31, cited in Gaëtan Puaud, *Olivier Messiaen* (Paris, 2021), p. 35.
5 Messiaen, interview with Goléa (1957); Rebecca Rischin, *For the End of Time: The Story of the Messiaen Quartet* (Ithaca, NY, 2003), p. 31; 'Régie Générale des Orchestres' (26 January 1942), listing French orchestral musicians in German POW camps. My thanks to Marc Bacon for this document.
6 Peter Hill and Nigel Simeone, *Messiaen* (New Haven, CT, and London, 2005), p. 132.
7 Peter O'Hagan, *Pierre Boulez and the Piano: A Study in Style and Technique* (London, 2017), p. 13; Jean Boivin, *La Classe de Messiaen* (Paris, 1995), pp. 410–11.
8 Messiaen in *Olivier Messiaen: la liturgie de cristal*, dir. Olivier Mille (Artline films–Arte France–INA Entreprise, 2002).
9 Rischin, *For the End of Time*, pp. 9–17; Yves Balmer and Christopher Brent Murray, 'Olivier Messiaen et la reconstruction de son parcours sous l'occupation: le vide de l'année 1941', in *La Musique à Paris sous l'occupation*, ed. Miriam Chimènes and Yannick Simon (Paris, 2013), pp. 154–5.
10 Pasquier in *Le Charme des impossibilités*. From 1927, Pasquier was a member of the Pasquier trio with his violinist brothers, Jean (1903–1992) and Pierre (1902–1986).
11 Messiaen in *Olivier Messiaen: la liturgie de cristal*.
12 See *Le Charme des impossibilités*; and 'Stalag VIIIA, Zgorzelec, Poland', www.youtube.com, accessed 15 February 2023, a modern guide of the camp. See also the website of the organization Meetingpoint Memory Messiaen, which describes itself as raising 'public awareness of the history and the fates of the prisoners of the former prisoner-of-war camp Stalag VIIIA on a world-wide scale together with its Polish partner, the Foundation Remembrance, Education, Culture. Next to the POWs the history of

National Socialism, the Shoah and the Second World War form the main pillars of the society's work.' They co-commissioned (with the Festival Messiaen au Pays de la Meije) Tristan Murail's *Stalag VIIIA* (2018), and they also published a short pamphlet written by Jerzy Stankiewicz in Polish and Russian on Messiaen, entitled (in Polish) *Człowiek i artysta w Stalagu VIII A w Görlitz* (2017).
13 Pierre Messiaen, *Images* (Paris, 1944), pp. 339–41.
14 Ibid., p. 340.
15 Messiaen in *Le Charme des impossibilités.*
16 Rischin, *For the End of Time*, pp. 27, 29–30.
17 Nardelli in *Le Charme des impossibilités.*
18 Rischin, *For the End of Time*, pp. 27–8.
19 Ibid., pp. 15, 32–42.
20 Antoine Goléa, *Rencontres avec Olivier Messiaen* (Paris, 1960), p. 63; Rischin, *For the End of Time*, p. 65.
21 Rischin, *For the End of Time*, pp. 62–70; see also Matthew 14:13–21; Mark 6:31–44; Luke 9:12–17; and John 6:1–14.
22 Goléa, *Rencontres*, p. 63.
23 Hill and Simeone, *Messiaen*, p. 101; Rischin, *For the End of Time*, pp. 139–41.
24 Messiaen in *Le Charme des impossibilités.*
25 Messiaen, preface to the score of *Quatuor pour la fin du Temps.*
26 Messiaen in *Olivier Messiaen et les oiseaux*, dir. Denise Tual and Michel Fano (Sofracima, 1973), at www.on-tenk.com, accessed 16 November 2023.
27 Leo Samama, interview with Messiaen, in *Messiaen: Quartet for the End of Time*, dir. Astrid Wortelboer (1993), quoted in Rischin, *For the End of Time*, p. 51.
28 I am indebted to the theologian Jeremy Begbie for this observation.
29 Philip Edgcumbe Hughes, *The Book of Revelation: A Commentary* (Leicester, 1990), p. 117.
30 'Sir Harrison Birtwistle in Conversation with Julian Anderson' (2019), www.youtube.com, accessed 24 April 2022; see also 'Harrison Birtwistle in Conversation' (2009), www.youtube.com, accessed 7 May 2022.
31 *TRCO*, tome I (1994), pp. 343–5.
32 Messiaen in *Le Charme des impossibilités.*
33 Messiaen, preface to *Quatuor.*
34 Messiaen, interview with Patrick Szersnovicz, *Le Monde de la musique* (July/August 1987), p. 33.
35 Tōru Takemitsu, *Confronting Silence: Selected Writings*, trans. and ed. Yoshiko Kakudo and Glenn Glasow (Berkeley, CA, 1995), p. 141.
36 See 'Messiaen: Quartet for the End of Time with GroundWorks Dance Theater' (2022), www.youtube.com, accessed 20 June 2023.
37 Alain Messiaen, *La Petite Lampe* [poem IV, from line 3 v. 5–7] (Paris, 1942), pp. 20–21 (Alain Messiaen's italics).
38 Nigel Simeone, *Olivier Messiaen: A Bibliographical Catalogue of Messiaen's Works, First Editions and First Performances* (Tutzing, 1998), p. 67; Hill and Simeone, *Messiaen*, p. 114.
39 BnF RES VMA MS-2183. See Nicholas James Capozzoli, 'Messiaen's Forgotten Mie: Rediscovering the Organ Music of Claire Delbos', DMus, McGill University, Montreal, 2020.

40 There is evidence of collaboration, correction and other editing for performance. See ibid., pp. 68–107.
41 Hill and Simeone, *Messiaen*, pp. 110–11, 119.
42 Lucie Kayas and Christopher Brent Murray, 'Olivier Messiaen and *Portique pour une fille de France*', in *Messiaen Perspectives 1: Sources and Influences*, ed. Christopher Dingle and Robert Fallon (Farnham, 2013), p. 46.
43 Hill and Simeone, *Messiaen*, pp. 103–6.
44 Lucie Kayas, 'Le groupe Jeune France à travers sa Correspondance', *Euterpe*, 35 (July 2020), p. 11. Hill and Simeone give the end date of March 1942 (*Messiaen*, p. 105).
45 Balmer and Brent Murray, 'Olivier Messiaen et la reconstruction de son parcours', pp. 157–8; Hill and Simeone, *Messiaen*, p. 109; Kayas and Brent Murray, 'Olivier Messiaen and *Portique pour une fille de France*', pp. 48, 61–3.
46 Messiaen (sometime between 1987 and 1991) with Loriod in *Yvonne Loriod: Pianist and Teacher*, dir. François Manceaux (Arte – La Sept/Radio France/Com'unimage, 1991) (Harmonia Mundi HMD 9909032, released 2011).
47 Hill and Simeone, *Messiaen*, pp. 125, 132, 126.
48 Balmer and Brent Murray, 'Olivier Messiaen et la reconstruction de son parcours', p. 159; Hill and Simeone, *Messiaen*, pp. 109–11.
49 Yves Balmer and Christopher Brent Murray, 'La classe d'Olivier Messiaen: retour aux sources', in *De la libération au Domaine musical: dix ans de musique en France, 1944–1954*, ed. Laurent Feneyrou and Alain Poirier (Paris, 2018), pp. 167–8.
50 Claude Samuel, *Olivier Messiaen, Music and Color: Conversations with Claude Samuel*, trans. E. Thomas Glasow (Portland, OR, 1986), p. 177.
51 O'Hagan, *Pierre Boulez and the Piano*, p. 14.
52 On Yvonne Loriod-Messiaen and pianism, see Matthew Schellhorn, 'Yvonne Loriod', in *Messiaen in Context*, ed. Robert Sholl (Cambridge, 2023), pp. 18–26.
53 Balmer and Brent Murray, 'Olivier Messiaen et la reconstruction de son parcours', pp. 158–9; Rischin, *For the End of Time*, p. 142.
54 Hill and Simeone, *Messiaen*, p. 112.
55 Ibid., pp. 119–20.
56 'Jean Langlais (Speaking in English) Remembers Vierne, Widor, Dupré, Messiaen, and Tournemire' (1982), www.youtube.com, accessed 20 June 2023.
57 Pierre Boulez, *Music Lessons*, trans. and ed. Jonathan Dunsby, Jonathan Goldman and Arnold Whittall (London, 2019), p. 81.
58 Rischin, *For the End of Time*, pp. 81–3, 93.
59 Hill and Simeone, *Messiaen*, p. 118.
60 Denise Tual, *Le temps dévoré* (Paris, 1980), pp. 194, 197.
61 Hill and Simeone, *Messiaen*, p. 118.
62 Messiaen in *Olivier Messiaen et les oiseaux*.
63 Balmer and Brent Murray, 'Olivier Messiaen et la reconstruction de son parcours', pp. 152–4.
64 Hill and Simeone, *Messiaen*, pp. 126–9.
65 Arthur Honegger, 'Concerts de Printemps', *Comoedia*, 101 (5 June 1943), p. 5, in *Écrits*, ed. Huguette Calmel (Paris, 1992), p. 571.
66 Hill and Simeone, *Messiaen*, p. 185.

67 Stephen Schloesser, *Visions of Amen: The Early Life and Music of Olivier Messiaen* (Grand Rapids, MI, 2014), pp. 294–456.
68 Charles Tournemire, *César Franck* (Paris, 1931), p. 73.
69 Claude Samuel, *Pierre Boulez: Éclats 2002* (Paris, 2002), pp. 21–2.
70 Messiaen, undated manuscript draft for the programme book for the première of *Visions de l'Amen* at the Concert de la Pléiade on 10 May 1943, BnF BN RES Vm. dos. 70 (11), pp. 5–6 (Messiaen's capitalization).
71 Preface to the score of *Visions de l'Amen* (Paris, 1950), and also Messiaen in 'Trois jours avec Olivier Messiaen: Une archive de 1962' (programme 2/3), conversation with Micheline Banzet recorded in March 1962, at www.radiofrance.fr, accessed 16 November 2023.
72 Steven Connor, '"On Such and Such a Day . . . In Such a World": Beckett's Radical Finitude', http://stevenconnor.com, accessed 3 March 2022.
73 Slavoj Žižek, *For They Know Not What They Do* (London, 2008), pp. 220–21.
74 Jacques Lacan, *Seminar III: The Psychoses*, ed. Jacques-Alain Miller, trans. Russell Grigg (New York, 1997), p. 17.
75 Hill and Simeone, *Messiaen*, p. 134; and Messiaen, 'Cahier vert', BnF RES VMA MS-1491, p. 50.
76 Messiaen, 'Cahier vert', pp. 15 and 51; and 'Cahier rouge', BnF RES VMA MS-1492, pp. 51 and 53.
77 Jacques Lacan, *Seminar XI: The Four Fundamental Concepts of Psychoanalysis*, ed. Jacques-Alain Miller, trans. Alan Sheridan (London, 2004), pp. 84, 115, 180, 188, 235.
78 Hill and Simeone, *Messiaen*, pp. 137 and 139.
79 Stephen Schloesser, 'Second Life of a Masterpiece', *Commonwealth*, 30 December 2020, available online at www.commonwealmagazine.org.
80 Messiaen in a masterclass with Loriod and Nicholas Angelich (1970–2022) in *Yvonne Loriod: Pianist and Teacher*.
81 Diary of Jeanne Demessieux for 22 June 1943, in *The Diaries and Selected Letters of Jeanne Demessieux*, ed. Lynn Cavanagh, trans. Stacey Brown and Lynn Cavanagh (n.d.), pp. 207–8, available at https://opentextbooks.uregina.ca, accessed 16 November 2023. See also the diary entry for 30 June 1943, when she relates her discussion with Dupré on the concert (pp. 208–9): 'JD: "I'm critical of his opaque harmonies, his lack of counterpoint, his formulas. His rhythms are obviously creative." MD: "Yes, although somewhat unstable."'
82 Diary of Jeanne Demessieux for 22 September 1945, in *The Diaries and Selected Letters of Jeanne Demessieux*, p. 328.
83 Antoine Goléa, *Vingt ans de musique contemporaine: de Messiaen à Boulez* (Paris, 1962), vol. I, p. 86.
84 Schloesser, 'Second Life of a Masterpiece'.
85 Francis Poulenc, letters to Paul Collaer, 26 April 1945, and Pierre Bernac, 24 June 1944, in Francis Poulenc, *Correspondance, 1910–1963*, ed. Myriam Chimènes (Paris, 1994), pp. 587 and 554.
86 Arthur Honegger, 'Y a-t-il un "Cas Messiaen?"' *Le Figaro littéraire* (13 April 1946), p. 4, in *Écrits*, ed. Calmel, p. 207.
87 Virgil Thomson, 'Olivier Messiaen', in *Virgil Thomson, A Reader: Selected Writings, 1924–1984*, ed. Richard Kostelanetz (New York and London, 2002), pp. 160–61.

88 Karlheinz Stockhausen, 'L'Avant-garde exclue' (18 October 1989), in *Écouter en découvrir: écrits de compositeurs*, ed. Imke Misch, trans. Laurent Cantagrel and Dennis Collins (Paris, 2016), p. 35; Samuel, *Pierre Boulez: Éclats 2002*, p. 23.
89 Messiaen in 'Trois jours avec Olivier Messiaen: Une archive de 1962' (programme 2/3).
90 *TRCO*, tome VII (2002), p. 193.
91 Ibid., p. 198.
92 Philippe Olivier, *Messiaen ou la lumière* (Paris, 2008), p. 38. 'Torrid eroticism' was Gabriel Dussurget's remark to Messiaen (Messiaen was writing *Vingt Regards* at his house). Francis Poulenc, 'Y a-t-il un "Cas Messiaen?"' (13 April 1946), in *J'écris sur que je me chant, écrits et entretiens*, ed. Nicholas Southon (Paris, 2011), p. 439.
93 Jean-Pierre Cauvin, 'Introduction: The Poethics of André Breton', in *Poems of André Breton: A Bilingual Anthology* (Austin, TX, 1982), p. xvii.
94 Darius Milhaud, *Notes without Music: An Autobiography* [1949], trans. Donald Evans, ed. Rollo H. Myers (New York, 1970), p. 236.
95 Francis Poulenc, letters to Darius Milhaud, 3 January 1945 and 27 March 1945, in *Correspondance*, ed. Chiménes, pp. 578, 585 (and p. 587, n. 2); Hill and Simeone, *Messiaen*, pp. 144–52; and the collection of critiques in 'Y-a-t-il un "Cas Messiaen?"' (13 and 20 April 1946), quoted in Hill and Simeone, *Messiaen*, pp. 165–8.
96 Poulenc, *Correspondance*, ed. Chiménes, p. 1037.
97 Hill and Simeone note that Messiaen was listening to rare recordings of Balinese music (possibly borrowed from the Musée de l'Homme) on the day he completed the *Liturgies* (15 March 1944). Hill and Simeone, *Messiaen*, p. 137.
98 Sigmund Freud, 'The "Uncanny"' (1919), in *The Standard Edition of the Complete Psychological Works of Sigmund Freud*, trans. James Strachey (London, 2001), vol. XVII, pp. 219–52.
99 'Set me as a seal' had been used for an a cappella wedding motet by the English composer William Walton (1902–1983) in 1938.
100 Thomson, 'Olivier Messiaen', p. 159.
101 Messiaen in 'Trois jours avec Olivier Messiaen: Une archive de 1962' (programme 2/3).
102 Lucie Kayas, 'From Music for Radio to a Piano Cycle: Sources for the *Vingt Regards sur l'Enfant-Jésus*', in *Messiaen Perspectives 1*, ed. Dingle and Fallon, pp. 85–100.
103 Messiaen, 'Cahier vert'; and four books of other sketches. See the first complete set of pieces, BnF VMA MS-1529. BnF RES VMA MS-1983 presents an earlier version of sketches, including an indication ('Vingt Regards sur l'Enfant-Jésus', p. 19). There is also BnF RES VMA MS -1533 (2), which contains a list of the twenty pieces, p. 10, and BnF MS-1533 (1), which contains six pages of birdsong sketches for piece XIV. Hill and Simeone also observe from Messiaen's diaries that 'some movements may have existed earlier in a more concise form.' Hill and Simeone, *Messiaen*, p. 135.
104 Messiaen, 'Cahier vert', pp. 62 and 78.
105 See BnF VMA MS-1529, unpaginated.
106 On the ordering of the final set see Hill and Simeone, *Messiaen*, pp. 134–5.

107 Messiaen (with Loriod and Angelich) in *Yvonne Loriod: Pianist and Teacher*.
108 Messiaen's memorial to the dead of the Second World War is the short *Chant de déportés*, for chorus and orchestra, performed at the Palais de Chaillot on 2 November 1945 and only rediscovered in 1991.
109 Messiaen in 'Trois jours avec Olivier Messiaen: Une archive de 1962' (programme 2/3); Boivin, *La Classe de Messiaen*, pp. 439, 442.
110 Messiaen (with Loriod and Angelich) in *Yvonne Loriod: Pianist and Teacher*.
111 Samuel, *Music and Color*, p. 121.
112 Loriod, *Programme du domain musical en homage à Olivier Messiaen* (1959), cited in *Panorama de l'art musical contemporain*, ed. Claude Samuel (Paris, 1962), pp. 309–10. See also Caroline Rae, 'Pianism and Virtuosity in Messiaen's *Vingt Regards sur l'Enfant-Jésus*', in *Messiaen in Context*, ed. Sholl, pp. 207–20.
113 Messiaen, 'Cahier vert', p. 10.
114 Poulenc, letters to Bernac, 14 July 1944 and May 1945, in *Correspondance*, ed. Chiménes, pp. 559 and 592.
115 *TMLM*, pp. 35, 48–50, 80–81; Yves Balmer, Thomas Lacôte and Christopher Brent Murray, *Le Modèle et l'invention: Messiaen et la technique de l'emprunt* (Lyon, 2017); and Robert Sholl, 'Review: Yves Balmer, Thomas Lacôte and Christopher Brent Murray, *Le Modèle et l'invention: Messiaen et la technique de l'emprunt*', *H-France Review*, XXIII/10 (January 2023), available online at https://h-france.net. See also Boulez, *Music Lessons*, pp. 29–32.
116 Boulez, *Music Lessons*, p. 469.

4 On Surrealism and Experimentation, 1945–51

1 Olivier Messiaen, 'Résponses à une enquête', *Contrepoints*, I/3 (March–April 1946), p. 73.
2 See Olivier Messiaen, 'Autour d'un oeuvre d'orgue', *L'Art sacré* (April 1939), p. 123; Stephen Broad, ed., *Olivier Messiaen: Journalism, 1935–1939* (Aldershot, 2012), pp. 73 and 135.
3 Olivier Messiaen, *Conférence de Notre-Dame* (Paris, 1978), p. 2.
4 Claude Samuel, *Olivier Messiaen, Music and Color: Conversations with Claude Samuel*, trans. E. Thomas Glasow (Portland, OR, 1986), p. 197; *TRCO*, tome II (1995), p. 235.
5 Arthur Honegger, 'Vue de present et d'avenir' (Paris, 1951), in *Écrits*, ed. Huguette Calmel (Paris, 1992), p. 718.
6 André Breton, *Oeuvres complètes* (Paris, 1992), vol. II, p. 164.
7 André Breton, *'Manifeste du Surréalisme'* (1924), in Breton, *Oeuvres complètes* (Paris, 1980), vol. I, p. 328.
8 Paul Guth, 'Nébuleuses spirales, stalactites et stalagmites suggèrent des rythmes à Olivier Messiaen', *Le Figaro littéraire* (14 February 1953), p. 4.
9 Claude Samuel, *Entretien avec Olivier Messiaen*, with Messiaen's *Turangalîla-symphonie*, 11–13 October 1961 (Véga 30 BVG 1363, released 1962).
10 *TRCO*, tome VII (2002), p. 194.
11 Francis Poulenc, *J'écris sur que je me chant: écrits et entretiens*, ed. Nicholas Southon (Paris, 2011), p. 441; and Poulenc, *Correspondance, 1910–1963*,

ed. Myriam Chimènes (Paris, 1994), p. 1037. Antoine Goléa, *Rencontres avec Olivier Messiaen* (Paris, 1960), p. 155.

12 Raffaele Pozzi, 'The Reception of Olivier Messiaen's Music in Italy: A Historical Interpretation', in *Messiaen Perspectives 2: Techniques, Influence and Reception*, ed. Christopher Dingle and Robert Fallon (Farnham, 2013), p. 288.

13 On the Surrealist map, see www.bigthink.com, accessed 20 June 2023.

14 'Convulsive beauty will be veiled-erotic, fixed-explosive, magic-circumstantial, or it will not be.' André Breton, *L'Amour fou*, in *Oeuvres complètes*, vol. II, p. 687.

15 Peter Hill and Nigel Simeone, *Messiaen* (New Haven, CT, and London, 2005), pp. 153–4; *TMLM* (2001), p. 7.

16 See Peter Asimov, 'Yvonne Loriod, Ultramodernist: Preliminary Glimpses of a Compositional Legacy', in *Women Composers in New Perspectives, 1800–1950: Genres, Contexts and Repertoire*, ed. Mariateresa Storino and Susan Wollenberg (Turnhout, 2023), pp. 265–90. Asimov provides a table of nine works from 1943 to 1947 (pp. 269–70) and describes some 'borrowing' of material between Messiaen and Loriod. She stopped composing mainly out of a desire to serve Messiaen's music. See also Loriod's interview with Bruno Serrou, 'Grands Entretiens de l'INA – Yvonne Loriod-Messiaen (2002)', www.youtube.com, accessed 26 June 2023.

17 Messiaen in 'Trois jours avec Olivier Messiaen: Une archive de 1962' (programme 1/3), conversation with Micheline Banzet recorded in March 1962, at www.radiofrance.fr, accessed 16 November 2023.

18 *TRCO*, tome I (1994), pp. 280–81.

19 Messiaen in 'Trois jours avec Olivier Messiaen: Une archive de 1962' (programme 1/3).

20 The 'Zero hour' (*Stunde Null*) refers to the end of the Second World War in Europe on 8 May 1945 in Germany.

21 Jean Barraqué, 'Olivier Messiaen', in *Écrits*, ed. Laurent Feneyrou (Paris, 2011), pp. 24, 58; Messiaen in Samuel, *Music and Color*, p. 186.

22 See Tim Themi, *Eroticizing Aesthetics: In the Real with Bataille and Lacan* (Lanham, MD, 2021), p. 4; see also Slavoj Žižek, *Surplus-Enjoyment: A Guide for the Non-Perplexed* (London, 2022).

23 See Samuel, *Entretien avec Olivier Messiaen* (1961); and Roger Scruton, *The Face of God: The Gifford Lectures* (London, 2012), pp. 102–6, 169–70.

24 Themi, *Eroticizing Aesthetics*, pp. 29 and 28. He states: 'Christianity . . . must preserve a space for an erotics,' because the 'erotic rituals of transgression . . . were once the very domain of religion'.

25 See Jean Laplanche and Jean-Bertrand Pontalis, *The Language of Psychoanalysis* (London, 1973), pp. 214–17; and Dylan Evans, *An Introductory Dictionary of Lacanian Psychoanalysis* (New York, 1996), pp. 33–4, 38.

26 Themi, *Eroticizing Aesthetics*, p. 17. Wagner first described what is known today as the 'Liebestod' as Isolde's *Verklärung*. See Roger Scruton, *Death-Devoted Heart: Sex and the Sacred in Wagner's Tristan and Isolde* (New York, 2004), p. 192.

27 *TRCO*, tome II (1995), p. 284; Marguerite Béclard and Raoul d'Harcourt, *La Musique des Incas et ses survivances*, 2 vols (Paris, 1925), vol. I, pp. 273–336. *TRCO*, tome III (1996), pp. 277–315.

28 See Robert Sholl, 'Messiaen and Surrealism', in *Messiaen in Context*, ed. Robert Sholl (Cambridge, 2023), pp. 257–66.
29 The woman in 'Seeing is believing' refers to the artwork *Dew Machine* (1937), a collaboration between Lee Miller and Penrose (the woman's hand in the painting is said to represent Lee's input in the work). The resemblance to Miller in both artworks makes reference to their collaborative creative process. Email to the author from Lori Inglis Hall (Lee Miller Archives), 8 August 2023.
30 *TRCO*, tome II, p. 152.
31 Hill and Simeone, *Messiaen*, pp. 164, 169–70.
32 *TRCO*, tome III, p. 279.
33 Ibid., p. 282 (Messiaen's italics).
34 For a summary of this see Stephen Schloesser, *Visions of Amen: The Early Life and Music of Olivier Messiaen* (Grand Rapids, MI, 2014), pp. 472–3.
35 Hill and Simeone, *Messiaen*, pp. 179, 209, 226, 228.
36 See Jean-Sébastien Béreau in Catherine Lechner-Reydellet, *Messiaen, l'empreinte d'un géant* (Paris, 2008), p. 269. The term 'villa' does not designate a large house. The Villa du Danube is one of a set of streets in the 19th arrondissement that is in fact like a lane (without the thoroughfare of cars) and that, somewhat unusually for central Paris, contains detached houses that have front and back gardens.
37 Hill and Simeone, *Messiaen*, pp. 239–41; and Robert Sholl, 'Messiaen and Jacques Charpentier', in *Messiaen in Context*, ed. Sholl, pp. 279–89.
38 Hill and Simeone, *Messiaen*, p. 241; and Roger Muraro, *Fauvettes de l'Hérault: Textes* (Paris, 2020), p. 35. There is no evidence of this blackbird in Messiaen's birdsong *Cahiers*.
39 Olivier Messiaen, 'Comment ils travaillent', *Musica*, XL (March 1958), p. 6; Hill and Simeone, *Messiaen*, p. 133.
40 James B. Sinclair, *A Descriptive Catalogue of the Music of Charles Ives* (New Haven, CT, and London, 1999), pp. 285, 294, 325, 333–4.
41 Nigel Simeone, 'Messiaen and the USA', in *Messiaen in Context*, ed. Sholl, pp. 46–53.
42 BnF RES VMA MS-1539, frontispiece.
43 Ibid., p. 117. Christopher Dingle notes another 'traditional' possibility: movements I, IV, VI and X, suggested by George Benjamin and Paul Crossley. Dingle, *The Life of Messiaen* (Cambridge, 2007), p. 118.
44 The live recording made of the European premiere of the work on 25 July 1950 was conducted by Roger Désormière with the Orchestre National de la RTF, Yvonne Loriod and Ginette Martenot (INA Musique), and the live radio broadcast of the work on 20 January 1959 (INA Musique) with Maurice Rosenthal conducting the Orchestre National de la RTF, Yvonne Loriod and her younger sister, Jeanne Loriod (1928–2001), on the ondes Martenot. The 1961 recording was conducted by Maurice Le Roux with the Orchestre National de la RTF, with Yvonne and Jeanne Loriod. The final revised version of the *Symphonie* was conducted by Myung-whun Chung with the Orchestre de l'Opéra Bastille, with Yvonne and Jeanne Loriod. The interval for the 1950 performance of the work is not included in the timing of movement V. *Pace* Messiaen, his timings for V and VI (*Symphonie-Tâla*) should surely be reversed.
45 See Hill and Simeone, *Messiaen*, p. 171.

46 Olivier Messiaen, letter to Klaus Schweizer, 23 March 1980, in Hill and Simeone, *Messiaen*, pp. 160–61.

47 Nigel Simeone, ed., *The Leonard Bernstein Letters* (New Haven, CT, and London, 2014), p. 261.

48 '*Turangalîla-symphonie* (Rehearsal)', www.youtube.com, accessed 2 June 2022. See also Andrew Shenton, *Olivier Messiaen's Turangalîla-Symphonie* (Cambridge, 2024).

49 Other composers who wrote for the ondes Martenot have included Boulez (who had lessons with Martenot), Darius Milhaud, Edgard Varèse, Marcel Landowski, Charles Koechlin, Florent Schmitt, Jacques Ibert, André Jolivet, who wrote a concerto for the instrument in 1947, Yvonne Loriod, Claire Delbos (two unpublished pieces), and later Tristan Murail, Hugues Dufourt and Jean-Pierre Leguay. See Messiaen, *TRCO*, tome II, pp. 155–6; and Peter O'Hagan, *Pierre Boulez and the Piano: A Study in Style and Technique* (London, 2017), pp. 34–7.

50 Francis Poulenc, letter to Darius Milhaud, 6 September 1950, in *Correspondance*, ed. Chiménes, p. 695.

51 Francis Poulenc, 'Vive Stravinsky!' (7 April 1945), in *J'écris sur que je me chant*, ed. Southon, p. 110; and Poulenc in an interview with the Portugese composer Fernando Lopes-Graça: 'Francis Poulenc' (1947), ibid., p. 590. See also Messiaen's response (28 October 1961) to a lost letter from Poulenc, in Poulenc, *Correspondance*, ed. Chiménes, pp. 983–4. Poulenc had visited Claude Samuel after rehearing the *Turangalîla-Symphonie* and confided to him that he had been mistaken about the work, which he had likely acknowledged to Messiaen in this (lost) letter, which was acknowledged by Messiaen with warmth and affection.

52 See Dominique Jameux, *Pierre Boulez*, trans. Susan Bradshaw (Cambridge, MA, 1991), p. 33; and Hill and Simeone, *Messiaen*, p. 173. See Jean-Claude Risset, *Du songe au son: entretiens avec Matthieu Guillot* (Paris, 2007), p. 68. My thanks to Nigel Simeone for this information about the BBC concert. The Messiaen movements were preceded in the concert by Ravel's suite *Ma Mère l'Oye*, Berlioz's *Les nuits d'été*, and the UK premiere of Boulez's *... explosante-fixe ...*, a work that drew its title from the first chapter of Breton's *L'Amour fou*, which had been an inspiration for Messiaen's 'Tristan trilogy'.

53 See Lewis and Susan Foreman, eds, *Felix Aprahamian: Diaries and Selected Writings on Music* (London, 2015), p. 302.

54 Messiaen in Aprahamian's score of *Turangalîla* (12 May 1968), in Melanie Daiken, 'À la recherche d'un festival Messiaen', *Royal Academy of Music Magazine*, 244 (Summer 1989), p. 9.

55 Jean Boivin, *La Classe de Messiaen* (Paris, 1995), p. 418.

56 Peter Maxwell Davies, 'Messiaen: *Turangalîla-Symphonie*' (12 March 1968), in *Peter Maxwell Davies, Selected Writings*, ed. Nicholas Jones (Cambridge, 2018), pp. 85–7.

57 Massimo Mila in Raffaele Pozzi, 'The Reception of Olivier Messiaen in Italy: A Historical Interpretation', in *Messiaen Perspectives 2*, ed. Dingle and Fallon, p. 292.

58 Igor Stravinsky and Robert Craft, *Themes and Episodes* (New York, 1967), p. 15.

59 Igor Stravinsky, *Themes and Conclusions* (London, 1972), pp. 27–8.
60 Stravinsky and Craft, *Themes and Episodes*, p. 199.
61 Craft, diary entry for 18 October 1958, in Robert Craft, *Stravinsky: The Chronicle of a Friendship, 1948–1971* (London, 1972), p. 72.
62 Sander van Maas, 'Messiaen's Saintly Naïveté', in *Messiaen the Theologian*, ed. Andrew Shenton (Farnham, 2010), pp. 41–59; Jacques Amblard, *Vingt Regards sur Messiaen* (Aix-en-Provence, 2015), p. 173.
63 Harry Halbreich, *Olivier Messiaen* (Paris, 1980), p. 503. See also Pierre Gervasoni, *Henri Dutilleux* (Paris, 2016), p. 1685, n. 163, which relates the Messiaens' naive reactions to the social uprisings in France of 1968 at a dinner party, in Dutilleux's *Journal 1* (23 May 1968): 'Dinner chez Darius and Madeleine Milhaud, with Messiaen, Y. Loriod and G[eneviève Joly – Dutilleux's wife]. The Milhauds were very aware of the situation. Astonishment from the Messiaens faced with all this youthful fermentation and our own reactions. Electric atmosphere due to the events.'
64 Samuel, *Entretien avec Olivier Messiaen* (1961).
65 Hill and Simeone, *Messiaen*, pp. 276–8; François-Bernard Mâche, 'Surréalisme et musique, remarques et gloses', *La Nouvelle Revue française* (December 1974), pp. 34–49.
66 *TRCO*, tome II, p. 151.
67 Stravinsky, *Themes and Conclusions*, p. 28.
68 Alain Messiaen, *Splendeurs et misères du concerto* (Rodez, 1978), p. 27; Caroline Potter, 'The Anxiety of Exoticism: André Jolivet's Relationship with Non-Western Musics', in *André Jolivet: Music, Art and Literature*, ed. Caroline Rae (Abingdon, 2019), pp. 163–5.
69 Michaël Levinas, 'De la polyphony de la *Turangalîla-Symphonie* (1948) d'Olivier Messiaen à *Rebonds* de Michaël Levinas', in Levinas, *Le Compositeur trouvère: écrits et entretiens, 1982–2002* (Paris, 2002), pp. 111–12.
70 *TRCO*, tome II, p. 275.
71 Ibid., p. 287.
72 Honegger, 'Vue de present et d'avenir', in *Écrits*, ed. Calmel, p. 719; *Jean-Louis Florentz: Olivier Messiaen, Comment l'entendez-vous?*, interview with Claude Maupomé (19 December 1979), France Musique, Paris, Inapro Documentary no. PHY03005044, accessed at www.inamediapro.com, 1 December 2023.
73 BnF RES VMA MS-1539, p. 183.
74 Messiaen, 'Cahier vert', BnF RES VMA MS-1491, p. 62.
75 *TRCO*, tome II, pp. 282–4.
76 Barraqué, 'Olivier Messiaen', p. 59.
77 *TRCO*, tome II, pp. 5–90.
78 Pierre Boulez, *Music Lessons*, trans. and ed. Jonathan Dunsby, Jonathan Goldman and Arnold Whittall (London, 2019), p. 50; *TRCO*, tome II, pp. 149–384.
79 Francis Poulenc, 'Entretiens avec Claude Rostand' (October 1953–April 1954), in *J'écris sur que je me chant*, ed. Southon, p. 830.
80 Betsy Jolas, 'Milhaud, Messiaen: Maître et Maître', in *Le Conservatoire de Paris, 1795–1995*, vol. II, ed. Anne Bongrain, Alain Poirier and Marie-Hélène Coudroy-Sagha (Paris, 1999), p. 373.

81 Michel Fano in *Olivier Messiaen: la liturgie de cristal*, dir. Olivier Mille (Artline films–Arte France–INA Entreprise, 2002). To Jeanne Demessieux, Dupré stated: 'Yet he has a legion of fans around him. Admitting that Messiaen is Messiaen, those who follow him will drag music along with them. He's dangerous. He made the big mistake of building a doctrine around himself and, especially, the mistake of proclaiming it. First, it becomes impossible for him to reinvent himself: he's painted himself into a corner. Second, people who hear him say, "St. John the Evangelist and me" think "Here's a man of the stature of St. John the Evangelist'; he treats him as an equal."' Diary of Jeanne Demessieux for 30 June 1943, in *The Diaries and Selected Letters of Jeanne Demessieux*, ed. Lynn Cavanagh, trans. Stacey Brown and Lynn Cavanagh (n.d.), p. 209, available at https://opentextbooks.uregina.ca, accessed 16 November 2023.

82 Ballif speaks of the 'ecstasy' of improvising on the organ. Catholicism is reflected in many of his works, including his *4 Sonates pour orgue*, op. 14 (1956). He regarded the organ as 'the religious instrument par excellence, in the sense that it "connects" the congregation to God by the sole medium of sound without words.' Claude Ballif, 'Mes musiques d'orgue: entretien avec Yves-Marie Pasquet' (n.d.), in *Écrits*, vol. II: *Voyage de mon oreille et autres textes*, texts collected, annotated and presented by Gabriel Ballif, Pierre-Albert Castanet, Alain Galliari and Michèle Tosi (Paris, 2015), pp. 407, 410.

83 Claude Ballif, 'L'habitant du labyrinth: entretiens avec Alain Galliari' (1992), in *Écrits*, vol. I: *Introduction à la métatonalité, Économie musicale et autres textes*, texts collected, annotated and presented by Gabriel Ballif, Pierre-Albert Castanet, Alain Galliari and Michèle Tosi (Paris, 2015), p. 477. Ballif attended Messiaen's class from 1948 to 1951 but was not officially enrolled in it. See Boivin, *La Classe de Messiaen*, pp. 413–15.

84 Ballif, 'L'habitant du labyrinth', p. 488.

85 'À chacun son chant', Jean-Pierre Leguay interviewed by François Sabatier (2004), in Leguay, *Jean-Pierre Leguay: portrait d'un compositeur et improvisateur* (Paris, 2019), p. 19.

86 Claude Ballif, 'Triste exotisme' (1959), in *Écrits*, vol. II, pp. 16–18.

87 Messiaen in 'Trois jours avec Olivier Messiaen: Une archive de 1962' (programme 2/3).

88 Samuel, *Music and Color*, p. 129.

89 *TRCO*, tome I, p. 355.

90 Jean Barraqué, 'Rythme et développement', in *Écrits*, ed. Feneyrou, pp. 87–114.

91 Henri Dutilleux, 'Les Dix chefs-d'oeuvre de la musique du XXe siècle' (1965), in Dutilleux, *L'Esprit de variation: écrits et catalogue établis par Pierre Gervasoni* (Paris, 2019), p. 145; Poulenc, letter to Messiaen, 1 August 1950, in *Correspondance*, ed. Chiménes, p. 690.

92 Honegger, 'Vue de present et d'avenir', p. 718; and André Hodier, *La Musique depuis Debussy* (Paris, 1961), p. 80.

93 Pierre Boulez, 'Olivier Messiaen: The Utopian Years' (October 1978), in Boulez, *Orientations: Collected Writings*, trans. Martin Cooper (London, 1986), pp. 412–16.

94 See René Leibowitz, 'Olivier Messiaen ou l'hedonisme empirique dans la musique contemporaine', *L'Arche*, 9 (September 1945), pp. 130–39.

95 Hill and Simeone, *Messiaen*, p. 190.
96 Goeyvaerts cited in Mark Delaere, 'Olivier Messiaen's Analysis Seminar and the Development of Post-War Serial Music', trans. Richard Evans, *Music Analysis*, XXI/1 (March 2002), p. 38. Quotation altered here for consistent spelling of Śārṅgadeva.
97 *TRCO*, tome VII, pp. 70–71; BnF RES VMA MS-1982 (A).
98 See Robert Sherlaw-Johnston, *Messiaen* (London, 1975), pp. 108–10.
99 Hill and Simeone, *Messiaen*, p. 180; Messiaen in Anik Lesure and Claude Samuel, eds, *Olivier Messiaen: le livre du centenaire* (Lyon, 2008), p. 55.
100 Messiaen finds three rows (one Prime form for each movement of the *Variations*). This is slightly different from Kathryn Bailey, who identifies a single row for the work (in *The Twelve-Tone Music of Anton Webern* (Cambridge, 1991), p. 24). Messiaen's row for movement I has an ingenious quasi-sequential quality and is divided into four trichords, his row for movement II has the same quasi-sequential quality but is comprised of four tetrachords (like Webern's practice for his *String Quartet*, op. 28, see Bailey, p. 25). His row for movement III agrees with Bailey. Perhaps curiously, Messiaen does not discuss rhythm (or register) in the Berg or Webern pieces, something that is a feature of Bailey's study.
101 *TRCO*, tome I, p. 44; BnF RES VMA MS-1982 (A).
102 Peter Hill, 'Messiaen Recorded: The *Quatre Études de rythme*', in *Olivier Messiaen: Music, Art and Literature*, ed. Christopher Dingle and Nigel Simeone (Aldershot, 2007), pp. 84–5, 87–90 and 81.
103 Boulez, *Music Lessons*, p. 231.
104 Barraqué, 'Rythme et développement', p. 104; Michaël Levinas, 'Ponctuation, musique et narrativité', in Levinas, *Le Compositeur trouvère*, p. 165; Boulez, *Music Lessons*, p. 109 (italics in source).
105 Messiaen, 'Cahier vert', p. 6.
106 Hill and Simeone, *Messiaen*, p. 178.
107 Boulez, *Music Lessons*, pp. 223–31, 235, 254–5, 397. See also Jonathan Goldman, *The Musical Language of Pierre Boulez* (Cambridge, 2011), pp. 63–70.
108 Samuel, *Music and Color*, p. 47.
109 *TRCO*, tome II, pp. 194–207, 289–92, 334.
110 *TRCO*, tome III, p. 126.
111 Boulez, *Music Lessons*, p. 607.
112 *TRCO*, tome II, pp. 99–101.
113 Messiaen, programme note (1994), in *Olivier Messiaen: le livre du centenaire*, p. 55.
114 *TRCO*, tome III, p. 131, and VII, p. 44.
115 Loriod gave the premiere of *Structures II chapitre I* with Boulez on 21 October 1961. See O'Hagan, *Pierre Boulez and the Piano*, pp. 163, 164, 242. Igor Stravinsky, *Selected Correspondence Edited with Commentaries by Robert Craft* (London, 1984), vol. II, p. 349.
116 Richard Toop, 'Messiaen/Goeyvaerts, Fano/Stockhausen, Boulez', *Perspectives of New Music*, XIII/1 (Autumn/Winter 1974), pp. 141–69; Boulez, *Music Lessons*, pp. 240–47.
117 Igor Toronyi-Lalic, 'Interview with Boulez', www.theartsdesk.com, accessed 11 June 2021.

118 Christopher Brent Murray, 'Olivier Messiaen's *Timbres-durées*', in *Messiaen Perspectives 1: Sources and Influences*, ed. Christopher Dingle and Robert Fallon (Farnham, 2013), p. 129.
119 Ibid., p. 134.
120 Messiaen in Hill and Simeone, *Messiaen*, p. 198.
121 Messiaen disowned the work to Samuel as 'so bad and such a failure that I'd rather not speak of it'. Samuel, *Entretien avec Olivier Messiaen* (1961).
122 *TRCO*, tome I, pp. 46–8, and IV, p. 44; BnF RES VMA MS-1493.
123 Barraqué, 'Rythme et développement', pp. 87–114.
124 *TRCO*, tome III, pp. 187–92; and *Olivier Messiaen: The Music of Faith*, dir. Alan Benson (London Weekend Television, 5 April 1985).
125 BnF RES VMB MS-128 (cote); and BnF RES VMC MA-179 (cote).
126 Hill and Simeone, *Messiaen*, p. 194. According to Loriod (private communication to Simeone), the work was performed complete on that date: Nigel Simeone, *Olivier Messiaen: A Bibliographical Catalogue of Messiaen's Works, First Editions and First Performances* (Tutzing, 1998), p. 113.
127 BnF RES VMA MS-1493, p. 39; BnF RES VMA MS-1496.
128 BnF RES VMA MS-1496, p. 11.
129 BnF RES VMA MS-1494; and the autograph, BnF RES VMA MS-1495.
130 Jean-Louis Florentz, letter to Gaëtan Puaud, 3 January 2002, cited in Michael Bourcier, 'Olivier Messiaen and Jean-Louis Florentz: A Filiation?', in *Messiaen in Context*, ed. Sholl, p. 313.
131 *TRCO*, tome IV, p. 84.
132 Ibid., pp. 86–8.
133 Barraqué, 'Rythme et développement', p. 102.
134 Yves Balmer, Thomas Lacôte and Christopher Brent Murray, 'Jolivet Revisited: Messiaen Borrowings from the Works of the 1930s', in *André Jolivet: Music, Art and Literature*, ed. Caroline Rae (Abingdon, 2019), pp. 184, 197–8.
135 BnF RES VMA MS-1493, p. 13; Adrian Foster, 'From Recorded Sound to Musical Notation: Reconstructing Olivier Messiaen's Improvisations on *L'Âme en bourgeon*', DMus, McGill University, Montreal, 2017, pp. 39–49.
136 *TRCO*, tome IV, p. 89.
137 BnF RES VMA MS-1493, p. 41.
138 *TRCO*, tome IV, pp. 99–102.
139 See Michel Bourcier, *Jean-Louis Florentz at l'orgue: essai analytique et exégétique*, 2 vols (Lyon, 2018), vol. I, pp. 218–19.
140 Messiaen in conversation with Claude Samuel (1988), *Messiaen Edition* (Warner Classics WA-11431930, 2005) [CD].
141 *TRCO*, tome IV, p. 113.
142 Hill and Simeone, *Messiaen*, p. 195; *TRCO*, tome IV, pp. 118, 115–16.
143 Yves Balmer, Thomas Lacôte and Christopher Brent Murray, *Le Modèle et l'invention: Olivier Messiaen et la technique de l'emprunt* (Lyon, 2017), pp. 305–8.
144 Hill and Simeone, *Messiaen*, p. 202.
145 *TRCO*, tome III, p. 177.
146 Ibid., p. 181.
147 Ibid., p. 188.
148 Ibid., p. 214.

149 Messiaen in 'Trois jours avec Olivier Messiaen: Une archive de 1962' (programme 1/3).
150 Ibid.
151 *TRCO*, tome III, p. 177.
152 Ibid., pp. 178–9.
153 Ibid., p. 195.
154 Brigitte Massin, *Olivier Messiaen: une poétique du merveilleux* (Aix-en-Provence, 1989), p. 74.
155 Stockhausen to Goeyvaerts in Herman Sabbe, 'Messiaen et Stockhausen: Enseignements et affinités', in *La Cité céleste: Olivier Messiaen zum Gedächtnis: Dokumentation einer Symposienreihe*, ed. Christine Wassermann Beirão, Thomas Daniel Schlee and Elmar Budde (Berlin, 2006), p. 308.
156 *TRCO*, tome III, p. 204 (Messiaen's italics).
157 Ibid., pp. 147–64, 196–8.
158 Sylvia Ons, 'Nietzsche, Freud, Lacan', in *Lacan: The Silent Partners*, ed. Slavoj Žižek (New York, 2006), p. 85, cited in Themi, *Eroticizing Aesthetics*, p. 100.

5 On Birdsong, 1952–63

1 Brigitte Massin, *Olivier Messiaen: une poétique du merveilleux* (Aix-en-Provence, 1989), p. 24.
2 Anna Murdoch, 'A Symphony from Deep in the Forest', *The Age* (11 June 1988), p. 3; and Claude Samuel, *Olivier Messiaen, Music and Color: Conversations with Claude Samuel*, trans. E. Thomas Glasow (Portland, OR, 1986), p. 33.
3 Messiaen in 'Trois jours avec Olivier Messiaen: Une archive de 1962' (programme 3/3), conversation with Micheline Banzet recorded in March 1962, at www.radiofrance.fr, accessed 16 November 2023; and Messiaen, 'Cahier vert', BnF RES VMA MS-1491, p. 82.
4 MS 23215, cited in Adrian Foster, 'From Recorded Sound to Musical Notation: Reconstructing Olivier Messiaen's Improvisations on *L'Âme en bourgeon*', DMus, McGill University, Montreal, 2017, pp. 56–9.
5 Messiaen, 'Préface', in Cécile Sauvage, *L'Âme en bourgeon* (Paris, 1987), p. 11. Sauvage's words are: 'Écoute l'alouette au fond du ciel perdue'; Messiaen in Anik Lesure and Claude Samuel, eds, *Olivier Messiaen: le livre du centenaire* (Lyon, 2008), p. 200.
6 *TMLM* (2001), p. 38.
7 Michaël Levinas, 'Imitations et ruptures dans la musique contemporaine: Boulez, le polyphoniste secret', in Levinas, *Le Compositeur trouvère: écrits et entretiens, 1982–2002* (Paris, 2002), p. 43.
8 Messiaen citing Delamain and speaking to Antoine Goléa, in 'André Jolivet et Olivier Messiaen', in Antoine Goléa, *La Musique de la nuit des temps aux aurores nouvelles* (Paris, 1977), vol. II, p. 730.
9 Samuel, *Music and Color*, pp. 91–2.
10 Messiaen (1969), in *Olivier Messiaen: la liturgie de cristal*, dir. Olivier Mille (Artline films–Arte France–INA Entreprise, 2002). See also *Olivier Messiaen: les couleurs du temps: trente ans d'entretiens avec Claude Samuel* disc 1, track 6 (1965) (Harmonia Mundi 211848, released 2000) [2-vol CD].

11 Robert Fallon, 'The Record of Realism in Messiaen's Bird Style', in *Olivier Messiaen: Music, Art and Literature*, ed. Christopher Dingle and Nigel Simeone (Aldershot, 2007), pp. 115–36; and François-Bernard Mâche, 'Messiaen Ornithologue', in *Olivier Messiaen: le livre du centenaire*, pp. 183–7.
12 Messiaen in *Olivier Messiaen: la liturgie de cristal.*
13 Ibid.
14 Ibid.
15 Ibid.
16 See Messiaen in *Olivier Messiaen et les oiseaux*, dir. Denise Tual and Michel Fano (Sofracima, 1973), at www.on-tenk.com, accessed 16 November 2023.
17 Robert Fallon, 'A Catalogue of Messiaen's Birds', in *Messiaen Perspectives 2: Techniques, Influence and Reception*, ed. Christopher Dingle and Robert Fallon (Farnham, 2013), pp. 113–46.
18 See the sketches for *Messe de la Pentecôte*, BnF RES VMA MS-1493, p. 49.
19 Giusy Caruso, 'Entretien avec Jacques Charpentier' (18 March 2015), in 'Mirroring the Gesture and Intentionality of a Piano Performance: An Interpretation of *72 Études Karnatiques pour piano*', Doctor of Arts, University of Ghent, 2018, p. 194. Other organist-composers to investigate serialism included Grunenwald, Langlais and Falcinelli.
20 Tristan Murail, 'Au fils des oeuvres', in Peter Szendy, *Tristan Murail: textes réunis par Peter Szendy* (Paris, 2002), p. 104.
21 Messiaen in *Olivier Messiaen et les oiseaux.*
22 Pierre Schaeffer, *In Search of a Concrete Music*, trans. Christine North and John Dack (Berkeley, CA, 2012), pp. 171–2.
23 Henri Dutilleux, 'Divers aspects d'un langage contemporain' (1960), in Dutilleux, *L'Esprit de variation: écrits et catalogue établis par Pierre Gervasoni* (Paris, 2019), p. 94; Elliott Carter, 'ISCM Festival, Rome' (1959), in *Collected Essays and Lectures, 1937–1995*, ed. Jonathan W. Bernard (Rochester, NY, 1997), p. 24.
24 Messiaen in *Olivier Messiaen: la liturgie de cristal.*
25 See Peter Hill and Nigel Simeone, *Olivier Messiaen: Oiseaux exotiques* (Aldershot, 2007), and Messiaen in 'Trois jours avec Olivier Messiaen: Une archive de 1962' (programme 3/3).
26 Hill and Simeone, *Messiaen* (New Haven, CT, and London, 2005), p. 209.
27 Messiaen (23 April 1979), in Almut Rössler, *Contributions to the Spiritual World of Olivier Messiaen*, trans. Barbara Dagg and Nancy Poland (Duisburg, 1986), p. 110.
28 BnF RES VMA MS-1526, pp. 13–14.
29 Messiaen in *Olivier Messiaen et les oiseaux.*
30 See Jean-Louis Florentz, 'Incidences de la bio-acoustique dans la composition musicale', *Journal de psychologie*, 1–2 (January–June 1983), pp. 83–110. Florentz identifies 'microformes' (forms within forms) as an aspect of 'human development', in Jean Boivin, *La Classe de Messiaen* (Paris, 1995), p. 389.
31 Messiaen in Tōru Takemitsu, 'Nature et musique' (1961–2), trans. Véronique Brindeau, in *Écrits*, trans. Véronique Brindeau and Wataru Miyakawa (Lyon, 2018), p. 184.
32 Samuel, *Music and Color*, p. 56.

33 Olivier Messiaen, 'La Nature, les chants d'oiseaux', *Le Guide du concert*, no. 229 (3 April 1959), p. 1093. For a plan from 1972 of a second *Catalogue* see Roger Muraro, *Fauvettes de l'Hérault: Textes* (Paris, 2020), p. 48.
34 Peter Hill, preface to the score of *La Fauvette passerinette* (London, 2015). See *Concert sur les garrigues et les oiseaux de l'Hérault* (*c.* 1960), written 'to the memory of Claude Debussy, lover of nature', for his centenary in 1962. See Muraro, *Fauvettes de l'Hérault: Textes*, p. 25, Muraro first performed it in Tokyo on 23 June 2017.
35 Messiaen in 'Trois jours avec Olivier Messiaen: Une archive de 1962' (programme 3/3).
36 Ibid.
37 Messiaen in 'Trois jours avec Olivier Messiaen: Une archive de 1962' (programme 1/3).
38 Messiaen in conversation with Claude Samuel (1988), *Messiaen Edition* (Warner Classics WA-11431930, 2005) [CD].
39 Messiaen in 'Trois jours avec Olivier Messiaen: Une archive de 1962' (programme 3/3).
40 Dutilleux, 'Divers aspects d'un langage contemporain', p. 96.
41 Pierre Boulez, 'Possibly . . .' (May 1952), in *Stocktakings from an Apprenticeship*, trans. Stephen Walsh (Oxford, 1991), p. 125 (Boulez's italics).
42 In the diary of Jeanne Demessieux for 30 June 1943, she responds to Dupré's prompt: 'MD: "His ideas on religion?" Me [JD]: "Mysticism . . . it's in fashion now. It's all people talk about. In fact, it's all a mask for paganism. Messiaen regards Christ's passion and bird song as two equal sources of inspiration." MD: "One cannot reproach him as not being sincere in his faith; he's a good fellow."' *The Diaries and Selected Letters of Jeanne Demessieux*, ed. Lynn Cavanagh, trans. Stacey Brown and Lynn Cavanagh (n.d.), p. 209, available at https://opentextbooks.uregina.ca, accessed 16 November 2023.
43 Olivier Messiaen, 'Résponses à une enquête', *Contrepoints*, 1/3 (March–April 1946), p. 73.
44 Claude Samuel, *Entretien avec Olivier Messiaen*, with Messiaen's *Turangalîla-Symphonie,* 11–13 October 1961 (Véga 30 BVG 1363, released 1962).
45 Olivier Messiaen (interviewed by Robert Siohan), '*Chronochromie* d'Olivier Messiaen', *L'Express* (21 September 1961), p. 43; Messiaen in 'Trois jours avec Olivier Messiaen: Une archive de 1962' (programme 3/3).
46 Messiaen, 'Cahier vert', pp. 6–7 and 53; *Quatre Études*, BnF RES VMA MS 1982 (A); and see *TRCO*, tome III (1996), pp. 320, 165–70.
47 *TRCO*, tome III, pp. 7–76.
48 BnF RES VMA MS-1551 (1–10).
49 *TRCO*, tome III, pp. 67–76.
50 Ibid., pp. 84–91.
51 Pierre Boulez, *Boulez on Music Today*, trans. Susan Bradshaw and Richard Rodney Bennett (London, 1975), p. 50.
52 *TRCO*, tome III, p. 79.
53 Gérard Akoka, *Entretiens avec Pierre Boulez* (Paris, 2019), p. 39.
54 Hill and Simeone, *Messiaen*, pp. 237–9.
55 Samuel, *Music and Color*, p. 197.
56 Hill and Simeone, *Messiaen*, pp. 243–5.

57 'Harrison Birtwistle in Conversation' (2009), www.youtube.com, accessed 7 May 2022.
58 'Sir Harrison Birtwistle in Conversation with Julian Anderson' (2019), www.youtube.com, accessed 24 April 2022.
59 Pierre Boulez, *Music Lessons*, trans. and ed. Jonathan Dunsby, Jonathan Goldman and Arnold Whittall (London, 2019), pp. 64–71.
60 See Julian Anderson, 'Messiaen and the Problem of Communication', in *Messiaen Perspectives 1: Sources and Influences*, ed. Christopher Dingle and Robert Fallon (Farnham, 2013), pp. 257–68.
61 Igor Stravinsky, *Selected Correspondence Edited with Commentaries by Robert Craft* (London, 1984), vol. II, p. 349, n. 6.
62 *TRCO*, tome V, vol. I (Paris, 1999), p. 603.
63 Muraro, *Fauvettes de l'Hérault: Textes*, p. 14.
64 Messiaen in *Olivier Messiaen: la liturgie de cristal.*
65 See Messiaen in *Olivier Messiaen et les oiseaux.*
66 Messiaen, BnF MS 22033, p. II.
67 See Catherine Lechner-Reydellet, *Messiaen, l'empreinte d'un géant* (Paris, 2008), pp. 47–8 and 50. Messiaen is referring to himself at the end of this letter, but 'I' here meant himself and Loriod.
68 *TRCO*, tome II (1995), p. 514 (Messiaen's italics).
69 Karlheinz Stockhausen, 'Telemusik', in *Écouter en découvrir: écrits de compositeurs*, ed. Imke Misch, trans. Laurent Cantagrel and Dennis Collins (Paris, 2016), pp. 109–10; Jonathan Harvey, 'An Approach to Church Music', *Musical Times*, CXXXI/1763 (January 1990), p. 55.
70 Boulez, *Music Lessons*, p. 495.
71 Messiaen's note in the score of the *Sept haïkaï: Esquisses Japonaises* (Paris, 1966), p. 58.
72 Boulez, 'Proposals', [1948], in *Stocktakings from an Apprenticeship*, p. 49.
73 Olivier Messiaen, preface to the score of *Couleurs de la Cité céleste* (Paris, 1966).
74 Olivier Messiaen, *Conférence de Notre-Dame* (Paris, 1978), pp. 7–13.
75 Messiaen in *Olivier Messiaen: The Music of Faith*, dir. Alan Benson (London Weekend Television, 5 April 1985).
76 Messiaen, score of *Couleurs de la céleste*, p. 50.
77 Hugues Dufourt, 'Les bases théoriques et philosophiques de la musique spectrale' (2003), in Dufourt, *La Musique Spectrale: une revolution épistémologique* (Paris, 2014), pp. 406 and 419.
78 Sander van Maas, *The Reinvention of Religious Music* (New York, 2014), p. 93.
79 Dufourt, 'Les bases théoriques', p. 414.
80 Olivier Messiaen, *Conférence de Kyoto* (Paris, 1988), pp. 5–9; on 'l'audition-intérieur', see Messiaen, 'Matière-lumière, espaces-temps, son-couleur . . .', *Prevues*, 179 (January 1966), p. 40.
81 Dufourt, 'Les bases théoriques', pp. 414–15.

6 On Influence

1 See Yves Balmer, Thomas Lacôte and Christopher Brent Murray, *Le Modèle et l'invention: Messiaen et la technique de l'emprunt* (Lyon, 2017); and Amy Bauer, 'An Explosive Confrontation: Messiaen and the Post-War Avant-Garde', in *Messiaen in Context*, ed. Robert Sholl (Cambridge, 2023), pp. 267–77.

2 Messiaen expressed his admiration for Bizet's *Carmen* in conversation with Claude Samuel (1988), *Messiaen Edition* (Warner Classics WA-11431930, 2005) [CD]. When asked about Verdi, Messiaen asked to pass over this and speak of other things, in 'Trois jours avec Olivier Messiaen: Une archive de 1962' (programme 2/3), conversation with Micheline Banzet recorded in March 1962, at www.radiofrance.fr, accessed 16 November 2023.
3 Pierre Boulez, 'Olivier Messiaen: Vision and Revolution' (13 May 1973), in Boulez, *Orientations: Collected Writings*, trans. Martin Cooper (London, 1986), p. 408 (italics in original).
4 See Nigel Simeone, 'Messiaen, Boulanger, and José Bruyr: Offrandes Oubliées 2', *Musical Times*, CXVII/1874 (Spring 2001), pp. 17–22.
5 Carolyn Shuster-Fournier, *Un siècle de vie musicale à l'église de la Trinité: de Théodore Salomé à Olivier Messiaen* (Paris, 2014), pp. 75–7, 118, 177.
6 Marie-Louise Langlais, *L'Ombre et lumière* (Paris, 1995), p. 163.
7 Diary of Jeanne Demessieux for 22 June 1941 in *The Diaries and Selected Letters of Jeanne Demessieux*, ed. Lynn Cavanagh, trans. Stacey Brown and Lynn Cavanagh (n.d.), p. 129, available at https://opentextbooks.uregina.ca, accessed 16 November 2023.
8 Messiaen's Mass is present in Messiaen, 'Cahier vert', BnF RES VMA MS-1491, pp. 32–9.
9 See essays by Julian Anderson, Caroline Rae and Yves Balmer, Thomas Lacôte and Christopher Brent Murray, in *André Jolivet: Music, Art and Literature*, ed. Caroline Rae (Abingdon, 2019).
10 Olivier Messiaen, 'Billet parisien: Le *Mana* de Jolivet', *La Sirène* (December 1937), pp. 8–10, in Stephen Broad, *Olivier Messiaen: Journalism, 1935–1939* (Farnham, 2012), pp. 34 and 96.
11 Messiaen, 'Introduction au "Mana" d'André Jolivet' (Paris, 1946, score) (Messiaen's italics).
12 Ibid.
13 Peter O'Hagan, *Pierre Boulez and the Piano: A Study in Style and Technique* (London, 2017), pp. 31–48.
14 Yves Balmer, Thomas Lacôte and Christopher Brent Murray, 'Jolivet Revisited: Messiaen Borrowings from the Works of the 1930s', in *André Jolivet: Music, Art and Literature*, ed. Rae, pp. 174–9.
15 See Christopher Brent Murray, 'Messiaen and the Paris Conservatoire', in *Messiaen in Context*, ed. Sholl, pp. 27–36.
16 Michaël Levinas, 'La Loi et le hors-la-loi', in *La Loi musicale: ce que la lecture de l'histoire nous (dés)apprend*, ed. Danielle Cohen-Levinas (Paris, 1999), p. 17.
17 Jean Boivin, *La Classe de Messiaen* (Paris, 1995), pp. 409–32.
18 Boulez in *Olivier Messiaen: la liturgie de cristal*, dir. Olivier Mille (Artline films–Arte France–INA Entreprise, 2002).
19 Messiaen in *Olivier Messiaen et les oiseaux*, dir. Denise Tual and Michel Fano (Sofracima, 1973), at www.on-tenk.com, accessed 16 November 2023.
20 George Benjamin, 'Olivier Messiaen parlait de la musique avec un tel enthousiasme!', episode 3/5, *Les Grandes Entretiens*, www.radiofrance.fr, 8 May 2019.
21 *TRCO*, tome IV (1997), pp. 5–40.
22 Messiaen, conversation with Samuel (1988).

23 Messiaen in Anik Lesure and Claude Samuel, eds, *Olivier Messiaen: le livre du centenaire* (Lyon, 2008), p. 60; Bob Gilmore citing the composer in liner notes for Horațiu Rădulescu CD Adda, 1993, available online at www.luceroprint.com/biography, accessed 16 November 2023.
24 Messiaen (7 December 1968), in Almut Rössler, *Contributions to the Spiritual World of Olivier Messiaen*, trans. Barbara Dagg and Nancy Poland (Duisburg, 1986), p. 35. See also Claude Samuel, *Olivier Messiaen, Music and Color: Conversations with Claude Samuel*, trans. E. Thomas Glasow (Portland, OR, 1986), pp. 175–90; and Boivin, *La Classe de Messiaen*.
25 *TRCO*, tome II (1995), pp. 99–101; Pierre Boulez, 'Stravinsky Remains', in *Stocktakings from an Apprenticeship*, trans. Stephen Walsh (Oxford, 1991), pp. 68–9.
26 *TRCO*, tome II, p. 99.
27 Pierre Boulez, *Music Lessons*, trans. and ed. Jonathan Dunsby, Jonathan Goldman and Arnold Whittall (London, 2019), p. 33; *TRCO*, tome II, pp. 112–13. See also Arnold Whittall, 'Messiaen and Boulez', in *Messiaen in Context*, ed. Sholl, pp. 290–97.
28 BnF RES VMA MS-2315 (28).
29 BnF RES VMA MS-1982 (A).
30 Pierre Boulez, *Boulez on Music Today*, trans. Susan Bradshaw and Richard Rodney Bennett (London, 1975), pp. 36–7, 42–4, 50.
31 Pierre Boulez, 'At the Edge of Fertile Land (Paul Klee)' (1955), in *Stocktakings*, pp. 167–8; Boulez, *Music Lessons*, p. 397.
32 *TRCO*, tome II, pp. 260–63.
33 O'Hagan, *Pierre Boulez and the Piano*, pp. 69–76.
34 Célestin Deliège, *Pierre Boulez: Conversations with Célestin Deliège*, trans. Robert Wangermee (London, 1976), pp. 40–42.
35 Samuel, *Music and Color*, p. 194.
36 Boulez's four studio recordings of this piece (1969, 1973, 1989 and 2002) are extremely different in terms of spacing, tempi, resonance (instrument and acoustic) and recording techniques.
37 *TRCO*, tome VI (2001), pp. 28–40.
38 *TRCO*, tome II, p. 423.
39 Ibid., pp. 424–7.
40 Ibid., pp. 407–34; and tome VI, pp. 1–11; Boulez, *Boulez on Music Today*, pp. 52–9.
41 Pierre Boulez, 'Proposals' (1948), in *Stocktakings*, p. 49. Boulez is pointing to a historical distinction between self-substantiating counterpoint that may have a firm harmonic basis, and the contrapuntal elaboration of harmony.
42 Jean Barraqué, 'Olivier Messiaen', in *Écrits*, ed. Laurent Feneyrou (Paris, 2011), p. 58.
43 Pierre Boulez, 'Olivier Messiaen: Vision and Revolution', in *Orientations: Collected Writings*, trans. Martin Cooper (London, 1986), p. 407.
44 Pierre Boulez, 'Sound, Word, Synthesis' (1958), in *Orientations*, p. 178.
45 Boulez, 'Proposals', p. 49; and Messiaen on melody in *Olivier Messiaen: The Music of Faith*, dir. Alan Benson (London Weekend Television, 5 April 1985).
46 Karlheinz Stockhausen, 'Every Day Brings New Discoveries', in *The Voice of Music: Conversations with Composers of Our Time*, ed. Anders Beyer

(Farnham, 2000), p. 169; Michel Fano in *Olivier Messiaen: le livre du centenaire*, p. 64.

47 Messiaen, 'L'Inspiration musicale', *Opéra* (19 December 1945), p. 10.

48 Michel Archimbaud, *Pierre Boulez: Entretiens avec Michel Archimbaud* (Paris, 2016), p. 99.

49 Deliège, *Pierre Boulez: Conversations with Célestin Deliège*, p. 37.

50 Boulez, *Music Lessons*, pp. 24–5, 27.

51 Samuel, *Music and Color*, pp. 103–4.

52 See Paul Griffiths, *Olivier Messiaen and the Music of Time* (London, 1985), p. 16. Peter Hill states that Messiaen's music 'accumulates [material], but it does not *develop* (in the accepted sense) or argue'. Anthony Pople supports this idea: 'Messiaen's music does not use its "language" to narrate, to dramatise, nor even to express, but rather to *represent*.' Anthony Pople, 'Messiaen's Musical language: An Introduction', in *The Messiaen Companion*, ed. Peter Hill (London, 1995), pp. 5, 16.

53 *TRCO*, tome I (1994), p. 7.

54 Boulez, 'Sound, Word, Synthesis', p. 178.

55 Arnold Schoenberg, *The Musical Idea: The Logic, Technique and Art of its Presentation*, trans. and ed. Patricia Carpenter and Severine Neff (New York, 1995); Boulez, *Boulez on Music Today*, pp. 17 (Boulez's italics), 18, 21, 28–34.

56 See Samuel, *Music and Color*, pp. 51, 52, 82, 182–4, 192.

57 Boulez, preface to *TRCO*, tome I, p. v.

58 James Harley, *Xenakis: His Life in Music* (London, 2004), p. 92.

59 Iannis Xenakis, programme notes, *Iannis Xenakis: Electro-Acoustic Music* (Nonesuch recording H-71246, released 1970).

60 Peter Hill and Nigel Simeone, *Messiaen* (New Haven, CT, and London, 2005), p. 226.

61 Iannis Xenakis, letter to Olivier Messiaen, 19 October 1958, in *Révolutions Xenakis*, ed. Makis Solomos (Paris, 2022), p. 216.

62 Nouritza Matossian, *Xenakis* (London, 1986), p. 48.

63 Gérard Grisey, 'La naïveté du Sage', Archives Radio France (30 May 1988), in *Olivier Messiaen: le livre du centenaire*, p. 224; and Tristan Murail, 'L'exigence vis-à-vis de l'acte artistique', *Le Monde de la musique*, no. 156 (June 1992), in *Olivier Messiaen: le livre du centenaire*, p. 225. See also Liam Cagney, *Gérard Grisey and Spectral Music: Composition in the Information Age* (Cambridge, 2023), p. 96; Grisey, 'Silences de Messiaen' (30 May 1988), in *Écrits* (édition augmentée) ed. Guy Lelong (Paris, 2018), pp. 227–8; Jeffrey Arlo Brown, *The Life and Music of Gérard Grisey: Delirium and Form* (Rochester, NY, 2023), pp. 70–91.

64 Bálint András Varga, *Conversations with Iannis Xenakis* (London, 1996), p. 31. See also Xenakis in *Olivier Messiaen et les oiseaux*.

65 Alexander Goehr, 'The Messiaen Class', in *Finding the Key: Selected Writings of Alexander Goehr*, ed. Derrick Puffett (London, 1998), p. 56.

66 Xenakis in *Olivier Messiaen et les oiseaux*.

67 Ibid.

68 Varga, *Conversations with Iannis Xenakis*, p. 31.

69 Xenakis's handwritten notes from Messiaen's class, in *Révolutions Xenakis*, pp. 218–21.

70 On Hindu rhythms see ibid., p. 220; and Xenakis, 'Les tendances actuelles de la musique Française', *Epitheorisi technis, 6: Athènes* (1955), pp. 468–9; on interversions see Xenakis, 'Pour saluer Olivier Messiaen', *Opéra de Paris*, 12 (November 1983), p. 6; and Xenakis, 'Un esprit universelle', *Le Monde de musique*, 156 (1992), p. 62.
71 Varga, *Conversations with Iannis Xenakis*, p. 32.
72 Makis Solomos and Peter Hoffmann, 'Xenakis et Messiaen: d'un respect mutuel', in *La Cité céleste: Olivier Messiaen zum Gedächtnis: Dokumentation einer Symposienreihe*, ed. Christine Wassermann Beirão, Thomas Daniel Schlee and Elmar Budde (Berlin, 2006), pp. 293–5.
73 Iannis Xenakis, 'La Crise de la musique sérielle', *Gravesaner Blätter*, 1 (1955), pp. 2–4; and Xenakis, 'Éléments sur les procédés probabilistes (stochastiques) de composition musicale', in *Panorama de l'art musical contemporain*, ed. Claude Samuel (Paris, 1962), pp. 416–25.
74 Varga, *Conversations with Iannis Xenakis*, p. 33; on sieve theory, see pp. 93–6. See also Solomos and Hoffmann, 'Xenakis et Messiaen: d'un respect mutuel', pp. 299–301.
75 Anne-Sylvie Barthel-Calvet, 'The Messiaen-Xenakis Conjunction', in *Messiaen Perspectives 2: Techniques, Influence and Reception*, ed. Christopher Dingle and Robert Fallon (Farnham, 2013), pp. 175–200.
76 Samuel, *Music and Color*, p. 181 (translation altered).
77 Ibid., p. 201 (translation altered).
78 Patrick Szersnovicz, interview with Messiaen (29 May 1987), *Le Monde de la musique* (July/August 1987), p. 33.
79 Levinas, 'La Loi et le hors-la-loi', p. 17. Levinas signals that Messiaen's thought gave him 'permission to develop' a form of 'polyphonic . . . superimposition of microintervals of mode 2 in various transpositions' in his *Rebonds* (1995), *Diaclase* (1993) and *Pardelà* (1994) ('La Loi et le hors-la-loi', p. 16).
80 BnF RES VMA MS-1493, BnF RES VMA MS-1496, BnF RES VMA MS-1494.
81 See Mark Delaere, 'Olivier Messiaen's Analysis Seminar and the Development of Post-War Serial Music', trans. Richard Evans, *Music Analysis*, XXI/1 (March 2002), pp. 36–8.
82 Karlheinz Stockhausen, 'Olivier Messiaen', in Stockhausen, *Texte zu eigenen Werken zur Kunst Anderer Aktuelles*, vol. II (Cologne, 1988), pp. 144–5.
83 Messiaen's recording of the work was released in October 1951. Martin Iddon, *Music and Darmstadt: Nono, Stockhausen, Cage, and Boulez* (Cambridge, 2013), pp. xv and 59, citing Michael Kurtz, *Stockhausen: A Biography*, trans. Richard Toop (London, 1992), p. 37. Goléa stated that Stockhausen played the work roughly thirty times back to back. Goevaerts in Delaere, 'Olivier Messiaen's Analysis Seminar', p. 47.
84 Iddon, *Music and Darmstadt*, p. 61; Boivin, *La Classe de Messiaen*, p. 416.
85 Jonathan Harvey, *The Music of Stockhausen* (London, 1975), pp. 16–19.
86 Karlheinz Stockhausen, 'Invention et découverte; essai de morphogenèse' (1961), cited in Paul Griffiths, *Modern Music and After*, 3rd edn (New York, 2010), p. 162.
87 Preface to the score of Stockhausen's *Kontra-Punkte* (1952).
88 Konrad Boehmer, 'Stockhausen's Spirituality', trans. Sander van Maas, *Contemporary Music and Spirituality*, ed. Robert Sholl and Sander van Maas

(London, 2017), pp. 185–203; Robin Maconie, 'Saving Faith: Stockhausen and Spirituality', *Tempo*, LXXII/283 (2017), pp. 7–20. Maconie had been in Messiaen's class of 1963–4.

89 Stockhausen in Robin Maconie, *Other Planets: The Complete Works of Karlheinz Stockhausen, 1950–2007* (Lanham, MD, 2016), p. vi; Szersnovicz, interview with Messiaen (29 May 1987), p. 34. See *Olivier Messiaen: The Music of Faith*.

90 Karlheinz Stockhausen, 'Six séminaires' (1970), in *Écouter en découvrir: écrits de compositeurs*, ed. Imke Misch, trans. Laurent Cantagrel and Dennis Collins (Paris, 2016), pp. 157–8. Boulez and Stockhausen were also interested in 'frequency shifting'; see Maconie, 'Boulez " . . . éventuellement . . ."', *Musical Times*, CLXII/1955 (Summer 2021), pp. 106–7.

91 Maconie, *Other Planets*, p. 73.

92 Karlheinz Stockhausen, 'Musique et graphisme' (1989), in *Écouter en découvrir*, ed. Misch, pp. 80–93.

93 *TMLM* (2001), p. 7; and Boehmer, 'Stockhausen's Spirituality.'

94 Messiaen (23 April 1979), in Rössler, *Contributions*, p. 104.

7 On the Monumental, 1964–83

1 Anik Lesure and Claude Samuel, eds, *Olivier Messiaen: le livre du centenaire* (Lyon, 2008), pp. 266–7; Peter Hill and Nigel Simeone, *Messiaen* (New Haven, CT, and London, 2005), p. 372.

2 *Olivier Messiaen: le livre du centenaire*, p. 178.

3 See George Parsons and Robert Sholl, eds, *James MacMillan Studies* (Cambridge, 2020).

4 See Alexander Rehding, *Music and Monumentality: Commemoration and Wonderment in Nineteenth-Century Germany* (New York, 2009).

5 See www.vatican.va, accessed 20 June 2023.

6 *SC*, article 121.

7 Messiaen (11 June 1972), in Almut Rössler, *Contributions to the Spiritual World of Olivier Messiaen*, trans. Barbara Dagg and Nancy Poland (Duisburg, 1986), p. 51.

8 Messiaen in conversation with Claude Samuel (1988), *Messiaen Edition* (Warner Classics WA-11431930, 2005) [CD].

9 Messiaen in *Olivier Messiaen: The Music of Faith*, dir. Alan Benson (London Weekend Television, 5 April 1985).

10 Hill and Simeone, *Messiaen*, p. 262.

11 Messiaen, preface ('Note de l'auteur') to the score of *Et exspecto* (Paris, 1966).

12 See Jennifer Newsome Martin, 'The Composition of Glory: Olivier Messiaen and Hans Urs von Balthasar', in *Messiaen in Context*, ed. Robert Sholl (Cambridge, 2023), pp. 135–42.

13 Messiaen, preface to *Et exspecto*.

14 Messiaen in 'Trois jours avec Olivier Messiaen: Une archive de 1962' (programme 2/3), conversation with Micheline Banzet recorded in March 1962, at www.radiofrance.fr, accessed 16 November 2023.

15 See *SC*, article 116: 'The Church acknowledges Gregorian chant as especially suited to the Roman liturgy: therefore, other things being equal, it should be given pride of place in liturgical services.'

16 Messiaen in *Olivier Messiaen: la liturgie de cristal*, dir. Olivier Mille (Artline films–Arte France–INA Entreprise, 2002).
17 Ibid.
18 Messiaen, score of *Et exspecto*, p. 17.
19 *TRCO*, tome VI (2001), pp. 67–9. See Messiaen teaching this in episode 3 of Luciano Berio's documentary *Verso la scuola ideale* (RAI, 1972), available online at www.raiplay.it, accessed 23 June 2023; see also *Olivier Messiaen et les oiseaux*, dir. Denise Tual and Michel Fano (Sofracima, 1973), at www.on-tenk.com, accessed 16 November 2023.
20 Pierre Boulez, *Boulez on Music Today*, trans. Susan Bradshaw and Richard Rodney Bennett (London, 1975), p. 61.
21 Messiaen in *Olivier Messiaen: la liturgie de cristal*; and in *Olivier Messiaen et les oiseaux*.
22 Messiaen, preface to *Et exspecto*.
23 Ibid.
24 See Jonathan Goldman, *The Musical Language of Pierre Boulez* (Cambridge, 2011), pp. 100–115.
25 Frédéric Blanc, ed., *Maurice Duruflé: souvenirs et autre écrits* (Paris, 2005), p. 127.
26 Pius X, *Tra le sollecitudini* (22 November 1903); and Pope Pius XI, *Divini cultus* (20 December 1928).
27 Duruflé, *Souvenirs*, p. 131.
28 Olivier Glandaz, *Messiaen à l'orgue* (Péronnas, 2014), p. 76.
29 Marie-Madeleine Duruflé-Chevalier, 'Entretien avec Marie-Madeleine Duruflé' (with Frédéric Denis on 7 April 1999), *Bulletin de l'Association Maurice et Marie-Madeleine Duruflé*, 17 (2019–20), p. 27.
30 Marie-Louise Langlais, *Jean Langlais Remembered* (2016), pp. 226–35, available online at www.agohq.org, accessed 16 November 2023. See also Marie-Louise Langlais, *L'Ombre et Lumière* (Paris, 1995), pp. 221–9.
31 Stéphane Detournay, *Rolande Falcinelli: une esthétique de la synthése, les enjeux d'une pensée humaniste à l'ère postmoderne* (Lille, 2001), p. 49, n. 34.
32 Olivier Latry, interview with Stéphane Friédérich, in Latry, *À l'orgue de Notre-Dame* (Paris, 2021), pp. 88, 94–5.
33 Claude Samuel, *Olivier Messiaen, Music and Color: Conversations with Claude Samuel*, trans. E. Thomas Glasow (Portland, OR, 1986), p. 30.
34 Messiaen in conversation with Samuel (1988).
35 Pierre Boulez, *Music Lessons*, trans. and ed. Jonathan Dunsby, Jonathan Goldman and Arnold Whittall (London, 2019), p. 412.
36 Olivier Messiaen, *Conférence de Notre-Dame* (Paris, 1978), p. 3. The Latin Mass continues to be an arena of debate; see Pope Francis II's Motu Proprio *Traditiones custodes* (16 July 2021), available online at www.vatican.va, accessed 20 June 2023.
37 Samuel, *Music and Color*, p. 146.
38 Olivier Messiaen, 'Cahier vert', BnF RES VMA MS-1491, p. 15 (Messiaen's underlining); Samuel, *Music and Color*, p. 145.
39 Hill and Simeone, *Messiaen*, pp. 264–75.
40 *Olivier Messiaen: The Music of Faith*; *TRCO*, tome VII (2002), pp. 19–20.
41 Cécile Sauvage, 'Pensées et fragments de lettres [Avignon, August–September 1908]', in *Cécile Sauvage, 20 juillet 1883–26 août 1927:*

études et souvenirs suivis de pages inédits de Cécile Sauvage (Saint-Étienne, 1928), p. 164.

42 George Steiner, *Errata: An Examined Life* (London, 1997), p. 22.

43 The philosopher Immanuel Kant stated that 'The feeling of the sublime is, therefore, at once a feeling of displeasure, arising from the inadequacy of imagination in the aesthetic estimation of magnitude to attain to its estimation by reason, and a simultaneously awakened pleasure, arising from this very judgement of the inadequacy of the greatest faculty of sense in accord with ideas of reason, so far as the effort to attain to these is for us a law.' Kant, *Critique of Judgement* [1790], trans. James Creed Meredith (Oxford, 1952), p. 88.

44 Messiaen stated: 'The truths of faith are terrible; they are fairy tales, by their turn mysterious, agonising, glorious, sometimes terrifying, always resting in a luminous, unchanging Reality,' in *Olivier Messiaen, le livre du centenaire*, p. 33.

45 Samuel, *Music and Color*, pp. 56–7; Virgil Thomson, 'Olivier Messiaen', in *Virgil Thomson, A Reader: Selected Writings, 1924–1984*, ed. Richard Kostelanetz (New York and London, 2002), p. 159.

46 Messiaen, *Conférence de Notre-Dame*, pp. 7–13. See Messiaen's improvisations on the organ of La Trinité (on 21 October 1985), 'Olivier Messiaen Improvisations', www.youtube.com, accessed 8 August 2023.

47 'Olivier Messiaen – L'Orgue de la Sainte-Trinité (Version Complète) [SUB JA] (1991)' (October 1985), www.youtube.com, accessed 12 February 2023.

48 Hill and Simeone, *Messiaen*, pp. 274–6; Samuel, *Music and Color*, pp. 125–8; and Messiaen (1969) in *Olivier Messiaen: la liturgie de cristal*. See also *Olivier Messiaen: les couleurs du temps: trente ans d'entretiens avec Claude Samuel*, disc 1, track 3 (16 December 1976) (Harmonia Mundi 211848, released 2000) [2-vol CD].

49 See Andrew Shenton, 'Messiaen and the Organ Recordings', *Messiaen in Context*, ed. Sholl, pp. 190–98.

50 Brigitte Massin, *Olivier Messiaen: une poétique du merveilleux* (Aix-en-Provence, 1989), p. 185. On *langage communicable*, see Andrew Shenton, *Olivier Messiaen's System of Signs: Notes Towards Understanding His Music* (Farnham, 2008).

51 Hajo Düchting, *Robert and Sonia Delaunay: The Triumph of Colour* (Cologne, 1994), p. 83.

52 See St Thomas Aquinas, *Summa Theologiae*, 'Question 107. The Speech of Angels' at www.newadvent.org/summa/1107.htm, accessed 21 November 2023.

53 *TRCO*, tome III (1996), pp. 360, 366–75. See Messiaen in conversation with Rössler on 23 April 1979 in Rössler, *Contributions*, pp. 69–70.

54 Glenn Watkins, *Proof through the Night: Music and the Great War* (Berkeley, CA, 2003), pp. 236–7.

55 Samuel, *Music and Color*, pp. 94–5.

56 Hugues Dufourt, 'Les bases théoriques et philosophiques de la musique spectrale' (2003), in Dufourt, *La Musique spectrale: une revolution épistémologique* (Paris, 2014), p. 385.

57 Tristan Murail, 'Tristan Murail Lecture (an Excerpt) (August 18)', www.ocnmh.cz, cited in Marilyn Nonken, *The Spectral Piano: From Liszt, Scriabin, and Debussy to the Digital Age* (Cambridge, 2014), p. 71.

58 Marcel Dupré, *Cours Complet d'Improvisation à l'Orgue* (Paris, 1925), vol. II, p. 27; Messiaen, 'Introduction au "Mana" d'André Jolivet', score (Paris, 1946).
59 Samuel, *Music and Color*, p. 163.
60 Messiaen in conversation with Samuel, on *Olivier Messiaen: les couleurs du temps: trente ans d'entretiens avec Claude Samuel*, disc 2, track 1 (16 December 1976).
61 *Olivier Messiaen: la liturgie de cristal*; and Fallon, 'Placing Mount Messiaen', in *Messiaen Perspectives 2: Techniques, Influence and Reception*, ed. Christopher Dingle and Robert Fallon (Farnham, 2013), pp. 323–39. See also Marie-Gabrielle Soret, 'Les Fonds Messiaen' (2016), p. 48, available online at www.iaml.info, accessed 16 November 2023.
62 Samuel, *Music and Color*, p. 170.
63 Hill and Simeone, *Messiaen*, p. 299.
64 Boulez, *Music Lessons*, p. 620.
65 Pierre Boulez, 'Sound, Word, Synthesis', in *Orientations: Collected Writings*, trans. Martin Cooper (London, 1986), p. 178.
66 Boulez, *Music Lessons*, p. 87.
67 See Michel Bourcier, 'Olivier Messiaen and Jean-Louis Florentz: A Filiation?', in *Messiaen in Context*, ed. Sholl, pp. 306–13. See also Christopher Dingle, *Messiaen's Final Works* (Farnham, 2013), p. 181.
68 *Des canyons aux étoiles...*, score, p. 14 (Paris, 1978). On these concepts see Stephen Schloesser, 'Fear; Sublimity, Transcendence: Notes for a History of Emotions in Olivier Messiaen', *History of European Ideas*, XL/6 (2014), pp. 1–31. See also Stephen Schloesser, *Visions of Amen: The Early Life and Music of Olivier Messiaen* (Grand Rapids, MI, 2014), pp. 189–93; and Christopher Dingle, 'Sacred Machines: Fear, Mystery and Transfiguration in Messiaen's Mechanical Procedures', in *Messiaen Perspectives 2*, pp. 13–31.
69 Hill and Simeone, *Messiaen*, pp. 286–7.
70 BnF VM Fonds 30 Mess OBJ 54; Soret, 'Les Fonds Messiaen', pp. 45–6.
71 Hill and Simeone, *Messiaen*, pp. 234, 304, 310.
72 Jean-Christophe Marti, interview with Olivier Messiaen (1992), in *Opera aujourd'hui, l'avant scène, programme du Festival de Salzbourg* (Paris, 1992), p. 15.
73 Messiaen in *Olivier Messiaen: la liturgie de cristal*.
74 Hill and Simeone, *Messiaen*, p. 310.
75 Ibid., pp. 334–5.
76 'Jean Langlais (Speaking in English) Remembers Vierne, Widor, Dupré, Messiaen, and Tournemire' (1982), www.youtube.com, accessed 20 June 2023.
77 Messiaen (16 December 1983), in Rössler, *Contributions*, p. 120.
78 Raymond Lyon, interview with Olivier Messiaen, *Le Courrier musicale de France*, 64 (1978), p. 132.
79 Samuel, *Music and Color*, p. 28.
78 Messiaen (16 December 1983), in Rössler, *Contributions*, p. 128.
81 See Robert Sholl, 'The Shock of the Positive: Olivier Messiaen, St Francis and Redemption through Modernity', in *Resonant Witness: Conversations between Music and Theology*, ed. Jeremy Begbie and Steve Guthrie (Grand Rapids, MI, 2011), pp. 162–89. For a detailed study of the opera,

see Vincent Benitez, *Olivier Messiaen's Opera, Saint François d'Assise* (Bloomington, IN, 2019).
82 Marti, interview with Messiaen (1992), p. 11.
83 Michel Fano in *Olivier Messiaen: le livre du centenaire*, p. 64.
84 See Roger Scruton, *Death-Devoted Heart: Sex and the Sacred in Wagner's Tristan and Isolde* (New York, 2004).
85 *SC*, section 121.
86 *SC*, sections 8 and 112.

8 On Final Works and Legacy

1 Theodor W. Adorno, 'Late Style in Beethoven' (1937), trans. Susan. H. Gillespie, and Adorno, 'Alienated Masterpiece: The *Missa Solemnis*' (1959), trans. Duncan Smith, modified by Richard Leppert, in *Essays on Music*, ed. Leppert (Berkeley, CA, 2002), pp. 564–8 and 569–83; Edward W. Said, *On Late Style: Music and Literature against the Grain* (London, 2006).
2 See Jason Ā. Josephson-Storm, *The Myth of Disenchantment: Magic, Modernity, and the Birth of the Human Sciences* (Chicago, IL, 2017). See also Christopher Dingle, *Messiaen's Final Works* (Farnham, 2013); and Sander van Maas, 'Late Style Messiaen', in *On Religion and Memory*, ed. Babette Hellemans, Willemien Otten and Burcht Pranger (New York, 2013), pp. 175–85.
3 Robert Sholl, 'The Shock of the Positive: Olivier Messiaen, St Francis and Redemption through Modernity', in *Resonant Witness: Conversations between Music and Theology*, ed. Jeremy Begbie and Steve Guthrie (Grand Rapids, MI, 2011), pp. 162–89.
4 See St Thomas à Kempis, *The Imitation of Christ*, trans. Leo Sherley-Price (London, 1952).
5 See Slavoj Žižek, 'If There Is a God then Anything Is Permitted' (2012), available online at www.abc.net.au, accessed 4 November 2022.
6 Messiaen (11 June 1972) in Almut Rössler, *Contributions to the Spiritual World of Olivier Messiaen*, trans. Barbara Dagg and Nancy Poland (Duisburg, 1986), p. 51.
7 See Robert Sholl and Sander van Maas, eds, *Contemporary Music and Spirituality* (New York, 2017).
8 Igor Stravinsky, *Themes and Conclusions* (London, 1972), p. 125.
9 Crumb in Gaëtan Puaud, *Olivier Messiaen* (Paris, 2021), p. 158.
10 Said, *On Late Style*, p. 7; Patrick Szersnovicz, interview with Messiaen (29 May 1987), *Le Monde de la musique* (July/August 1987), p. 34.
11 *TMLM* (2001), p. 35.
12 Olivier Messiaen, 'Résponses à une enquête', *Contrepoints*, 1/3 (March–April 1946), p. 73.
13 'Sir Harrison Birtwistle in Conversation with Julian Anderson' (2019), www.youtube.com, accessed 24 April 2022.
14 Pierre Boulez, *Music Lessons*, trans. and ed. Jonathan Dunsby, Jonathan Goldman and Arnold Whittall (London, 2019), p. 51.
15 See Stefan Keym, '"The Art of the Most Intensive Contrast", Olivier Messiaen's Mosaic Form Up to Its Apotheosis in *Saint François d'Assise*',

in *Messiaen Studies*, ed. Robert Sholl (Cambridge, 2007), pp. 188–205. Boulez, *Music Lessons*, pp. 568–9.

16 Jacques Amblard, 'The Simplicity of Messiaen', in *Messiaen in Context*, ed. Robert Sholl (Cambridge, 2023), pp. 233–9.

17 Said, *On Late Style*, pp. 23–4.

18 Père Francis Cohn, 'Olivier Messiaen, un homme de foi', *Du côté de la Trinité*, 7 (June 1992), p. 1, citing *Du côte de la Trinité*, 2 (March 1991).

19 Brigitte Massin, *Olivier Messiaen: une poétique du merveilleux* (Aix-en-Provence, 1989), p. 201.

20 Rolande Falcinelli, letter to Stéphane Detournay, November 1981, in Detournay, *Rolande Falcinelli: une esthétique de la synthése, les enjeux d'une pensée humaniste à l'ère postmoderne* (Lille, 2001), p. 272.

21 On Messiaen in Israel and the West Bank, see Peter Hill and Nigel Simeone, *Messiaen* (New Haven, CT, and London, 2005), pp. 338, 345–6; Messiaen in *Olivier Messiaen: la liturgie de cristal*, dir. Olivier Mille (Artline films–Arte France–INA Entreprise, 2002); Massin, *Olivier Messiaen: une poétique du merveilleux*, p. 74.

22 Messiaen, *Diaries* (manuscript), cited in Adrian Foster, 'From Recorded Sound to Musical Notation: Reconstructing Olivier Messiaen's Improvisations on *L'Âme en bourgeon*', DMus, McGill University, Montreal, 2017, p. 13.

23 See Jean-Christophe Marti and Olivier Messiaen, 'C'est un secret d'amour: un entretien avec Olivier Messiaen', in *Messiaen: Saint François d'Assise*, CD liner notes (Deutsche Grammophon, 20/21 Series, 1999), p. 69; Massin, *Olivier Messiaen: une poétique du merveilleux*, p. 202; Hill and Simeone, *Messiaen*, p. 343.

24 Massin, *Olivier Messiaen: une poétique du merveilleux*, p. 74; Messiaen in *Olivier Messiaen: la liturgie de cristal*.

25 Massin, *Olivier Messiaen: une poétique du merveilleux*, p. 74.

26 These sacraments are: Baptism, Eucharist (Communion), Confirmation, Reconciliation (Confession), Anointing of the Sick (Extreme Unction), Marriage and Ordination.

27 James D. Herbert, 'The Eucharist in and Beyond Messiaen's *Book of the Holy Sacrament*', *Journal of Religion*, LXXXVIII/3 (July 2008), pp. 331–64.

28 George Steiner, *Errata: An Examined Life* (London, 1997), p. 22.

29 Massin, *Olivier Messiaen: une poétique du merveilleux*, p. 86.

30 Olivier Messiaen, preface to the score of *Livre du Saint Sacrement* (Paris, 1989).

31 *Olivier Messiaen Live: improvisations inédites* (La Praye DLP 0209, 2001 [2-vol CD]).

32 Private communication with Carolyn Shuster Fournier (7 and 8 May 2022); Melanie Daiken, 'À la recherche d'un festival Messiaen', *Royal Academy of Music Magazine*, 244 (Summer 1989), p. 5.

33 Two years before his death Messiaen expressed the wish, in a letter to the builder Olivier Glandaz, to add chamades to the instrument in La Trinité, a 32' Bombarde to the pedal, and on the Récit (Swell), a Septième, a Neuvième and a 32' Douçaine. See René Verwer, 'Messiaen's Organ at Ste-Trinité, Paris' (2008), www.hetorgel.nl/en, accessed 2 August 2023.

34 Dutilleux, diary entry (undated, but from on or after June 1971), in Pierre Gervasoni, *Henri Dutilleux* (Paris, 2016), p. 924; Michel Bourcier, 'Olivier Messiaen and Jean-Louis Florentz: A Filiation?', in *Messiaen in Context*, ed. Sholl, pp. 306–13.
35 Olivier Messiaen, letter to Louis Florentz, 7 July 1991, in Marie-Louise Langlais, *Jean-Louis Florentz: l'oeuvre d'orgue: témoignages croisés* (Lyon, 2009), p. 86.
36 Hill and Simeone, *Messiaen*, p. 259; *TRCO*, tome IV (1997), pp. 125–99; see also Olivier Messiaen, *Les 22 concertos pour piano de Mozart* (Paris, 1987).
37 Olivier Messiaen, 'Introduction to the Programme for Paris, 1978', in Rössler, *Contributions*, p. 10. See this text in *Hommage à Olivier Messiaen*, programme booklet for the Messiaen festival, artistic direction: Claude Samuel (November–December 1978), p. iii (unpaginated). This festival included concerts in Paris, Angers, Bordeaux, Cannes, Chambéry, Enghien, Évry, Fréjus, Grenoble, La Rochelle, Le Pecq, Lille, Lyon, Metz, Nantes, Nice, Orléans, Saint-Tropez, Toulouse, Versailles and Villejuif. My thanks to Roderick Chadwick and Richard Shaw for showing me the programme.
38 Messiaen's preface to the score of *Un Vitrail et des oiseaux* (Paris, 1992).
39 Thomas Merton, *Contemplative Prayer* (London, 1973), p. 115. Merton is often cited by Messiaen as one of his great influences.
40 Paul Klee, 'Kunst gibt nicht das Sichtbare wieder, sondern macht sichtbar,' in Klee, *Inward Vision* (London, 1958); *Creative Credo* (1920), cited in *The Oxford Dictionary of Quotations*, ed. Angela Partington, 4th edn (Oxford, 1996), p. 402.
41 See Robert Sholl, 'Making the Invisible Visible: The Theology, Culture and Practice of Olivier Messiaen's Improvisations', originally published at www.oliviermessiaen.net (2007), available at www.yumpu.com, 5 February 2013.
42 The players commence at the direction of the conductor.
43 Messiaen, Preface to the score of *La Ville d'En-Haut* (Paris, 1994).
44 Ibid.
45 See Maynard Solomon, *Mozart: A Life* (London, 1995); and H. C. Robbins Landon, *1791: Mozart's Last Year* (London, 1999).
46 Jean Boivin, *La Classe de Messiaen* (Paris, 1995), p. 420.
47 A discarded third movement, *Un oiseau des arbres de vie (Oiseau tui)*, was orchestrated by Christopher Dingle and premiered at the BBC Proms on 7 August 2015 (score published in Paris, 2022).
48 Daiken, 'À la recherche d'un festival Messiaen', p. 10; comment confirmed by the pianist and musicologist Jonathan Dunsby to the author (25 January 2023).
49 Lewis and Susan Foreman, eds, *Felix Aprahamian: Diaries and Selected Writings on Music* (London, 2015), p. 304; Daiken, 'À la recherche d'un festival Messiaen', p. 11.
50 Communication from Tony Way, Director of Music at St Francis' Church, Lonsdale St, Melbourne.
51 See Dingle, *Messiaen's Final Works*, p. 182.
52 Massin, *Olivier Messiaen: une poétique du merveilleux*, pp. 79–81 and 96–103.
53 Anna Murdoch, 'A Symphony from Deep in the Forest', *The Age*, Saturday Extra (11 June 1988), p. 3.

54 Charles Bodman Rae, 'Messiaen and Australia: The Composer as Lyrebird', in *Messiaen in Context*, ed. Sholl, pp. 76–86. See also Hollis Taylor, 'Messiaen's Australian Birds: The Impact of H. Sydney Curtis', *Musicology Australia*, XLIV/1 (2022), pp. 58–78.
55 See BnF MS 23158.
56 See also David Rothenburg, 'The Opposite of Time: What Birds Meant for Messiaen', in *Messiaen in Context*, ed. Sholl, pp. 248–56.
57 Adorno, 'Alienated Masterpiece', pp. 575, 578, 579.
58 Ibid., p. 580.
59 Ibid.
60 See Henri Dutilleux, *Mystère et mémoire des sons, entretiens avec Claude Glayman* (Paris, 1997), p. 200, on what he calls 'l'expression l'incantatoire' in the music of Messiaen, Maurice Ohana and Jean-Louis Florentz; see also Julian Anderson, 'Jolivet and the Style Incantatoire: Aspects of a Hybrid Tradition', in *André Jolivet: Music Art and Literature*, ed. Caroline Rae (Abingdon, 2019), pp. 15–40.
61 Jacques Amblard, 'Messiaen in France Today', in *Messiaen in Context*, ed. Sholl, pp. 314–21.
62 See Anne Bongrain, 'Envois d'élèves', pp. 159–64, and 'Envois de pairs: Rayonnement de Messiaen', pp. 165–74, in *Messiaen 2008: Messiaen au Conservatoire: contributions du Conservatoire national supérieur de musique et de danse de Paris aux célébrations de la naissance d'Olivier Messiaen*, ed. Anne Bongrain (Paris, 2008).
63 Robert Fallon, 'The Tombeaux of Messiaen: At the Intersection of Influence and Reception', in *Messiaen Perspectives 2: Techniques, Influence and Reception*, ed. Christopher Dingle and Robert Fallon (Farnham, 2013), pp. 243–73.
64 Robert Sholl, 'Jean Louis Florentz and Spectralism' and 'Olivier Messiaen: Spectralist', in *The Oxford Handbook of Spectral Music*, ed. Amy Bauer, Liam Cagney and Will Mason (New York, 2023), at www.academic.oup.com, accessed 23 November 2023. See also Marilyn Nonken, 'Messiaen and Spectralism', in *Messiaen in Context*, ed. Sholl, pp. 298–305.
65 See www.auditorium-lyon.com, accessed 26 April 2022.
66 See 'Toul Inauguration Rue Olivier MESSIAEN VI', www.youtube.com, accessed 21 June 2023.
67 For pictures of the house, and details of the competitions (piano and organ) and festivals associated with the Fondation Messiaen, see www.maisonmessiaen.com, accessed 21 June 2023.
68 *Hommage à Olivier Messiaen* (November–December 1978).
69 Alain Messiaen, 'Olivier, mon frère . . .', *Diapason*, 234 (December 1978), p. 40.
70 Antoine Goléa, *Rencontres avec Olivier Messiaen* (Paris, 1960), p. 17; Philippe Olivier, *Messiaen ou la lumière* (Paris, 2008), p. 38.
71 'Les Dérives sonores de Gérard Grisey: entretien avec Guy Lelong', in Gérard Grisey, *Écrits ou l'invention da la musique spectrale* (Paris, 2008), p. 235.
72 Unnamed former Conservatoire student in Catherine Lechner-Reydellet, *Messiaen, l'empreinte d'un géant* (Paris, 2008), p. 232; Messiaen (7 December 1968) in Rössler, *Contributions*, p. 35. See the list of tributes to Messiaen by students in Bongrain, 'Hommages', in *Messiaen au Conservatoire*, pp. 177–261.

73 Olivier, *Messiaen ou la lumière*, pp. 47–9.
74 Michaël Levinas, 'Rupture et Système', in *Le Temps de l'écoute: Gérard Grisey, ou la beauté des ombres sonores*, ed. Danielle Cohen-Levinas (Paris, 2004), p. 34.
75 See Jonathan Cross, *Harrison Birtwistle: Man, Mind, Music* (London, 2000), p. 57, cited in Arnold Whittall, 'Messiaen and Twentieth-Century Music', in *Messiaen Studies*, ed. Sholl, p. 232.
76 'Harrison Birtwistle in Conversation' (2009), www.youtube.com, accessed 7 May 2022.
77 Paul Éluard, 'Notes sur la poésie en collaboration avec André Breton' (1936), in Éluard, *Oeuvres Complètes* (Paris, 1968), vol. I, p. 477; Michaël Levinas, 'Olivier Messiaen: Le Fondateur', in Levinas, *Le Compositeur trouvère: écrits et entretiens, 1982–2002* (Paris, 2002), p. 59. On Messiaen, Birtwistle and Carter, see Whittall, 'Messiaen and Twentieth-Century Music', pp. 232–53.
78 Paul Ricoeur, 'The Addressee of Religion: The Capable Human Being' and 'Epilogue: Personal Capacities and Mutual Recognition', in *Philosophical Anthropology: Writings and Lectures*, vol. III, ed. Johann Michel and Jérôme Porée, trans. David Pellauer (Cambridge, 2016), pp. 269–89, 290–95.
79 See André Hodeir, *La musique depuis Debussy* (Paris, 1961), p. 85.
80 Andrew Shepherd, *The Gift of the Other: Levinas, Derrida, and a Theology of Hospitality* (Eugene, OR, 2014); see also Samuel, *Music and Color*, pp. 168–9.
81 John D. Caputo, *Truth: The Search for Wisdom in the Postmodern Age* (London, 2013), pp. 60–101.
82 See Messiaen (11 June 1972), in Rössler, *Contributions*, p. 51.
83 Paul Ricoeur, 'Naming God', in *Figuring the Sacred: Religion, Narrative, and Imagination*, trans. David Pellauer, ed. Mark I. Wallace (Minneapolis, MN, 1995), p. 225.

Select Discography

1 See my review of Messiaen organ recordings made at La Trinité (for Jade) following a festival of Messiaen's organ music from 8 March to 12 April 1995 by various artists in Robert Sholl, 'The True Way?', *Musical Times*, CXXXVII/1839 (May 1996), pp. 35–7. See also Shenton on Messiaen's recordings and tempi in 'Composer as Performer, Recording as Text: Notes towards a "Manner of Realization" for Messiaen's Music', *Messiaen Studies*, ed. Robert Sholl (Cambridge, 2007), pp. 168–87; and 'Messiaen and the Organ Recordings', in *Messiaen in Context*, ed. Robert Sholl (Cambridge, 2023), pp. 190–98.
2 See Peter Hill, 'Messiaen Recorded: The *Quatre Études de rythme*', in *Olivier Messiaen: Music, Art and Literature*, ed. Christopher Dingle and Nigel Simeone (Aldershot, 2007), pp. 79–90.
3 See Christopher Dingle, 'Yvonne Loriod Discography', in *Messiaen Perspectives 1: Sources and Influences*, ed. Christopher Dingle and Robert Fallon (Farnham, 2013), pp. 323–34.
4 The *Monodie*, *Offrande au Saint Sacrement* and the *Prélude* were recorded at the Katharinenkirche in Oppenheim, Germany.
5 See D'Arcy Trinkwon, 'Jeanne Demessieux 1921–1968', liner notes to *Jeanne Demessieux: The Decca Legacy* (London, 2021), pp. 38–9, Eloquence 484 1424. See also *The Diaries and Selected Letters of Jeanne Demessieux*,

ed. Lynn Cavanagh, trans. Stacey Brown and Lynn Cavanagh (n.d.), p. 447, available at https://opentextbooks.uregina.ca, accessed 16 November 2023.

6 Private email from Père Jean-Rodolphe Kars, 30 November 2020.

7 See Jean Boivin, *La Classe de Messiaen* (Paris, 1995), pp. 427–8.

8 *Hommage à Olivier Messiaen pour son 70ème anniversaire*, France Musique, recorded at the Théâtre d'Orsay (19 November 1978), document no. PHD86003807, accessed at www.inamediapro.com, 1 December 2023.

9 For a list of these, see Dingle, 'Yvonne Loriod Discography'.

10 See the discussion of eight interpretations and a discography for *Oiseaux exotiques* in Peter Hill and Nigel Simeone, *Olivier Messiaen: Oiseaux exotiques* (Aldershot, 2007), pp. 93–104 and 121–2. This book includes a CD reissue of the first performance.

Select Bibliography

Messiaen's Writings

Conférence de Bruxelles (Paris, 1958)
Conférence de Kyoto (Paris, 1988)
Conférence de Notre-Dame (Paris, 1978)
'Préface', in Cécile Sauvage, *L'Âme en bourgeon* (Paris, 1987), pp. 7–15
Ravel: Analyses of the Piano Works of Maurice Ravel, ed. Yvonne Loriod-Messiaen, trans. Paul Griffiths (Paris, 2004)
The Technique of My Musical Language (*TMLM*), 2 vols, trans. John Satterfield (Paris, 1956); single-volume edition published 2001
Traité de rythme, de couleur, et d'ornithologie (*TRCO*), 7 tomes (Paris, 1994–2002)

Conversations with Messiaen

Goléa, Antoine, *Rencontres avec Olivier Messiaen* (Paris, 1960)
Massin, Brigitte, *Olivier Messiaen, une poétique du merveilleux* (Aix-en-Provence, 1989)
Rössler, Almut, *Beiträge zur geistigen Welt Olivier Messiaens* (Duisberg, 1984), trans. Barbara Dagg and Nancy Poland as *Contributions to the Spiritual World of Olivier Messiaen* (Duisburg, 1986)
Samuel, Claude, *Olivier Messiaen: les couleurs du temps: trente ans d'entretiens avec Claude Samuel* (Harmonia Mundi 211848, released 2000) [2-vol CD]
—, *Olivier Messiaen: musique et couleur, nouveaux entretiens avec Claude Samuel* (Paris, 1986), trans. E. Thomas Glasow as *Olivier Messiaen: Music and Color, Conversations with Claude Samuel* (Portland, OR, 1986)
—, *Permanances d'Olivier Messiaen: dialogues et commentaires* (Paris, 1999)

Writings on Messiaen

Amblard, Jacques, *Vingt Regards sur Messiaen* (Aix-en-Provence, 2015)
Anderson, Julian, 'Messiaen and the Notion of Influence', *Tempo*, LXIII/247 (January 2009), pp. 2–18
Asimov, Peter, 'Yvonne Loriod, Ultramodernist: Preliminary Glimpses of a Compositional Legacy', in *Women Composers in New Perspectives,*

1800–1950: Genres, Contexts and Repertoire, ed. Mariateresa Storino and Susan Wollenberg (Turnhout, 2023), pp. 265–90

Balmer, Yves, 'La Classe d'Olivier Messiaen: retour aux sources', in *De la Libération au Domaine musical: dix ans de musique en France, 1944–1954*, ed. Laurent Feneyrou and Alain Poirier (Paris, 2018), pp. 162–79

—, and Christopher Brent Murray, 'Olivier Messiaen et la reconstruction de son parcours sous l'Occupation: Le vide de l'année 1941', in *La Musique à Paris sous l'Occupation*, ed. Myriam Chimènes and Yannick Simon (Paris, 2013), pp. 149–60

—, Thomas Lacôte and Christopher Brent Murray, 'Messiaen the Borrower: Recomposing Debussy through the Deforming Prism', *Journal of the American Musicological Society*, LXIX/3 (December 2016), pp. 699–791

—, —, and —, *Le Modèle et l'invention: Messiaen et la technique de l'emprunt* (Lyon, 2017)

Benitez, Vincent, *Olivier Messiaen's Opera, Saint François d'Assise* (Bloomington, IN, 2019)

Boivin, Jean, *La Classe de Messiaen* (Paris, 1995)

Bongrain, Anne, *Messiaen 2008: Messiaen au Conservatoire: contributions du Conservatoire national supérieur de musique et de danse de Paris aux célébrations de la naissance d'Olivier Messiaen* (Paris, 2008)

Broad, Stephen, ed., *Olivier Messiaen: Journalism, 1935–1939* (Aldershot, 2012)

Bruhn, Siglind, *Messiaen's Contemplations of Covenant and Incarnation: Musical Symbols of Faith in the Two Great Piano Cycles of the 1940s* (Hillsdale, NY, 2007)

—, *Messiaen's Explorations of Love and Death* (Hillsdale, NY, 2008)

—, *Messiaen's Interpretations of Holiness and Trinity* (Hillsdale, NY, 2008)

Chadwick, Roderick, and Peter Hill, *Olivier Messiaen's Catalogue d'oiseaux: From Conception to Performance* (Cambridge, 2017)

Delaere, Mark, 'Olivier Messiaen's Analysis Seminar and the Development of Post-War Serial Music', trans. Richard Evans, *Music Analysis*, XXI/1 (2002), pp. 35–51

Dingle, Christopher, *The Life of Messiaen* (Cambridge, 2007)

—, and Nigel Simeone, eds, *Olivier Messiaen: Music, Art and Literature* (Aldershot, 2007)

Ericsson, Hans-Ola, Anders Ekenberg and Markus Rupprecht, 'Approaching the Ineffable: On the Organ Music of Olivier Messiaen', in *Historical Performance Practice in Organ Playing*, Part 3: *Modern and Contemporary Music*, ed. Jon Laukvik, trans. Henry Fairs and Sonya Freter (Stuttgart, 2022), pp. 69–216

Fallon, Robert, and Christopher Dingle, eds, *Messiaen Perspectives*, 2 vols (London, 2013)

Glandaz, Olivier, *Messiaen à l'orgue* (Péronnas, 2014)

Griffiths, Paul, *Olivier Messiaen and the Music of Time* (London, 1985)

Halbreich, Harry, *Olivier Messiaen* [1980] (Paris, 2008)

Hill, Peter, ed., *The Messiaen Companion* (London, 1995)

Hill, Peter, and Nigel Simeone, *Messiaen* (London and New Haven, CT, 2005; French edn Paris, 2008)

—, *Olivier Messiaen: Oiseaux exotiques* (Aldershot, 2007)

Johnson, Robert Sherlaw, *Messiaen* (Berkeley, CA, 1975; Oxford, 1989; London, 2009) with an additional chapter and edited by Caroline Rae
Latry, Olivier, and Loïc Mallié, *L'Oeuvre d'orgue d'Olivier Messiaen: oeuvres d'avant-guerre* (Stuttgart, 2008)
Lechner-Reydellet, Catherine, *Messiaen, l'empreinte d'un géant* (Paris, 2008)
Lesure, Anik, and Claude Samuel, eds, *Olivier Messiaen: le livre du centenaire* (Lyon, 2008)
Maas, Sander van, *The Reinvention of Religious Music: Olivier Messiaen's Breakthrough toward the Beyond* (New York, 2009)
Marchal, Béatrice, *Les Chants du silence: Olivier Messiaen, fils de Cécile Sauvage ou la musique face à l'impossible parole* (Le Vallier, 2008)
—, ed., *Cécile Sauvage: écrits d'amour* (Paris, 2009)
Massip, Catherine, ed., *Portrait(s) d'Olivier Messiaen* (Paris, 1996)
Nichols, Roger, *Messiaen*, 2nd edn (Oxford, 1986)
Olivier, Philippe, *Messiaen ou la lumière* (Paris, 2008)
Puaud, Gaëtan, *Olivier Messiaen* (Paris, 2021)
Reverdy, Michèle, *L'Oeuvre pour orchestre d'Olivier Messiaen* (Paris, 1988)
—, *L'Oeuvre pour piano d'Olivier Messiaen* (Paris, 1978)
Rischin, Rebecca, *For the End of Time: The Story of the Messiaen Quartet* (Ithaca, NY, 2004)
Sauvage, Cécile, *Oeuvre complètes* (Paris, 2002)
Schloesser, Stephen, *Jazz Age Catholicism: Mystic Modernism in Postwar Paris, 1919–1933* (Toronto, 2005)
—, *Visions of Amen: The Early Life and Music of Olivier Messiaen* (Grand Rapids, MI, 2014)
Shenton, Andrew, *Olivier Messiaen's Turangalîla-Symphonie*, Elements in Music since 1945 series (Cambridge, 2024)
—, ed., *Messiaen the Theologian* (Farnham, 2010)
Simeone, Nigel, *Olivier Messiaen: A Bibliographical Catalogue of Messiaen's Works* (Tutzing, 1998)
Sholl, Robert, 'Olivier Messiaen: Spectralist', in *The Oxford Handbook of Spectral Music*, ed. Amy Bauer, Liam Cagney and Will Mason (New York, 2023)
—, 'The Shock of the Positive: Olivier Messiaen, St Francis and Redemption through Modernity', in *Resonant Witness: Conversations between Music and Theology*, ed. Jeremy Begbie and Steve Guthrie (Grand Rapids, MI, 2011), pp. 162–89
—, ed., *Messiaen in Context* (Cambridge, 2023)
—, ed., *Messiaen Studies* (Cambridge, 2007)
Taylor, Hollis, 'Whose Bird Is It? Messiaen's Transcriptions of Australian Songbirds', *Twentieth Century Music*, XI/1 (2014), pp. 63–100

Other Literature

Adorno, Theodor W., *Essays on Music*, ed. Richard Leppert, trans. Susan H. Gillespie et al. (Berkeley, CA, 2002)
Akoka, Gérard, *Entretiens avec Pierre Boulez* (Paris, 2019)
Ballif, Claude, *Écrits*, texts collected, annotated and presented by Gabriel Ballif, Pierre-Albert Castanet, Alain Galliari and Michèle Tosi, 2 vols (Paris, 2015)

Barraqué, Jean, *Écrits*, ed. Laurent Feneyrou (Paris, 2011)
Boulez, Pierre, *Boulez on Music Today*, trans. Susan Bradshaw and Richard Rodney Bennett (London, 1975)
—, *Music Lessons*, trans. and ed. Jonathan Dunsby, Jonathan Goldman and Arnold Whittall (London, 2019)
—, *Orientations: Collected Writings*, trans. Martin Cooper (London, 1986)
—, *Pierre Boulez: Conversations with Célestin Deliege*, trans. Robert Wangermee (London, 1976)
—, *Pierre Boulez: entretiens avec Michel Archimbaud* (Paris, 2016)
—, *Stocktakings from an Apprenticeship*, trans. Stephen Walsh (Oxford, 1991)
Bourcier, Michel, *Jean-Louis Florentz et l'orgue* (vol. I: *L'Unvers florentzien*; vol. II: *Une tétralogie pour l'orgue*) (Lyon, 2018)
Catechism of the Catholic Church (London, 1995)
Corbier, Christophe, *Maurice Emmanuel: lettres choisies* (Paris, 2017)
—, and Sylvie Douche, eds, *L'Enseignement de Maurice Emmanuel* (Paris, 2020)
Davies, Brian, *The Thought of Thomas Aquinas* (Oxford, 1992)
—, *Thomas Aquinas's Summa Theologiae: A Guide and Commentary* (Oxford, 2014)
d'Indy, Vincent, *Cours de Composition musicale, rédigé avec la collaboration de Auguste Sérieyx d'après les notes prises aux Classes de Composition de la Schola Cantorum en 1899–1900*, 2 vols (Paris, 1909)
Donelson, Jennifer, and Stephen Schloesser, eds, *Mystic Modern: The Music, Thought, and Legacy of Charles Tournemire* (Richmond, VA, 2014)
Dufourt, Hugues, *La Musique Spectrale: une revolution épistémologique* (Paris, 2014)
Dupré, Marcel, *Traité d'improvisation à l'orgue* (Paris, 1925)
Dutilleux, Henri, *L'Esprit de variation: écrits et catalogue établis par Pierre Gervasoni* (Paris, 2019)
Emmanuel, Maurice, *Histoire de la langue musicale* (Paris, 1911)
Falcinelli, Rolande, *Souvenirs et regards: entretiens avec Stéphane Detournay* (Tournai, 1985)
Gervasoni, Pierre, *Henri Dutilleux* (Paris, 2016)
Gillock, Jon, *Performing Messiaen's Organ Music: 66 Masterclasses* (Bloomington and Indianapolis, IN, 2010)
Goehr, Alexander, *Finding the Key: Selected Writings of Alexander Goehr*, ed. Derrick Puffett (London, 1998)
Goldman, Jonathan, *The Musical Language of Pierre Boulez: Writings and Compositions* (Cambridge, 2011)
Grosset, Joanny, 'Inde: histoire de la musique depuis l'origine jusqu'à nos jours', in *Encyclopédie de la musique et dictionnaire du conservatoire*, ed. Albert Lavignac, 2 vols (Paris, 1913), vol. I, pp. 257–376
Harvey, Jonathan, *The Music of Stockhausen: An Introduction* (Berkeley, CA, 1975)
Jolivet-Erlih, Christine, ed., *André Jolivet: écrits*, 2 vols (Sampzon, 2006)
Josephson-Storm, Jason Ā., *The Myth of Disenchantment: Magic, Modernity, and the Birth of the Human Sciences* (Chicago, IL, 2017)
Kayas, Lucie, *André Jolivet* (Paris, 2005)

Levinas, Michaël, *Le Compositeur trouvère: écrits et entretiens, 1982–2002* (Paris, 2002)
Murail, Tristan, *Tristan Murail: textes réunis par Peter Szendy* (Paris, 2002)
Nonken, Marilyn, *The Spectral Piano: From Liszt, Scriabin and Debussy to the Digital Age* (Cambridge, 2014)
O'Hagan, Peter, *Pierre Boulez and the Piano: A Study in Style and Technique* (London, 2017)
Pople, Anthony, *Quatuor pour la fin du Temps* (Cambridge, 1998)
Poulenc, Francis, *Correspondance, 1910–1963*, ed. Myriam Chimènes (Paris, 1994)
—, *J'écris sur que je me chant: écrits et entretiens*, ed. Nicholas Southon (Paris, 2011)
Rae, Caroline, ed., *André Jolivet: Music, Art and Literature* (Abingdon, 2019)
Risset, Jean-Claude, *Du song au son: entretiens avec Matthieu Guillot* (Paris, 2007)
Rothenberg, David, *Why Birds Sing* (New York, 2005)
Samuel, Claude, *Pierre Boulez: Éclats 2002* (Paris, 2002)
—, ed., *Panorama de l'art musical contemporain* (Paris, 1962)
Sholl, Robert, and Sander van Maas, eds, *Contemporary Music and Spirituality* (Abingdon and New York, 2017)
Shuster-Fournier, Carolyn, *Un siècle de vie musicale à l'église de la Trinité: de Théodore Salomé à Olivier Messiaen* (Paris, 2014)
Solomos, Makis, ed., *Révolutions Xenakis* (Paris, 2022)
Stockhausen, Karlheinz, *Écouter en découvrir*, ed. Imke Misch, trans. Laurent Cantagrel and Dennis Collins (Paris, 2016)
Takemitsu, Tōru, *Écrits*, trans. Véronique Brindeau and Wataru Miyakawa (Lyon, 2018)
Taylor, Hollis, and Philip Kitcher, *Is Birdsong Music? Outback Encounters with an Australian Songbird* (Bloomington, IN, 2017)
Tournemire, Charles, *Mémoires de Charles Tournemire, édition critique*, *L'Orgue*, ed. Jean-Marc Leblanc, nos 321–4 (2018)
Varga, Bálint András, *Conversations with Iannis Xenakis* (London, 1996)

Filmography

Le Charme des impossibilités, dir. Nicholás Buenaventura Vidal (Les Films du Rat, Gloria Films, INA, 2008)
La Liturgie de cristal, dir. Olivier Mille (Idéale Audience International DVD9DS44, 2009)
Olivier Messiaen: The Music of Faith, dir. Alan Benson (London Weekend Television, broadcast 5 April 1985, transcript 1986)
Olivier Messiaen et les oiseaux, dir. Denise Tual and Michel Fano (Sofracima, 1973), available online at www.on-tenk.com
Olivier Messiaen: Quartet for the End of Time/Improvisations, dir. Georges Bessonnet (Image Entertainment, 1999)
Yvonne Loriod: Pianist and Teacher (with Olivier Messiaen), dir. François Manceaux (Arte – La Sept/Radio France/Com'unimage, 1991) (Harmonia Mundi HMD 9909032, released 2011)

Other Media

Langlais, Marie-Louise, *Jean Langlais Remembered* (2016), available online at www.agohq.org
Messiaen, Olivier, *L'Âme en bourgeon*, recorded in Église de la Sainte-Trinité, Paris (1977) (French Erato, Stereo LP STU 71104, released 1978)
Olivier Messiaen Live: improvisations inédites (La Praye DLP 0209, 2001 [2-vol CD])

Acknowledgements

Many people have contributed to this book. I would like to thank Anna McCready and Nigel Simeone, especially for their comments on the manuscript, and other friends and colleagues for imparting their wisdom over the years: Julian Anderson, Felix Aprahamian, for his hospitality and generosity with materials, Marc Bacon, Amy Bauer, Jeremy Begbie, Michel Bourcier, Timothy Bowers, Ian Brearey, Christopher Brent Murray, Harlin Butterley, Roderick Chadwick, Daniel K. L. Chua, Simon Colvin, Geoffrey Cox, Rosalind Cyphus, John Deathridge, Stéphane Detournay, Laurence Dreyfus, Jonathan Dunsby, Christopher Elton, Michel Fischer, David Foster, Anthony Gritten, Adrian Gunning, Peter Hicks, Christine Jolivet-Erlih, Timothy Jones, Agnès Klingenberg, Thomas Lacôte, Olivier Latry, Sophie Levy, Béatrice Marchal, Sander van Maas, Andrew McCrea, Andrew Neilson, Christine Petch, Daniel-Ben Pienaar, Francis Pott, Caroline Rae, Matthew Schellhorn, Stephen Schloesser, Richard Shaw, Andrew Shenton, Caroline Shuster-Fournier, Michael Maxwell Steer, Elizabeth Stratford, David Trendell, D'Arcy Trinkwon, Nicholas Walker, Tony Way and Arnold Whittall. Special thanks to the Royal Academy of Music and the University of West London for their financial support, Catherine Massip of La Fondation Messiaen, and to Marie-Gabrielle Soret, Catherine Vallet-Collot and the staff of the Bibliothèque Nationale de France for their invaluable help and advice. Thanks also to the editors at Reaktion, especially Michael Leaman, Ben Hayes (for commissioning the book), Emma Devlin and Susannah Jayes. Lindsay O'Neill and Dennis Hunt have nurtured my work on Messiaen from the beginning, and my gratitude to them is inexhaustible. Thank you above all to Ann and Peter, my parents, to my sisters Edwina and Diana, and to Daphne, Amynta and Atticus for their love and support.

Photo Acknowledgements

The author and publishers wish to thank the organizations and individuals listed below for authorizing reproduction of their work.

Published in *The Age* (1 June 1988): p. 178 (Photograph by Mark Wilson); Collection of Felix Aprahamian: p. 145; Bibliothèque nationale de France (BnF), Fonds Messiaen: pp. 17, 18 left and right, 19, 20, 21, 25, 26, 27, 32, 40, 59, 60, 65, 73, 89, 97, 120, 121, 122, 153, 156, 160 (Photograph by Claude Langlais), 171, 175, 181, 183; Archives de CNSMDP (Conservatoire National Supérieur de Musique et de Danse de Paris). Reproduced by permission: pp. 28, 155 (Photograph by André Papillon); Henning Lohner, Archive Stockhausen-Stiftung für Musik, Kürten, Germany (www.karlheinzstockhausen.org): p. 141; Courtesy of Dennis Hunt: p. 6; © Maison Messiaen – AIDA/Bruno Moussier: p. 184; Roland Penrose © Lee Miller Archives, England 2023 (www.leemiller.co.uk). All rights reserved: p. 88; Roger-Viollet: pp. 56 (Photograph by Boris Lipnitzki), 106 (Photograph by Boris Lipnitzki), 139; Courtesy of the private collection of Nigel Simeone: p. 50; Courtesy of Joëlle Vouaux (with permission): p. 90.

Index

Page numbers in *italics* refer to illustrations